PANDEMIC PANIC

HOW CANADIAN GOVERNMENT RESPONSES TO COVID-19 CHANGED CIVIL LIBERTIES FOREVER

JOANNA BARON *AND* **CHRISTINE VAN GEYN**
FOREWORD BY **PRESTON MANNING**

OPTIMUM
PUBLISHING
INTERNATIONAL
LONDON I MONTRÉAL I TORONTO

Pandemic Panic How the Canadian Governments responses to Covid 19 changed Civil Liberties forever
©Toronto, 2023 Joanna Baron and Christine Van Geyn

First Edition published in Canada and United States
Published by Optimum Publishing International.

LIBRARY AND ARCHIVES CANADA CATALOGUING IN PUBLICATION
Title: Pandemic Panic How the Canadian Governments responses to Covid 19 changed Civil Liberties Forever Joanna Baron and Christine Van Geyn

Subjects: Public Health, Civil Liberties, Canadian Law, Government Policy, Covid-19
Description: Optimum Publishing International, Canada edition
ISBN 978-0-88890-349-5 (Trade Paperback)
ISBN 978-0-88890-350-1 (ePub)

Jacket and interior design by Jessica Albert

Printed and bound in Canada.
Marquis Printing

For information on rights or any submissions, please e-mail to
Optimum: deanb@opibooks.com
Optimum Publishing International
Dean Baxendale, President & CEO
Toronto, Canada

www.optimumpublishinginternational.com
www.opibooks.com
Twitter @opibooks | Instagram @opibooks

OPTIMUM
PUBLISHING
INTERNATIONAL
LONDON I MONTRÉAL I TORONTO

CONTENTS

*For Asher, Georgia, Harrison, Dash, Dahlia,
Aksel, Ariela, and for all children, who are the
future guardians of our civil liberties.*

FOREWORD

Preston Manning PC CC AOE

The COVID-19 pandemic of 2019–2022 was an event of unprecedented magnitude that threatened to adversely affect the health of millions of Canadians of all ages and in all walks of life.

But the response measures adopted by Canada's governments—including vaccine and masking mandates, social distancing requirements, school closures, and economic lockdown measures—had ramifications well beyond their health impacts, significantly affecting the social and economic well-being of millions of Canadians regardless of whether or not they had contracted the virus.

All of these response measures, as the authors of *Pandemic Panic* meticulously document, also significantly impacted the constitutionally guaranteed rights and freedoms of Canadians—severely limiting rights to privacy and equality of treatment under the law and dramatically limiting freedom of expression, assembly, religion, and movement.

The official government narrative, accepted and communicated by most of the mainstream media and largely accepted by the courts, was that all these limitations on rights and freedoms were, under emergency circumstances, reasonable and justifiable even in a professedly free and democratic society.

In *Pandemic Panic,* Joanna Baron and Christine Van Geyn of the Canadian Constitution Foundation, challenge, chapter by chapter, this official and widely accepted narrative.

They establish the facts that virtually every right and freedom supposedly guaranteed by the *Charter of Rights and Freedoms* was violated one way or another by the COVID-19 response measures. They then lament that the pandemic response not only showed the weakness of the courts in responding quickly to rights violations, but more seriously, that "it revealed the weakness of Canada's culture of civil liberties and may have permanently weakened that culture."

They rightly observe that: "Many Canadians would like to forget the three pandemic years. To throw them into a 'memory hole' and move forward." But they also strongly warn that we must not forget or ignore the major lesson taught by the pandemic panic—that crises always present "the greatest opportunity for government to seize new powers and limit rights"—and that if we ignore this lesson, "the governments of this country will be even better positioned to do this to us again."

Baron and Van Geyn conclude their introduction to *Pandemic Panic* by inviting each of us to read their analysis of the response to COVID-19 with an open mind, to be prepared to have our own personal interpretations of the crisis challenged, and to become much more watchful of and resistant to whatever limitations on our rights and freedoms the next public emergency might bring.

In extending this invitation and providing us with the information required to evaluate it, the authors of *Pandemic Panic* have rendered an important public service to Canada and Canadians. I personally have accepted their invitation and would urge you, the reader, to do likewise.

Preston Manning PC CC AOE
Calgary, Alberta
September 2023

CHAPTER 1
INTRODUCTION[1]

In October 2022, economist Emily Oster wrote a plea for a "pandemic amnesty." After detailing various ill-conceived public health policies cobbled together throughout the pandemic, Oster concluded that "The standard saying is that those who forget history are doomed to repeat it. But dwelling on the mistakes of history can lead to a repetitive doom loop as well." She reasoned that many admittedly poor public health decisions were made in an information vacuum and that the salubrious thing to do going forward would be to forgive and forget.[2]

Oster was concerned about the social fabric fraying as a result of polarizing online discourse and urged the need to move forward. However, our anecdotal experience has shown a second common response to pandemic mishaps—going blank entirely on what occurred during that time.

We have observed a phenomenon whereby the surreal, sometimes inane, often unprecedented and unusual public health measures taken over the roughly three-year pandemic period were "memory holed," i.e., the mind completely fogged over. Many times in the course of writing this book we messaged one another after unearthing yet another public policy absurdity: the City of Toronto taping off cherry blossoms or Quebec requiring unvaccinated people to be chaperoned in plexiglass carts through the essential aisles of big-box stores.

We are not psychologists, but we can see that there must be an evolutionary benefit to allowing a collective trauma to dissolve into the slipstream: it's unproductive to dwell on how we got by and how our government coped in real time. Our memories are warped, first, by the "primacy effect"—our tendency to remember "firsts," exemplified by people universally naming George Washington when asked to recall former U.S. presidents.

Most people have a crystal-clear memory of the moment their plague year started in earnest. For us and for many others, it was March 11, 2020, the day the National Basketball Association suspended games for the rest of the season. Joanna was in bed eating takeout in a hotel in Montreal, watching the feed of escalating bad news roll in with increasing unease, knowing she had to get on a plane back to Toronto the next day. She got home and more or less barricaded herself in her condo. Within a few days, the entire world had changed. Christine was visiting her family in northern Ontario with her husband and kids. They would remain up north for weeks. Such an extraordinary and immediate change to virtually every aspect of daily life is indelibly etched in our memories.

As the pandemic dragged on, however, most of the various lockdowns, reopenings, stay-at-home orders, regulations, and ordinances melted into a grey area that has less significance for our individual recollections. To take just one of infinite examples, you probably don't remember: an incident in December 2020. At this point it was well established that COVID-19 very rarely[3] spread outdoors. Two Calgary police officers arrested a twenty-one-year-old man for skating outdoors. When the man asked why he was being grabbed, one officer warned him "Get on the ground before I f**cking taser you."[4] To watch the video is to be reminded of the grotesque occurrences that, for a period of time, became normalized. This book aims to serve as something of a corrective to the frailties of our collective memories. *The British Medical Journal* recently called[5] for a national inquiry into Canada's public health response to COVID-19, declaring that "the world expected more of Canada." We respectfully claim the same is merited with regards to Canada's treatment of constitutional rights.

The Fathers of Canadian Confederation placed a high premium on liberty. But unlike the American revolutionaries, who often spoke of liberty as an *a priori* concept found in the laws of nature itself and rooted in individual rights, Canada's founders were inspired by Anglo-Irish philosopher Edmund Burke's notions of liberty. For them, liberty was not an individual endeavour but was formed in "social freedom," which is "secured by well-constructed institutions." For this reason, Burke famously decried the French Revolution as causing more destruction and suffering than freedom. Canada's founders and early statesmen saw liberty as a function of political society and human experience, and thus to be defined and limited by the people themselves through their elected representatives.

When liberty doesn't emerge from the laws of nature but instead must be mediated through the people's representatives, groupthink and political exigencies can do a lot of damage. From the outset of the pandemic, Canadians witnessed an extraordinary—and mainly uncontested—outgrowth of governmental powers and assaults on individual liberties. The Macdonald-Laurier Institute, in its COVID Misery Index,[6] ranked Canada's pandemic misery in unemployment and excess inflation as among the worst in the world.

Any way you calculate it, there was plenty of misery to go around. Canada's most populous provinces, Ontario and Quebec, endured some of the world's longest lockdowns. Restaurants in Toronto were shut down for more than 360 days over the course of the pandemic, the longest period of any city in the world. Schools in Ontario were shut for more than seven months between March 2020 and January 2022. As for the economic and social consequences, the worst may still be to come.

The book moves sequentially through the fundamental freedoms guaranteed by the Canadian Constitution, primarily its *Charter of Rights and Freedoms*, but also the rights guaranteed by the *Constitution Act, 1867*. In Chapter 2, we look at the right to freedom of assembly and the democratic lifeblood that is the right to protest. Chapters 3 and 4 take a sober look at the epoch-defining Freedom Convoy and subsequent invocation of the federal *Emergencies Act*, which saw the Trudeau government, for the first time in history, invoke an extraordinary portfolio of draconian state powers.

In Chapter 5, we discuss movement restrictions, going back to the early days of the first wave of the pandemic, when the Maritime provinces put in place a flurry of interprovincial travel restrictions. We also have a lengthy deep dive into the ultimately misconstrued federal quarantine hotels program and the challenge the CCF led against it.

Chapter 6 looks at the various privacy implications of the pandemic measures, including the notoriously expensive COVID Alert app, vaccine passports, snitch lines, and cellphone data tracking. Chapter 7 highlights the asymmetrical effects public health measures had on Canadians, including disabled Ontarians who were barred from accessing mobility therapy due to gym lockdowns and individuals who suffered known medical complications from a COVID-19 vaccine and were left unaccommodated by British Columbia's vaccine passport program.

One of the areas most ravaged by pandemic policies was freedom of expression, with staggering restrictions placed on individuals' abilities to share information and engage in debate—including a case where a judge imposed one of the most extreme compelled-speech orders of any country in the world during the pandemic. We discuss this case and other restrictions on speech in Chapter 7.

Chapter 8 covers the devastating effects lockdowns had on the ability of religious congregations to gather in worship, and discusses why religious freedom attracts unique constitutional protections, looking at various court challenges to lockdown orders.

In Chapter 9, we review one of the most intensely polarizing issues of the pandemic: vaccine mandates, passports, and the differential treatment of unvaccinated individuals which, at times, even raised the spectre of imposing a special "unvax tax."

Finally, public emergencies often go hand in hand with politicians skirting ordinary legislative procedures with the goal of defending public safety, and Canada's experience during the COVID-19 pandemic was no different. In Chapter 11, "COVID-19, Democracy and the Rule of Law," we look at extended states of emergency, legislative power grabs, and other worrying irregularities that occurred at various levels of government.

As you go through the book, we ask that you read with an open mind. Over the course of the pandemic, we saw the world views of many thoughtful, intelligent friends ossify into uniform narratives. The underlying reality of how the pandemic affected our rights is uneven and complex. So whether you fall into the camp that believes the pandemic constituted a generational health threat and most public health measures intended to blunt its impact were justified, or you think that governments lurched towards unjustified power grabs, prepare to have your narrative challenged.

CHAPTER 2
THE RIGHT TO FREEDOM
OF ASSEMBLY

Robert Bristol is a bit of a gym rat from Kingston, Ontario, and a big supporter of small businesses. As the COVID-19 pandemic wore into its second year in 2021, Robert grew increasingly frustrated by sustained lockdowns. He saw how the lockdown measures were destroying the small businesses his friends and neighbours had poured their lives into.

"I know several people in the city of Kingston who have lost their businesses due to this," Robert told the *Quinte News*, a local news outlet serving the Bay of Quinte region of southern Ontario. "There was no point to this lockdown. It is getting to a point where it is becoming extreme."[1]

Spring of 2021 was a challenging time in Canada. On April 7, Ontario Premier Doug Ford had declared a third state of emergency and announced a second stay-at-home order that took effect at midnight. The order closed retailers except for grocery stores, pharmacies, and garden centres, but it permitted big box stores to remain open with capacity limits and restrictions that permitted only the sale of "essential goods." Gyms were ordered shut.

A few days later, on April 12, Premier Ford announced that all schools in the province would stop in-person classes following spring break, and on April 16 he announced that the stay-at-home order would be extended at least until May 20. The extended stay-at-home order also included additional capacity restrictions for retail and the closing of all outdoor recreation amenities such as parks, and prohibited non-essential interprovincial land travel into Ontario. Yet at roughly the same time, some public health experts were publicly commenting that the risk of outdoor transmission of COVID-19 was low.[2]

At his wit's end, Robert attended a "No More Lockdowns" rally in nearby Belleville on the day Ford announced the extended stay-at-home order. Encouraged and inspired by that rally, he wanted to plan his own demonstration in Kingston a few days later.

April 21 was one of those late April days when Canadians are still somehow surprised by the cold and shocked by a spring snow. Undeterred, Robert marched to Kingston City Hall with a sign that said: "End Lockdowns." He was alone, and he wore a mask.

It is hard to imagine how Robert's one-man masked protest could have spread COVID-19 to anyone. However, shortly after arriving at City Hall, he was approached by Kingston police and ticketed for breaching the stay-at-home order. Robert filmed his encounter with the police, which attracted attention on social media, including from the lawyers at the national civil liberties group that wrote this book: the Canadian Constitution Foundation (CCF).

The CCF assisted Robert with his case, retaining lawyer Asher Honickman to represent him.[3] Ultimately, the Crown withdrew the ticket. Ticketing a man for standing outside alone in a mask is outrageous. In conducting his protest, Mr. Bristol was expressing his political views against government actions, which is his constitutionally protected right. We at the CCF were pleased that the Crown prosecutors agreed to drop the charge, and we said that the government should take this case as an example. In a news release, the CCF wrote "We urge the Crown to drop other similar tickets that have been issued to Ontarians across the province who have been ticketed for exercising their right to protest."[4]

Robert's protest may or may not have constituted an "assembly" under the *Canadian Charter of Rights and Freedoms*, section 2(c) of which guarantees the right to peaceful assembly.[5] After all, Robert was protesting alone, so was he really "assembling"? This may seem like an unusual anecdote with which to begin this chapter. But it is also an excellent anecdote to begin with, because it reveals the weaknesses in the law. One of the challenges with *Charter* claims for breaches of freedom of assembly is that the law on this right is underdeveloped.

The CCF was preparing an argument that Robert's conduct engaged the right to freedom of assembly because his conduct constituted an invitation to assemble. We hoped this would be an interesting opportunity for development of the law. However, because the charge was dropped, ultimately in Robert's best interest, the novel argument could never be attempted.

The lack of development of the law on freedom of assembly is a problem because it means there is very little case law to back up arguments before the courts. So claims against pandemic-related ordinances such as the stay-at-home orders and the tickets associated with them can only rely on scant case law to make an argument that the right to freedom of assembly was violated. Courts have almost always treated cases involving freedom of assembly as part of the right to freedom of expression, religion, or association. But a unique feature of the government response to the COVID-19 pandemic was that the mere act of assembling, either in public or in private, was prohibited. There have not really been other instances in Canada where the simple act of assembling was viewed as dangerous by the government and subject to restrictions. This should have created an opportunity to develop the law in this area, but this opportunity was dodged by the courts.

We believe that Robert's protest invited assembly, and that his rights to both assembly and expression were violated, but that ultimately no useful precedent emerged from his case. The courts evading the novel rights issues emerging from the pandemic is an unfortunate theme throughout this book. This chapter will aim to add to our underdeveloped jurisprudence on freedom of assembly by exploring how COVID-19 restrictions on private and public assemblies should be seen as engaging and restricting our right to freedom of assembly.

In this chapter, we will consider:

- the lack of case law on freedom of assembly alone;
- a proposed legal framework for freedom of assembly claims;
- restrictions on private gatherings;
- restrictions on public gatherings such as protests; and
- the Freedom Convoy (although this is considered in greater detail in Chapters 3 and 4).

THE LAW OF FREEDOM OF ASSEMBLY: LITTLE CONSIDERATION BY THE COURTS

Canadians had never really considered the risk that their governments would prohibit family Christmas dinners, baby birthday parties, summer barbeques, or in fact any kind of private social gatherings. This was a unique feature of the pandemic, but when at various points throughout the pandemic laws restricting assemblies were challenged, there was little case law on freedom of assembly as a standalone right to draw on. Canadian courts have rarely dealt with the right to peaceful assembly independently of other fundamental freedoms. For that reason, the right has been referred to by some scholars as one of our "forgotten freedoms."[6]

The scant existing case law on freedom of assembly appears to indicate that the right is "geared towards protecting the physical gathering together of people."[7] In

In *Roach v. Canada (Minister of State for Multiculturalism and Citizenship)* Justice Linden explained in a partially dissenting opinion that "there is scant case law on the guarantee of freedom of peaceful assembly. However, what little there is would appear to indicate that freedom of peaceful assembly is geared towards protecting the physical gathering together of people."

In the 2019 Quebec Court of Appeal case of *Bérubé c. Ville de Québec*,[8] the unanimous court held that the authors of the *Charter* chose to protect expression and assembly separately and that this itself is revealing. While the court called section 2(c) "the least judicially explored freedom," it also said that "this does not make it an accessory or second-order freedom, the protection of which should be less robust."[9] The court went on to say that while it is often joined by other rights, such as freedom of expression, the right to freedom of assembly on its own "has its inherent virtues, which mark the importance of regrouping and assembly, in this case peaceful, regardless of the object or purpose of that meeting [. . .]"[10]

But for the most part, cases where the *Charter*'s section 2(c) guarantee of the right to freedom of assembly has been argued have almost always engaged other rights, such as freedom of expression or freedom of religion. Because the courts can refer to a much richer body of case law related to those other rights, it is easier for them to make decisions based on those other rights. In fact, some courts entirely subsume the freedom of assembly analysis into other rights.

For example, the case of *Ontario (Attorney-General) v. Dieleman* dealt with anti-abortion protests and the government's move to stop such protests close to hospitals and free-standing abortion clinics, as well as physician offices and homes. In that 1994 case, the Ontario Supreme Court[11] subsumed freedom of assembly analysis into the already well-established freedom of expression analysis. "Freedom of assembly is subject to the same analysis as freedom of expression," the court held in that case. And that "freedom of assembly is 'speech in action.'"[12]

From a rights-protecting perspective, the approach in Quebec's *Bérubé* case is preferable to the approach in *Dieleman*. In fact, since the text of the *Charter* makes it clear that the right to freedom of peaceful assembly protects more than religious or expressive gatherings (such as protests), freedom of assembly should not be viewed as a second-order right. Using the *Dieleman* approach, purely social gatherings would not receive *Charter* protection because they do not fit neatly into the box of freedom of expression or freedom of religion.

This is a problem, because COVID-19 public health restrictions affected all gatherings, not just protests or religious gatherings. Governments imposed restrictions on purely small and private social gatherings. There were periods across Canada when home gatherings were limited to immediate family only, or to groups of ten or less, and even small outdoor public gatherings were restricted.[13] Never before had courts considered the possibility of such a thing, and they lacked a framework to consider the problem.

THE LAW OF FREEDOM OF ASSEMBLY: A PROPOSED FRAMEWORK

While there is some acknowledgment from courts in cases like *Bérubé* that freedom of assembly is a stand-alone right, courts have not developed an analytical framework to examine when the right is engaged. In other words, there is no legal test for violations of freedom of assembly.

In this void, some scholars have proposed frameworks. In a 2018 paper, "Exploring a More Independent Freedom of Peaceful Assembly in Canada,"[14] Basil Alexander suggests that the "substantial interference" framework used for freedom of religion and freedom of association claims could be repurposed into a new test for freedom of assembly. This new test would recognize that certain constitutional guarantees are subject to "degrees of infringement," allowing for contextually driven legal results that "better account for peaceful assembly's unique features and character." Under Alexander's proposed test, courts could ask whether the interference with the freedom of assembly is "more than trivial or insubstantial," permitting a case-by-case analysis to determine whether the *Charter* has been limited.

Building on this point, Kristopher Kinsinger writes in "Restricting Freedom of Peaceful Assembly During Public Health Emergencies"[15] that courts do not need to decide if a gathering was social or political when deciding if the right is engaged. Rather, differentiating between the purpose of the gatherings happens at a later stage, when courts consider whether a limit on a right is justified under section 1 of the *Charter*, which allows for rights to be limited if the limit is demonstrably justified in a free and democratic society.[16] The upshot is that using Alexander's proposed "substantial interference" test will ensure that merely trivial or insubstantial claims of restrictions on assembly will not make it to the stage where courts consider whether a limit is justified.

In the context of how this analysis might apply to COVID-19 public health restrictions, Kinsinger writes that it will likely be unnecessary to distinguish too rigidly between these different types of assemblies at the scope-defining stage of the analysis. There is ample room under section 1 to recognize that a higher threshold of justification ought to apply to core exercises of freedom of peaceful assembly.[17]

From our perspective, applying Kinsinger's proposed framework to pandemic-related restrictions on gatherings is likely to engage our section 2(c) *Charter* right to freedom of assembly, whether those gatherings are expressive, religious, or purely social. We want to emphasize that there is no bright line that differentiates between when a social gathering turns into an expressive gathering. Consider your own Thanksgiving dinners, which if they are anything like ours, commonly turn into some type of political or religious debate. Or consider the fact that prohibited social gatherings that occurred during periods of lockdown may in fact express a subversive political sentiment about government responses to COVID-19, even if those assemblies were for social purposes. Under Kinsinger's framework, the question of whether those limits to our rights were justified occurs during the section 1 analysis.

There was some interest at a hearing in the summer of 2023 about adopting a test for violations of freedom of assembly. Kinsinger's proposed paper was referenced during the oral arguments by Justice Callaghan in *R v Hillier*.[18] That Ontario case involved former Lanarck-Frontenac-Kingston MPP Randy Hillier. Hillier, a vocal opponent of COVID-19 lockdowns, was issued a ticket by the Smiths Falls Police Service for organizing a "No More Lockdowns" rally in May of 2021, contrary to a COVID-19 restriction on gatherings. The decision had not been released at the time of this writing, and this remains a good opportunity to develop a test on freedom of assembly that was missed by earlier courts.

FREEDOM OF ASSEMBLY CASES IN THE COVID-19 CONTEXT: PRIVATE GATHERINGS

During the pandemic the courts had opportunities to develop a test on freedom of assembly, to consider freedom of assembly as a standalone right, as well as consider the difference in how the right applies to private social gatherings versus public expressive gatherings. Earlier case law has increasingly recognized freedom of assembly as a standalone right. As discussed, it has been considered in cases like *Bérubé*, and scholars have proposed workable frameworks like those developed by Alexander and Kinsinger for interpreting this little-considered right. This could help courts interpret the right in a meaningful and coherent way. Unfortunately, these opportunities were missed.

Koehler v. Newfoundland and Labrador

The issue of pandemic restrictions on private gatherings was considered in the case of *Koehler v. Newfoundland and Labrador*.[19] In that case, the Newfoundland Supreme Court relied on case law that led them to both narrow and restrict the freedom of assembly in the context of COVID-19.

In *Koehler*, Ontario residents Werner and Sharon Koehler wanted to move to Newfoundland to live in their residential property there and operate their seasonal business. However, a Special Measures Order adopted by the provincial government to prevent the spread of COVID-19 prevented them from entering Newfoundland. The Order, made by the Newfoundland Chief Medical Officer of Health and effective May 4, 2020, prohibited anyone from entering the province unless they were subject to an exemption.

In addition to raising section 6 *Charter* mobility rights and equality rights issues, the couple challenged the travel restrictions based on the freedom of peaceful assembly. The purpose of their planned assembly was purely social—they did not argue that they intended to gather for any purposes other than to have friends over to their residence in Newfoundland to socialize. The purpose of their assembly was not to protest, express political views, or to engage in religious worship. The province countered that section 2(c) only protects the freedom to gather in public places to express opinion. This case was an opportunity for the court to answer the question of whether or not section 2(c) protects purely social gatherings.

In interpreting section 2(c), the Supreme Court of Newfoundland and Labrador used the approach laid out by the Ontario court in *Dieleman*, the case described earlier as subsuming the right of freedom of assembly into other rights, such as freedom of expression. The court found that "The right to peacefully assemble is one that furthers the other fundamental freedoms. It protects the right of citizens to gather to express views concerning matters related to the functioning of a civil society."[20]

In our view, this approach unduly narrows the otherwise broad language of section 2(c), which does not explicitly say that freedom of peaceful assembly is only related to the exercise of these other freedoms. It only says that people have a freedom of peaceful assembly, yet the Newfoundland court chose to continue the trend from cases like *Dieleman* of treating section 2(c) as a subordinate freedom to these other freedoms.

The Newfoundland court also cited the case of *Attorney General of Ontario v. 2192 Dufferin Street*,[21] which said that the freedom of peaceful assembly protects people, not places, meaning the Koehlers' private residence was not protected as a place by freedom of peaceful assembly. The two cases are quite different, however. In *2192 Dufferin Street*, the court was concerned with the forfeiture of several properties being used as clubhouses by the Outlaws Motorcycle Club, which the government asserted were being used as proceeds of crime or instruments of unlawful activity. In contrast, the Koehler family simply wanted to move to Newfoundland to live in their own home and run their business. There was not a whiff of impropriety let alone criminality.

While it may be true that section 2(c) protects people not places, it is unclear why freedom of assembly would not apply to people who choose to exercise that freedom in a private place such as a personal residence. Regardless, on the narrow issue of whether the Newfoundland travel restrictions infringed the Koehlers' section 2(c) freedoms, the court found that the Koehlers were "merely saying that because Special Measures Order 11 prohibited them from coming here they couldn't socialize here"[22] and therefore concluded that they had not sufficiently pleaded a breach of their right to freedom of peaceful assembly.

In other words, the *Koehler* court considered only whether the travel restrictions preventing the Koehlers from entering Newfoundland infringed their section 2(c) rights and not whether gathering restrictions internal to the province infringed those rights.

FREEDOM OF ASSEMBLY CASES IN THE COVID-19 CONTEXT: PUBLIC GATHERINGS AND PROTESTS

The right to peaceful assembly, including the right to protest, is a core right of liberal democracies. If we accept too many restrictions on the fundamental right to protest, we silence the voices of many in our society, especially those whose ways of making their views known may be limited. A democratic society welcomes debate and disagreement on the key issues of the day, and protest is a big part of this process. Protests can be messy and disruptive, but they are also good for our society.

At various times during the pandemic, however, protests were not permitted. Several provinces, including Ontario, imposed gathering limits that included restrictions on outdoor gatherings. Some protests continued despite the restrictions. In some of those protests, tickets were handed out to protest organizers for violating public health restrictions, including the case of Robert Bristol, who received a ticket for protesting alone.

Tickets were issued at all kinds of public protests, but there was a perception that protests over COVID-19 restrictions were more likely to result in tickets. It is difficult to measure whether or not this perception was accurate, but anecdotally there was great inconsistency in ticketing. For example, in 2020 several people were given $1,200 tickets when they took part in anti-restriction demonstrations at the Alberta legislature. Those tickets were ultimately withdrawn.[23] Yet during other periods, protests occurred in spite of gathering restrictions and no tickets were issued. During one period in Ontario, large weekly protests in downtown Toronto took place opposing lockdowns. Other protests were held in the prairies over farming policy in India. There were protests in many major cities related to the Black Lives Matter movement and police violence. In many instances, these protests took place without fines and without police shutting them down, even in cases where the protests were in violation of public health restrictions.

At times there was some bizarre doublespeak from public health officials condemning protests related to COVID-19 restrictions while encouraging other types of protest. In particular, Black Lives Matter protests in the wake of the horrific murder of George Floyd proceeded, with some public health officials commending the protests and politicians even participating.[24] To be sure, George Floyd's murder warranted public outrage and protest. However, the condemnation of protests against COVID-19 restrictions as "super-spreader" events while BLM protests were celebrated and attended by politicians was hypocritical. If the government is to prohibit public assemblies on the grounds of public health risk, it can't pick and choose between assemblies on the basis of the cause, no matter how worthy it is.

Beaudoin v. British Columbia

Public protests and the right to peaceful assembly were both issues in the case of *Beaudoin v. British Columbia*. Alain Beaudoin, an activist who had organized public protests in British Columbia, was protesting what he called unnecessary and "draconian" restrictions by the government in the name of safety during the pandemic. At each of his protests on December 1, 5, and 12, 2020, Beaudoin was issued a ticket for violating public health gathering restrictions. He subsequently argued that the protests were peaceful political events that took place outdoors. He further argued that the government orders prohibiting gatherings (in this case, protests), violated several of his rights, including the rights to freedom of assembly, expression, and religion.[25]

The *Beaudoin* case was important because the government conceded that Beaudoin's right to freedom of assembly was violated. The court accepted this concession and found that the violation was not saved by section 1 of the *Charter*. The violation could not be justified in a free and democratic society. The concession by the government appears to have been made because in February of 2021 the provincial government amended the public health orders so that they no longer prohibited outdoor assemblies for protests. In changing the order, B.C.'s public health officer, Dr. Bonnie Henry, included a new preamble to the updated public health order, which said:[26]

> When exercising my powers to protect the health of the public from the risks posed by COVID-19, **I am aware of my obligation to choose measures that limit the Charter rights and freedoms of British Columbians less intrusively,** where this is consistent with public health principles. **In consequence, I am not prohibiting outdoor assemblies for the purpose of communicating a position on a matter of public interest or controversy,** subject to my expectation that persons organizing or attending such assembly will take the steps and put in place the measures recommended in the guidelines posted on my website in order to limit the risk of transmission of COVID-19. [emphasis added]

The court granted Mr. Beaudoin a declaration that the orders he was ticketed under were of no force and effect. For procedural reasons, however, the court did not adjudicate on the validity of the tickets themselves.

While this judgment could be seen as a partial victory for the right to freedom of assembly, its usefulness as a precedent is limited. While freedom of assembly was treated and acknowledged as its own right, not just as a second-order right to freedom of expression or religion, there was no further analysis by the court because the government had conceded that the right had been violated.[27] While ultimately this was a rare win for freedom of assembly during the COVID-19 pandemic, the decision did not lead to any interesting findings about how section 2(c) claims should be considered by the courts. In short, the court yet again avoided an opportunity to develop section 2(c) jurisprudence.

One interesting point to note about the revised preamble to the B.C. order is that it contains an acknowledgment of the right to assembly, and that explicit statement by Dr Henry that outdoor protests would be permitted. Yet while this change was made in British Columbia, other provinces still maintained gathering restrictions, including for outdoor protests. Other provinces, notably Ontario, had orders containing no such preamble affirming the right to protest. These Ontario orders were challenged in a case called *Baber v. Ontario (Attorney General)*.

Baber v. Ontario (Attorney General)

On January 15, 2021, Ontario Member of Provincial Parliament Roman Baber was ejected from the Progressive Conservative caucus following his public release of a letter[28] sent to Premier Doug Ford titled "The lockdown is deadlier than COVID." In the letter, Baber called on the premier to end the lockdown, citing the "catastrophic toll" it was taking on Ontarians. Baber wrote that "the lockdown isn't working [. . .] It's causing an avalanche of suicides, overdoses, bankruptcies and divorces, and takes an immense toll on our children."

In a statement announcing Baber's ejection from the PC caucus, Premier Ford described his statements as "irresponsible" and "misinformation," and said "there is no room for political ideology in our fight against COVID-19."[29]

In March 2021, as a newly independent MPP for York Centre, Baber began a legal challenge to certain gathering restrictions together with a group that he incorporated, called Lift the Lockdowns. Baber is a lawyer and practised civil litigation before being elected to the Ontario legislature. In his application, he argued that the fifty-person outdoor gathering restriction in place at the time under the *Reopening Ontario*

Act was a violation of the *Charter* rights to freedom of religion, expression, assembly, and association, and hampered the ability of citizens to "protest, pray and gather outdoors."[30]

The application was heard in May 2021 by Justice Vella at the Ontario Superior Court of Justice, and the decision was released in August.[31] While acknowledging that Baber's application raised important issues about whether Ontario's various public health restrictions violated fundamental freedoms guaranteed in the *Charter*, including the right to freedom of assembly, Justice Vella dismissed the case because she found that Mr. Baber and Lift the Lockdown had not met the test for public interest standing.

And so another opportunity to clarify the law on freedom of assembly in the unique context of the pandemic was lost on procedural grounds.

THE FREEDOM CONVOY AS A PUBLIC PROTEST

The most high-profile protests in Canada related to pandemic restrictions involved the Freedom Convoy that took place in late January and early February 2022. The legal issues around the protests and the Freedom Convoy are distinguishable from the other protest cases mentioned earlier in this chapter because the overwhelming question in those cases was how government restrictions on public gatherings affect the right to protest. In contrast, the legal questions about the Freedom Convoy are more typical questions about the right to protest, including the acceptable level of disruption a protest may cause and questions about physical blockades.

From the outset, it is important to know that there are internal limits on the right to freedom of assembly. The *Charter* protects the right to *peaceful* assembly; it does not protect riots and gatherings that seriously disturb the peace.[32] The right to freedom of assembly, along with freedom of expression, does not include the right to physically impede or blockade lawful activities.[33]

In addition to those internal limits, the *Charter* allows for rights to be limited under section 1 if those limits can be demonstrably justified in a free and democratic society. So the place, time, and manner of restrictions on protests can be justified.

This has several implications for the Convoy, which consisted of hundreds of big-rig trucks that blockaded roads in downtown Ottawa and at several key border crossings across Canada. The first is the question of whether a blockade is even protected by the right to freedom of assembly (the case law suggests it is not).[34] Second, to the extent that the Freedom Convoy protests violated federal and provincial laws governing blockades and impeding traffic, as well as municipal bylaws about noise and parking, those laws were in all likelihood reasonable limits on the right to freedom of assembly.

For example, blocking highways has long been illegal under provincial legislation. In Ontario the *Highway Traffic Act* allows police officers to order the removal of vehicles from highways (which the Act defines to include all public roadways) where they believe the removal is necessary to ensure the orderly movement of traffic or to prevent injury or damage to persons and property. Section 134.1 of the Act grants police the power to remove those vehicles at the cost of the owner, operator, and driver of the vehicle.[35]

There is a balance to be struck here, of course. Protests may violate bylaws and regulations governing the use of public space. But while these bylaws and regulations may be completely proper and justifiable in most contexts, in others, such as a demonstration, they may not be reasonable limits. It may even be improper for police to try to shut down a protest for a minor bylaw infraction, depending on the circumstances. Law Professor Ryan Alford has written that bylaws and regulations may sometimes need to give way so that demonstrators can have their voices heard.[36] Political demonstrations should not be suppressed in the name of minor bylaws that may not be a reasonable limit on the right to assembly and expression. For example, parking a vehicle on a public street as part of a public demonstration is a commonly accepted tactic—and was used by the trucks parked in downtown Ottawa as part of the Convoy. However, the balancing under section 1 of the *Charter* to determine whether a limit is reasonable is fact-based. For example, a vehicle cannot remain parked on a public street indefinitely as part of a protest. Ultimately, in our view, the city was justified in having the Freedom Convoy trucks removed.

There were also major complaints raised by residents of Ottawa who had their lives disrupted by the noisy and extended Freedom Convoy protests. The fact is, protests can interfere with bystanders' rights, including their ability to walk unimpeded on a sidewalk or even the quiet enjoyment of their home. The Freedom Convoy protests were extremely disruptive, with loud air horns honking and even occasional fireworks being let off at night. This went on for a long time, and there is no doubt it was distressing for people who lived in Ottawa. One can have sympathy for this situation, but the fact is, protests can be disruptive, and even disruptive protests are constitutionally protected.

The question about the noise comes down to section 1 of the *Charter*. In our view, the government would have been justified in enforcing noise restrictions. Ultimately, however, it was not the government, but the residents of downtown Ottawa, who stopped the horns by obtaining an injunction. The police then enforced this injunction (with varying levels of success).

Another important consideration is that enforcing existing laws has implications for the rule of law in Canada. As we will explore in Chapter 11, one of the underlying principles of Canadian law is that everyone is governed by the same law. While peaceful assembly is protected by the *Charter*, protests can sometimes go too far and stray into constitutionally unprotected forms of assembly, such as blockades. Canadians who may have supported the Freedom Convoy ought to ask themselves how they feel about highway blockades of logging roads in British Columbia, or the prolonged rail blockades by Indigenous protesters that occurred throughout Canada in early 2020.[37] Likewise, supporters of those blockades should ask themselves if they viewed the blockades of the Freedom Convoy the same way as the blockades they supported. Canada has one law that applies to all Canadians equally, and the law should be enforced consistently without regard to ideology.

It is also important to acknowledge that individuals who participate in protests may commit offences. While the act of protesting is protected, individuals who break laws may be prosecuted. While civil disobedience can be a form of expression that communicates a political message, it can still attract the possibility of prosecution. Protesters need to be aware of this when they choose to engage in civil disobedience, especially if some of that disobedience involves behaviour that violates the *Criminal Code*, such as the destruction of property. The ability of the police to enforce the *Criminal Code* during a protest is important for the rule of law in Canada. The best way of doing this is for police to prioritize the prevention of violence and destruction of property by enforcing the law against individuals. Not by attempting to shut down non-violent protests wholesale.

In the context of the Freedom Convoy, the protests were constitutionally protected speech and assembly as long as they were peaceful. The blockades were likely not a protected form of assembly. However, in our view the protracted nature of the demonstrations ultimately did justify enforcement, and that enforcement was a reasonable limit on Convoy protesters' right to freedom of assembly and expression.

The conduct of some individual protesters also likely warranted criminal charges for mischief, although certainly the police had this power to enforce bylaws and the *Criminal Code* all along. Most significantly, there was no need for the government to invoke the *Emergencies Act* in order to lay charges or end the protests. The use of that extraordinary law and the lead-up to its use will be considered in the next two chapters.

CHAPTER 3
THE FREEDOM CONVOY

Tamara Lich and her husband lost their jobs on the same day. She worked in an oil and gas services company in Alberta, and because of pandemic hardships her employer needed to lay off a large number of staff. Her parents' business in the trucking industry was also being impacted by restrictions. Tamara began to fear that provinces would restrict travel and she would not be able to visit her parents and grandmother in Saskatchewan or her daughter in Manitoba. After just under two years of dealing with restrictions, for Lich and many others, enough was enough.

Tamara Lich is an unlikely leader of a group of rowdy truckers. A petite blonde fitness enthusiast and grandmother, she plays guitar and seems taller than her barely five-foot height thanks to her favourite heeled boots. Her charisma is undeniable. She rose as one of the most prominent figures in the Freedom Convoy of January and February 2022, a group of long-haul truckers and their supporters who travelled to Ottawa to protest the two years of pandemic restrictions. Lich has said that while many people viewed her as the Convoy's leader, she didn't feel that she was. But Lich ultimately managed the Freedom Convoy's $10 million GoFundMe donations that had been sent in by supporters across Canada[1] and was a lead speaker in many of the Convoy-organized press conferences. When the protests ended, she was criminally charged with mischief, obstructing police, and counselling others to commit mischief and intimidation.[2] She also had her bank account frozen by orders made under the Trudeau government's use of the *Emergencies Act*, which was invoked in February 2022.

Months after the Convoy ended, Lich wept as she talked about why she got involved in the movement. She explained how she had heard from families that became homeless and were living in their vehicles because they had lost their jobs and homes as a result of pandemic-related lockdowns. She had also heard from families who were barred from visiting their elderly loved ones in care homes—and the horror of knowing that their loved ones could die alone in isolation. She heard from families who had lost loved ones to suicide, and from thousands of people who found hope in the Convoy movement.[3] Lich said the Convoy protests were "the biggest love fest I've ever participated in."[4]

For Lich and her supporters, their time in Ottawa felt like a carnival. There were blaring horns, blasting music, bouncy castles, and inflatable hot tubs in the street. There was a flatbed truck that served as an impromptu stage for concerts, speeches and church services. There was frantic and ecstatic socialization of people who had spent the last two years isolated.

But not everyone saw the same things. Two people walking through the Freedom Convoy in downtown Ottawa in early 2022 could easily have come away with wildly different interpretations of the event.

Victoria De La Ronde is a retired federal government employee.[5] She lives in downtown Ottawa and is visually impaired and uses a guide cane. During the protest she experienced anxiety and sleep deprivation from the constant noise of honking and idling trucks. The smell of diesel fuel permeated her downtown apartment. She lost some of her hearing as a result of the extended and inescapable noise of the trucks. To lose hearing on top of her existing vision loss is tragic.

Ms. Lich's experience with the Freedom Convoy was dramatically different from Ms. De La Ronde's experience, and we should be careful to avoid painting the protest with a broad brush. It was not purely a family-friendly love fest, but it was also not a hate-motivated insurrection intent on overthrowing the government. The most accurate way to describe the Freedom Convoy is as a large and unusually long and disruptive protest about COVID-19 restrictions that was poorly managed by police.

In this chapter we will examine:

- the background of the Freedom Convoy;
- what the protests involved once they were under way;
- the police response to the Freedom Convoy;
- the border blockades;
- the contrasting views of the Freedom Convoy; and the end of the protests.

BACKGROUND OF THE FREEDOM CONVOY

The Freedom Convoy emerged as a protest movement following nearly two years of pandemic-related restrictions across Canada. At the most basic level, the protests can be understood as sparked by a newly imposed vaccine mandate for cross-border commercial truckers. But this policy is better understood as the straw that broke the camel's back. The protest was in fact motivated by widespread exhaustion with public health measures and restrictions in the name of COVID-19 prevention, and vaccination mandates in particular. This was also all in the context of rising populism in Canada and globally.[6]

In late 2021 various health measures were still in force across Canada. In Ontario businesses were still dealing with shutdowns. Border restrictions on unvaccinated travellers were still in force. And the federal government was publicly contemplating a vaccine mandate for previously exempt cross-border truckers.[7] This policy would put an estimated 10 to 15 per cent of cross-border commercial truckers off the road, according to the Canadian Trucking Alliance.[8]

On November 16, 2021, a trucker named Brigitte Belton posted a video on TikTok complaining about an interaction she'd had with border officials over masking. The fifty-two-year-old Ontario trucker was alone in her truck with her dog, and unmasked. A Canadian border agent threatened to arrest her for being unmasked, even though Belton was alone and shared that she was medically exempt from masking on the basis of asthma and psychological trauma as a domestic violence survivor.[9] Belton was let go with a warning, but shaken by the experience, she recorded a TikTok describing what happened.

Belton's video went viral. Three days later, on November 19, when the federal government announced it was considering a vaccine mandate for truckers, Belton ended up connecting with several other individuals who, because of that video, went on to become Convoy organizers. She recounted her experience to author and journalist Andrew Lawton in his book *The Freedom Convoy*, saying "At that point I was done. I was done with life. I just knew I couldn't live in Canada in an open-air jail."[10]

The federal government went back and forth on whether the mandate for truckers would be imposed. Ultimately, on January 13, 2022, Canadian officials announced that the new measures would come into effect on January 15, 2022.[11] Following the government announcement, Belton participated in a Facebook Live event with several other people, including two men, Chris Barber and James Bauder. During this Facebook Live discussion they planned a route and logistics for a convoy to Ottawa. On January 14, Tamara Lich set up a GoFundMe page for the protest.

On January 22 and 23, Freedom Convoy participants began departing from British Columbia and making their way to Ottawa, picking up participants along the way. By January 28 the first trucks began to arrive in Ottawa. Ottawa police Chief Peter Sloly had anticipated the convoy lasting for a weekend at most, or a few days more. However, Ontario Provincial Police (OPP) intelligence reports (called Henden Reports) anticipated a longer duration for the protests.[12] The Ottawa Hotel Association and Ottawa business groups also raised concerns with Ottawa police and city hall early on that the protests would last longer.[13]

During televised remarks on January 27, Prime Minister Justin Trudeau discussed the new trucker mandate and described the Freedom Convoy as a "small fringe minority" with "unacceptable views."[14] This statement incensed many in the movement, and it continues to be frequently cited by those who were involved in or supported the Convoy. Not only were the remarks incendiary, they were condescending, ignored the frustrations of many thousands of Canadians who were fed up with pandemic restrictions, and demonstrated a kind of elitism and intolerance to any divergence from the government's approved viewpoints. The phrase #WeTheFringe became a rallying cry for the Convoy, with branded hoodies and touques even appearing for sale online.[15] Over a year later, the Public Order Emergency Commission (POEC) that looked into the government's use of the *Emergencies Act* in response to the Freedom Convoy was critical of the prime minister for this divisive language,[16] and the prime minister subsequently said he regretted making these statements.[17] Following the release of the POEC report, Prime Minister Trudeau conceded "Yeah, I wish I had said that differently. As I look back on that, and as I've reflected on it over the past months, [. . .] I wish I had phrased it differently."[18]

THE PROTESTS WERE UNDER WAY

The arrival of the first Convoy protesters in Ottawa on January 28 was chaotic. Initially, Ottawa Police Service managed to facilitate the orderly arrival of protesters, directing vehicles onto Wellington Street, which is runs directly in front of Parliament and the Prime Minister's Office. Protesters on arrival were initially cooperative and followed the directions given by the police.[19] But this would soon change.

The Ottawa Police Service's traffic plan quickly collapsed, and they lost the ability to manage the protests in the downtown core.[20] At the protest's peak there were more than five hundred trucks occupying downtown Ottawa, especially around government buildings including Parliament.[21] According to the Ottawa Police Service, there were 5,000 to 18,000 protesters on January 29.[22] Heavy equipment was able to enter downtown, including a boom truck, which is a heavy flatbed truck used to lift and deliver construction equipment.[23] The police were unable to issue tickets, lay charges, or make arrests, which contributed to a sense of lawlessness.

Once the protests were under way they were highly disruptive. Big rig horns rang late into the night, until they were (mostly) stopped on February 7 by an injunction obtained by Ottawa residents.[24] Trucks were parked in residential neighbourhoods and even on sidewalks. Large stages were set up on the truck beds of the vehicles parked on Wellington Street. On some nights, fireworks were set off. The protests included a broad cross-section of Canadians, motivated to attend for a variety of reasons. For many, attendance at the protests went far beyond the new trucker mandate and represented more widespread frustration and opposition to the government's extended COVID-19 restrictions. On weekends, many more protesters would join, while the more hard-core and committed group stayed throughout the week. Some truckers slept in their vehicles while others stayed at local hotels.

There were also reports of upsetting incidents. One protester climbed the cenotaph at the National War Memorial,[25] and another danced on the Tomb of the Unknown Soldier. While the woman who danced on the Tomb expressed regret later and did not face charges,[26] this incident was widely condemned and contributed to public animosity towards the Convoy. Some protesters reportedly harassed a local homeless shelter demanding food, and others crowded the largest mall in Ottawa (the Rideau Centre) unmasked, and ultimately the mall was forced to shut down.[27] And as we will discuss in more detail later, some protesters reportedly displayed extremist symbols, including swastikas.

The trucks themselves were the unique and powerful feature of the Freedom Convoy protests, because by their nature they are large, intrusive, and difficult to move. This presented a unique challenge for police, who had instructed the trucks to park in the downtown core, where they became entrenched for weeks. This was just the first of many apparent policing miscalculations and failures.

POLICE RESPONSE TO THE FREEDOM CONVOY

The response by the Ottawa Police Service to the Freedom Convoy has been criticized by many, including politicians from all levels of government (municipal, provincial, and federal) as well as the POEC, which issued its report one year after the protests.

Part of the lack of enforcement can be explained as a good-faith effort by police to respect the protesters' constitutionally protected right to freedom of expression. Ottawa Chief of Police Peter Sloly testified during the Rouleau Commission that he believed the police could not prevent the protesters from coming into Ottawa because the truckers had a *Charter*-protected right to protest. "I'm a police officer, not a lawyer," he said.[28]

Although it is laudable that the police were cognizant of the importance of protecting the *Charter* rights of protesters, the protests were also violating a number of laws (as discussed in Chapter 2). And to the extent that protesters were acting unlawfully, Ottawa police should have ended the extended blockades. But for weeks the police failed to use the available legal tools to do so.

The hands-off enforcement response to the protests by the Ottawa police also needs to be understood in the historical context of modern policing. In particular, the G20 anti-globalization protests of 2010 were a crucial impetus for a change in modern policing policy. The G20 protests in Toronto were extremely wild, with windows in the downtown core smashed by black-masked protesters and a police cruiser lit on fire at the intersection in the heart of the city's financial district. But equally wild was the government response.

Canadians saw news clips of police officers with obscured badge numbers beating a defenceless man. They saw footage of police harassing journalists. They saw interviews with bystanders who were swept up by police in a strategy called "kettling," which is used to box people in on public streets. Toronto police kettled protesters on Toronto streets for hours. This police conduct thoroughly shocked the public. In the end, the Toronto Police Services Board was sued by some of the people who were arrested and settled the lawsuit for $16.5 million.[29]

According to Professor Ryan Alford,[30] the public backlash against police brutality during the Toronto G20 protests set a pattern for a decade of hands-off approaches to protests, with police focusing instead on de-escalation. The experience with the G20 was likely formative for Ottawa Police Chief Peter Sloly in particular. He was Deputy Chief in Toronto during the G20 protests, and documents from the POEC suggest that he was hesitant with the Freedom Convoy because of his experience with those G20 protests.[31]

There was another reason for the delayed response to the protests by Ottawa police: the internal power struggle between Ottawa police and the RCMP. To begin, Chief Sloly and other senior officers failed to review crucial intelligence about the protests contained in the OPP Henden reports.[32] Those reports clearly indicated that the protesters planned to stay far longer than Chief Sloly had anticipated. As well, testimony from the POEC revealed that Chief Sloly acted territorially over sharing decision-making authority with the RCMP and OPP officers who were sent to assist the Ottawa Police Service. One senior Ottawa police officer recounted how Sloly had described these officers from other forces as being controlled by their "political masters."[33] The Rouleau Report released one year after the invocation of the *Emergencies Act* also found that Chief Sloly had a "mixed" attitude towards integrating forces, and that he seemed concerned that an integrated OPP/RCMP planning cell was being used to "undermine" him and the Ottawa Police Service.[34]

In addition, the Ottawa Police Service's request for 1,800 additional officers from across Canada lacked specific and crucial details. For example, RCMP Commissioner Brenda Lucki testified that the public demand for 1,800 officers made by Sloly and Ottawa Mayor Jim Watson caught the RCMP off guard.[35] She testified at the POEC that "we didn't have those discussions with chief Sloly up to that time,"[36] and that they didn't know that the Ottawa Police Service was looking for such a large number of officers until the demand was made public.

What is more, the Ottawa Police Service did not even initially explain why the 1,800 additional officers were needed in Ottawa, or provide a plan for what those officers would be doing.[37] OPP Superintendent Caron Pardy testified that the request by the Ottawa police effectively amounted to saying "just send us 1,800 officers" without detailing what they would do, where they would stay, or even what they would eat.[38] Pardy explained that members of other police forces cannot just be taken away from their own communities to sit around in Ottawa waiting for a plan.[39]

The Ottawa Police Service also failed to effectively negotiate with the Freedom Convoy protesters and undermined their own negotiation team, a group called the Police Liaison Team. The negotiating units were not properly deployed and spent a lot of time just sitting around waiting for direction.[40] And once they were deployed the conduct of other officers in the Ottawa Police Service would undermine negotiated agreements with the protesters.

For example, on February 6 the negotiating unit had made an agreement with protest leaders to remove fuel that was being stockpiled at the Freedom Convoy logistics site at Coventry Road. The police believed that stockpiling thousands of litres of fuel created a major safety risk. The Ottawa police negotiating unit was able to reach an agreement to move the fuel, but two hours into the negotiations they learned that the Ottawa Police Public Order Unit was going to conduct an enforcement operation. The negotiators tried to stop the operation, but it proceeded anyway. The result was that the Ottawa police moved into the area and arrested protesters as they were removing fuel, pursuant to the agreement they'd made with the negotiators. The protesters viewed this as a betrayal, and the negotiating teams were demoralized.[41]

This was not the only time the Ottawa police undermined their own negotiation unit. On another occasion, a faction of protesters had agreed with the Ottawa police negotiators to move trucks off residential streets and onto Wellington Street. Once the trucks were prepared to move, however, they were blocked by other Ottawa police.[42] These experiences undermined trust and the ability of those negotiating units to function effectively. This matters because the effective use of negotiating units could have been key in resolving the entrenched protest.

Making matters worse was the fact that this was also an especially difficult time for the Ottawa police. There was infighting among senior officers; some senior officers had recently retired, leaving leadership gaps. The police force was short-staffed as a result of the pandemic, which placed a greater burden on the officers who were working the protests.[43] The sheer exhaustion of many good Ottawa officers was obvious.

With all that said, the Ottawa Police Service was not the only party to be blamed for allowing the Freedom Convoy protests to establish illegal blockades that persisted for weeks: the federal and provincial governments as well as other police forces were also responsible. First, although there were problems with how Ottawa police made their request for 1,800 officers, there was a real need for additional officers and that need was not effectively met. The RCMP sent only 250 officers, who ended up guarding the governor general's residence and the prime minister's cottage.[44] Second, the failure of Ontario political leaders to come to a tripartite planning table of senior government officials from the federal, provincial, and municipal governments made coordination between Ontario and Ottawa police even more difficult. Ontario's absence made coordination among the governments organizing a response even more of a challenge. The report of the POEC accused the province of "abandoning" Ottawa.[45]

Further, all levels of police misunderstood the Ontario *Police Services Act*. RCMP Commissioner Lucki testified at the POEC that she was told by OPP Commissioner Carrique that Ottawa's requests for more officers needed to go to the OPP first, and when exhausted it could go to another local police service, all before the RCMP could respond to it.[46] The problem was that these understandings by the RCMP and OPP commissioners were wrong. The *Police Services Act* does not require a municipal police force like the Ottawa Police Service to seek help first from the OPP and then from the RCMP. Nothing in the text of the Act prohibits the Ottawa police from asking for help from the OPP and RCMP simultaneously. Had police correctly understood the Act, Ottawa police would have been positioned to obtain help from other forces without getting a bureaucratic runaround and could have been better able to clear the protests.

There were also tools available under the Ontario *Emergency Management and Civil Protection Act* and the *Criminal Code* that were not effectively used. For example, the legislation could have empowered the government to gain access to tow trucks and compensate and indemnify the drivers. The province could also have created a restricted zone in Ottawa using this legislation. Although the province of Ontario invoked this emergency legislation on February 11, these tools were not used. All of this matters because there were many ways in which Ottawa could have effectively cleared the Convoy protests without invoking the *Emergencies Act*.

BORDER BLOCKADES

The protests were not limited to Ottawa. There were also significant protests at borders and major cities in other parts of Canada. The metropolitan protests were well attended but did not cause the same level of disruption as they did in Ottawa. Notably, the Toronto police prevented large vehicles from entering the downtown core.

The border protests presented a significant problem. These protests took place in border towns in Ontario (Windsor), Manitoba (Emerson), and Alberta (Coutts). There was no official connection between protesters at borders and the protesters in Ottawa, in part due to the organic nature of the Freedom Convoy protests.

The border blockades had a serious economic impact. According to Bill Anderson, director of the University of Windsor's Cross Border Institute, the blockade prevented anywhere from $3 to $6 billion worth of goods from crossing the border over the course of just one week.[47] Blockades of such magnitude, while sending a strong signal to federal and provincial governments regarding the resolve of the Convoy, also risked putting out of work many Canadians who rely on cross-border trade for their livelihood. The BBC reported that some major car manufacturers, including Toyota and Ford, temporarily shut down several plants in Canada as a result of disruptions relating to the cross-border Freedom Convoy blockades.[48]

Coutts, Alberta

On January 29, as the Ottawa protests were just beginning, a group of about one hundred protesters and truckers in Alberta blockaded the border crossing at Coutts, one of the busiest ports of entry west of the Great Lakes. In response to the blockade, Alberta Premier Jason Kenney affirmed the right to engage in lawful protest[49] but asked the protesters to avoid creating road hazards. "Canadians have a democratic right to engage in lawful protests. I urge those involved in this truck convoy protest to do so as safely as possible, and not to create road hazards which could lead to accidents or unsafe conditions for other drivers,"[50] Kenney said. Additionally, Premier Kenney noted that Alberta's *Critical Infrastructure Defence Act* gives police and prosecutors additional penalties they could levy to address blockades of highways and other infrastructure.[51]

On February 1, police stopped negotiations with the Coutts protesters and demanded that protesters leave the highway. On February 14, the RCMP stepped in and arrested thirteen people, seizing long guns, handguns, body armour, a large quantity of ammunition, and high-capacity magazines.[52] Four men were subsequently charged with conspiracy to murder RCMP officers.[53] Plans to clear Coutts were well under way before the *Emergencies Act* was invoked on the 14th, and ultimately the blockade was completely cleared by February 15.

The Ambassador Bridge, Ontario

There was also a major blockade in Ontario, at the Ambassador Bridge connecting Windsor and Detroit. This is one of Canada's busiest and most important trade crossings, and it was completely blocked by protesters on February 7.

Ontario Premier Doug Ford was deeply concerned about the Ambassador Bridge blockade. On a call with Prime Minister Trudeau about the protests and border blockades, Ford told Trudeau that the police had a plan, but that he could not direct them. "They'll act, but without directing them it's hard to describe their game plan," Ford said of the OPP. "This is critical, I hear you. I'll be up their a** with a wire brush."[54] The contrast between Ford's involvement in the resolution of the Ambassador Bridge blockade and the situation in Ottawa, which was also in his jurisdiction, was apparent.

On the morning of February 12, aided by the OPP and the RCMP, Windsor police began to clear out the blockade using new powers under Ontario's emergency legislation. Despite the heavy police presence of joint forces in Windsor, by the end of the day on February 12, most protesters remained, albeit in a smaller area further away from the bridge. On the morning of February 13, joint police forces took control of the area and began to make arrests, and by evening the bridge was cleared and reopened.[55] In total, forty-two arrests related to the Windsor blockage were made, and thirty-seven vehicles were seized.[56]

FAMILY-FRIENDLY STREET PARTY OR IDEOLOGICALLY MOTIVATED EXTREMISTS? THE CONTRASTING VIEWS OF THE FREEDOM CONVOY

As discussed in the introduction, it is impossible to paint the Ottawa Freedom Convoy protests with one brush. It is not accurate to say that the protest was just a "love fest"[57] or that the protesters were all ideologically motivated extremists with "unacceptable views."[58] Like any protest, the Freedom Convoy protests attracted a broad range of individuals for different reasons. Journalist Matt Gurney wrote "depending on which person you're using as your explainer for the local vibe, you could reasonably walk away convinced that most of what was happening in Ottawa was a pretty big party, or a hostile invasion by thugs and harassers."[59]

As we have seen in this chapter, some protesters were cheerful and played music, set up barbeques, inflatable hot tubs, and bouncy castles for children, and danced in the streets. The protests were described by some observers as having a "carnival atmosphere"[60] and some protesters brought their children and families. Many people were happy to be together and socializing after many months of isolation. Gurney visited the downtown Ottawa site of the protest and wrote that "the overall vibe was quite friendly . . . The protesters are eager to make eye contact and to chat about everything—the weather (warmer!), the Super Bowl, and, oh, how Trudeau has to go and the pandemic is a lie. And how about those Maple Leafs!"[61]

It was also true that some protesters conducted themselves badly. Gurney explained that "if you want to find evidence that the protesters are peaceful, ordinary, frustrated Canadians who came to Ottawa to make their displeasure known, you can find those folks. And if you want evidence that the protesters are angry, racist, far-right agitators here to attempt to overthrow the government, you can find that, too."[62]

Some protesters were highly aggressive towards local Ottawa residents. Ottawa City Councillor Mathieu Fleury alleged that some protesters pulled masks off the faces of members of the public.[63] As discussed above, one protester danced on the Tomb of the Unknown Soldier,[64] and there were reports that some protesters looking for food had harassed the staff at a local Ottawa homeless shelter.[65] Some of the protesters, including the high-profile protester Pat King, had a track record of making racist and xenophobic comments. King also had a record of making violent and inflammatory comments; for example, stating that the pandemic and protests would end "with bullets."[66] King has subsequently said that this particular comment was hyperbolic.[67] However one of the concerns raised by police intelligence was that this type of violent rhetoric could inspire others to engage in violent acts as "lone wolves."[68] There were many flags saying "Fuck Trudeau," and some protesters carried symbols of hate, including Nazi swastikas. In some cases, the use of the swastika symbol appeared to intend to draw a false and offensive equivalency between the Trudeau government as a perceived authoritarian government and the Nazi regime.[69] In other cases, the swastika was displayed without such context. And even in cases where racist symbols were being used to make some poorly articulated political statement about the prime minister, these symbols are very frightening and disturbing to many (indeed most) Canadians.

The fact that the Freedom Convoy protest attracted some individuals with extreme, ignorant, or offensive views is not unique. This is a feature of every protest and does not necessarily reflect the vast majority of people who participated in the protests. The protests went on for three weeks, and there was no rioting, no significant property damage, and not a single person seriously injured. In fact, in his testimony at the POEC former Police Chief Sloly stated that the protests were noteworthy for their absence of violence.[70]

This is all to say that the Convoy protests were messy and complicated, and any attempt to characterize their motives simplistically would be a mistake. Simply put, the protests were highly disruptive, and they were designed to be disruptive, both to gain media and political attention and so that the disruptiveness could be used as a kind of leverage. This is not unique and is a feature of most protests. What made this protest particularly unique was the use of big-rig trucks and the failure of police.

THE PROTESTS END

The right to freedom of expression does not include the right to indefinitely block public roads, and reasonable limits on the right mean protesters may not blare horns for days on end. The right to assembly comes with the caveat that it is the right to *peaceful* assembly. While the right to freedom of expression encompasses more than standing quietly in a park with a protest sign, Canada is also governed by the rule of law. No one is above the law, and the law applies equally to all Canadians. While peaceful assembly is protected by the *Charter*, protests can sometimes go too far and stray into constitutionally unprotected forms of assembly when they restrict the freedoms of others. And the rights are subject to reasonable limits under section 1 of the *Charter*.

Blocking highways has long been illegal under provincial legislation. Police and officials were within their authority to end the protests and clear out the streets. Especially as the protests wore on. However, the police response was badly lacking. This failure played into the rationale for what became one of the largest and most unjustified government acts of the pandemic, and that was the prime minister's illegal invocation of the *Emergencies Act*. That is what we will explore next.

CHAPTER 4
THE EMERGENCIES ACT

On Valentine's Day of 2022, Prime Minister Justin Trudeau held a news conference where he announced that his government was invoking the extraordinarily powerful federal *Emergencies Act* in response to the 2022 Freedom Convoy. Standing with four masked senior cabinet ministers in front of a row of Canadian flags, the prime minister announced that "The scope of these measures will be time limited, geographically targeted, as well as reasonable and proportionate to the threats they are meant to address."[1] "This is about keeping Canadians safe, protecting jobs, and restoring faith in our institutions."[2]

The *Emergencies Act* is an extraordinary law. It vests tremendous power with the federal cabinet, including the power to make new criminal law by executive order, without parliamentary debate or advance notice. In the decades since the *Emergencies Act* was passed in 1988, Canada has weathered terrorist attacks, economic hardship, and an unprecedented global health pandemic, all without ever resorting to the incredible powers contained in the *Emergencies Act*. Such powers must be exercised with restraint in a liberal democracy. The prime minister's February 14 announcement ended those years of restraint. The law was invoked not in response to a natural disaster or the outbreak of war, but to a series of disruptive but largely peaceful protests.

Using the powers of the *Emergencies Act*, cabinet created two new categories of criminal prohibitions by regulation, in short, making it a crime to participate in or materially assist a public assembly that could

38

reasonably lead to a breach of the peace. What is more, cabinet created new criminal powers related to financial matters that required banks to monitor bank accounts and freeze the accounts of anyone participating in or assisting the Convoy, and also to report information about these accounts to the Canadian Security Intelligence Service (CSIS) and the RCMP. Anyone who violated these prohibitions potentially faced up to five years of imprisonment.

Yet the context in which the *Emergencies Act* was invoked smacked of political motivation rather than a true national crisis. When the *Emergencies Act* was invoked, the border blockades had already been cleared. Windsor had been cleared on February 13, and Coutts was being cleared as the *Emergencies Act* was being invoked. Although only the Ottawa protest site remained, and the prime minister had committed to the powers being geographically limited, the declaration of a public order emergency and the powers under it existed nationwide.

In the days following the invocation of the Act, some 290 bank accounts were frozen. The RCMP has said that it only gave banks the names of people directly involved in the Ottawa protests for asset freezing, not the names of *supporters* who donated to the Freedom Convoy.[3] But in a troubling statement about the political targeting of financial accounts, Justice Minister David Lametti told CTV's *Power Play* "If you are a member of a pro-Trump movement who is donating hundreds of thousands of dollars and millions of dollars to this kind of thing, then you ought to be worried."[4]

The push by heavily armoured police to clear the Ottawa blockades began in earnest on February 18. The day before, Convoy organizers Tamara Lich and Chris Barber were arrested. On February 18, Pat King was arrested. And by Sunday February 20, downtown Ottawa was clear.

The Trudeau government's use of the *Emergencies Act* is and was controversial and may be the most severe example of overreach and violation of civil liberties that was seen during the pandemic. It was, in the view of civil liberties organizations like the Canadian Constitution Foundation, an unauthorized use of an extraordinarily powerful law because the legal threshold to use the law was not met. Accordingly, the powers to prohibit assembly and freeze bank accounts were unconstitutional. The normalization of this type of governing by emergency power has the potential to be the greatest and most dangerous threat to civil liberties arising out of the COVID-19 pandemic.

Many civil liberties organizations in Canada, including the Canadian Constitution Foundation, have raised alarms about the use of the *Emergencies Act* in response to the Freedom Convoy, calling the invocation of the Act illegal and unconstitutional. The CCF participated in the public inquiry that followed the declaration of the emergency and also launched a separate court challenge to the use of the Act.

In this chapter we will examine:

- how the protests were cleared;
- the arrest and bail of protest leader Tamara Lich;
- the implications of freezing bank accounts;
- the threshold for invoking the *Emergencies Act*;
- the Public Order Emergency Commission;
- the court challenge to the use of the Act.

POLICE CONDUCT CLEARING THE PROTESTS

By February 18, when the police operation to clear the protests began, most of the Convoy had been consolidated onto Wellington Street. This is the street that runs in front of the lawn of parliament, with government buildings like the Privy Council Office, Senate offices, and the Prime Minister's Office on the other side. It is bookended by the luxury hotel the Chateau Laurier at one end and the National Archives at the other.

The police operation began slowly, on the bitterly cold afternoon of the 18th. Officers gathered in front of the posh Chateau Laurier hotel, forming a line shoulder to shoulder that gradually marched towards the protesters, and the protesters were pushed back into the shrinking area in front of parliament. Every ten to fifteen minutes, the police would press in shouting "Move! Move! Move!"[5] The most noteworthy incident took place on the 18th, when the police brought in horses to push back the crowd and some protesters were trampled in the commotion. During this incident police pepper sprayed the crowd, including independent journalist Andrew Lawton, who was standing to the side.[6] However, aside from this incident, the early police operation seemed to move at a glacial pace. Canadians watching at home had few moments of excitement. Christine was watching live television coverage late at night on the 18th as an undercover CBC reporter walked back and forth in the so-called "red zone" in front of Wellington Street. The footagewas was dull, merely showing people standing around idly in the snow.

At 3:30 a.m. on the morning of February 19, protesters began shovelling snow onto fence barricades in an attempt to resist further advancement by the police.[7] Speaking to Vice News, one young protester was asked if he believed a snow wall would help the Convoy stave off police. He quickly replied "no" before pausing and adding "but we have to do something."[8]

On the morning of Saturday February 19, Ottawa police took a more militant approach, brandishing batons as they advanced on the crowd. As they passed the trucks still parked on Wellington Street, they broke the windows and arrested those inside the trucks.[9] Police moved down Wellington arresting protesters who remained. Protester Chris Deering, a wounded combat veteran who served in Afghanistan, described his experience of being arrested.[10] On that Saturday, he stood with a group of around twenty other veterans lined up with linked arms by the War Memorial on Wellington Street. As police closed in on the group, Deering gave a heads-up to the police officers and told them about the injuries he'd sustained serving in the Canadian Armed Forces in Afghanistan. He told the police, "If you arrest me, keep in mind I have a bad back." But he was nevertheless arrested in rough fashion:[11]

> As the police took me down, he kneed me in my side,
> and kicked me in my back. I was laying down. I was
> in the fetal position on my back. He kicked me in my
> ankle and my foot. As I was laying down, I had my

hands completely up. I'm saying, "I'm very peaceful. I'm peaceful. I'm not resisting." I was then punched four or five times in my head. I had a knee on my back to keep myself down. I was on the ground for one-and-a-half to two minutes.

Once Deering got up, he was sent by the police to a processing line where he stood without gloves in the bitter cold for two hours. "I asked the policemen on both sides of me, I said, 'Do you mind, you know my condition, is it okay if I sit or kneel because I'm in chronic pain?' It was obvious. My face was flushed, and I had cried multiple times, and I don't cry ever," said Deering. "It was the worst pain I had felt since I'd been blown up. The fact that I couldn't sit, or stand was, to me, cruel and unusual punishment."[12] After processing, Deering was put in a squad car and told he was being charged with mischief.

By noon on February 19, most protesters had been pushed off Wellington Street, which marked the *de facto* end of the Freedom Convoy. While some protesters remained on side streets, they no longer had access to the large vehicles that had made this protest so unique and entrenched. Some of the Convoy organizers issued a statement[13] asking for time to remove any remaining trucks. By the end, police laid 393 charges against 122 people, charges that included mischief, assault, assaulting an officer, possession of a weapon, and dangerous operation of a motor vehicle.[14] Police also towed away more than 70 vehicles.[15]

ARREST AND DETENTION OF TAMARA LICH

The arrest of Tamara Lich, one of the primary organizers of the 2022 Freedom Convoy, is worthy of some special attention because of her experience being denied bail despite her status as a non-violent first-time offender arrested on minor charges. Her experience should be concerning to civil libertarians. In pure medieval fashion, Lich, a non-violent and first-time offender, was brought into court in shackles.[16]

According to an article published by *The National Post*, Lich was denied bail because of her role in organizing the protests and Lich's "obstinate and disingenuous" statements to the court. This decision was made by Justice Bourgeois, who presided over Lich's first bail hearing. This was a remarkable decision to deny her bail and keep her detained following her arrest.[17] A court can deny bail only in circumstances where it is necessary to assure the accused's attendance in court, to prevent her from reoffending, or due to her offence being especially serious or a strong case against her. Lich did not raise any of these concerns.

Then why did Justice Bourgeois deny Lich's bail? It appears that Justice Bourgeois perceived a risk that if Lich were released, she might have continued to advise people to attend the protests in Ottawa, thereby reoffending by continuing to counsel mischief. The denial of Lich's bail raises deeper questions regarding just how dangerous her mischief actually was. Mischief is not an especially serious charge in comparison to other *Criminal Code* offences that warrant a denial of bail, such as murder or assault causing bodily harm. Justice Bourgeois' decision is even more curious given that the Freedom Convoy protests were non-violent, generally peaceful, and had been cleared by the time of the bail hearing (there were no more protests to encourage). Nonetheless, the Justice appeared satisfied that bail should be denied.

On March 7, 2022, a new judge—Justice Johnston—reviewed Lich's case and decided to grant her bail. According to *Global News*, Justice Johnston found several errors in Justice Bourgeois' judgment, but rejected Lich's argument that these errors were a result of personal bias by Justice Bourgeois against Lich. According to Justice Johnston, the severity of Lich's charges needed to be considered against other *Criminal Code* offences (for example, murder), not based on their impact on Ottawa communities. He also held that although mischief carries a hefty ten-year maximum sentence, it was unlikely that Lich would actually be given such a serious penalty.[18]

While the government's position is that the Freedom Convoy leaders committed serious offences by counselling people to blockade the U.S.-Canada border and downtown Ottawa, the approach taken with Lich looks especially punitive and vindictive in nature. Instead of considering that Lich and others had been charged with non-violent offences such as mischief, the government has tried to treat them as though they are serious, malicious criminals. In Lich's case, the government was walking a tightrope act, moving as close as they could to abuse their discretionary authority without clearly stepping over the boundaries courts would enforce.

THE IMPACT OF FROZEN BANK ACCOUNTS

Perhaps the most novel law-enforcement tools created by the government's use of the *Emergencies Act* were included in the *Emergency Economic Measures Order*. These measures, created by cabinet and without any advance notice or parliamentary debate, allowed bank accounts to be frozen by the federal department of Finance (called Finance Canada) without a court order. They also enabled federal and provincial governments to share information with financial institutions about individuals or entities funding the protests or blockades. That information could also be shared with the RCMP and CSIS.

The *Economic Measures* required banks, crowdfunding websites, and other financial entities to disclose "without delay" to the RCMP and CSIS the existence of property in their possession or control that they had "reason to believe" was held on behalf of someone who was a "designated person." A "designated person" is defined as, among other things, any person participating in an "unlawful assembly." The measures also further required those same financial institutions to disclose any information they had about any transactions that "relate[d]" to the property of designated persons.

Approximately 290 accounts were frozen, most of them targeted by the RCMP.[19] The total value of those accounts was around $8 million.[20]

It is well established that when government authorities like the police or CSIS request private electronic data from non-state entities such as banks, that request can constitute a search under section 8 of the *Charter*, which requires that such searches be reasonable. In this case, we are of the view that the *Economic Measures* constituted an unreasonable search and therefore violated section 8 of the *Charter*. By requiring financial institutions to disclose this information, the state mandated that financial institutions conduct warrantless searches on its behalf. There is no scenario in which the government can justify creating a search power that requires a wholesale financial disclosure to the police and the RCMP—especially when it is predicated on a loose and unconstitutional standard of "any reason to believe" and subject to no system of prior authorization, such as a warrant requirement.

During the Public Order Emergency Commission (POEC) there was a full week of testimony from the Convoy protesters themselves, including its leaders. What stood out most from the protester testimony was the impact of the government orders to freeze bank accounts.

Testimony from protesters revealed that joint spousal bank accounts were frozen. As a result, the spouses of some protesters were unable to buy groceries. One protester testified that his family was unable to pay for necessary medication.[21] Some protesters were unable to make loan payments related to their businesses. Others couldn't make child support payments. There could also be long-term credit implications for people who had their accounts frozen, which was an additional punitive measure. In fact, if the goal was to force the protesters to leave the protests, freezing their accounts actually made this harder, since they had no money for travel.[22]

In freezing the bank accounts of Freedom Convoy protesters, Finance Canada bureaucrats conceded the harmful impact the orders had on the protesters and their families and said that they did not intend to hurt the ability of protesters' families to buy groceries or pay child support. But they admitted that this harm ultimately happened. In hindsight, Finance Canada Assistant Deputy Minister Isabelle Jacques said the department could have done a better job of restricting the power to freeze Freedom Convoy organizers' bank accounts because "the intent was not to unduly affect payments of child support or other payments."[23]

The long-term implications of freezing bank accounts are serious. It created a chilling effect among Canadians. For the CCF, this became clear when we received numerous emails and phone calls from donors who were concerned that their own bank accounts could be frozen if they made donations to our legal challenge to the government's use of the *Emergencies Act*.[24] Even Canadians who may have disagreed with the aim of the Freedom Convoy or the behaviour of its protesters should be concerned about the ways in which the government froze bank accounts and denied citizens access to money for travel, medication, groceries, and child support. Lest it happen to them.

THE THRESHOLD FOR INVOKING THE EMERGENCIES ACT

Invoking the *Emergencies Act* creates a *de facto* constitutional amendment that hands the federal cabinet the most expansive executive powers known to Canadian law. Under the *Emergencies Act*, Cabinet is empowered to unilaterally proclaim a public order emergency. Once Cabinet does so, vast legislative authority is delegated to the Cabinet itself, including the power to create new criminal offences and police powers, without recourse to parliament, advance notice, or public debate.

The *Emergencies Act* creates powers that collide with basic features of Canada's federal constitutional democracy. Canada's past, including our experience with the discredited *War Measures Act*,[25] teaches us that these powers should never be used except as a last resort. Being a power of last resort is in fact built into the language and legal threshold of the *Emergencies Act*. The law is only available when there is a "national emergency," which is defined as a situation that cannot be dealt with effectively under any other law of Canada. Parliament cannot use the *Emergencies Act* as a tool of convenience. It can only be used when there is a national emergency and there are no other laws at the federal, provincial, and/or municipal levels that can address the situation.[26]

THE LAST RESORT CLAUSE: THE HISTORY

This requirement of the "last resort" clause was intentionally put into the *Emergencies Act*. When the law was originally proposed in the 1980s as Bill C-77, it did not contain the last resort clause and it did not even have a statutory definition of "national emergency." At the committee stage, Bill C-77 came under attack for omitting this statutory definition because critics were concerned that adequate safeguards to prevent the unnecessary declaration of an emergency had not been included in the legislation. The government of the day responded to this criticism by proposing a statutory definition of national emergency. But committee members and witnesses were still worried.

As a result, a government member moved to add what became section 3 of the *Emergencies Act*, including the last resort clause. The amendment was supported by the New Democratic Party (NDP). The Chair of the committee, Mr. Derek Blackburn of the NDP, had an exchange about the proposed amendment at committee with a witness, Mr. Bill Snarr, Executive Director of Emergency Preparedness Canada:[27]

> **Mr. Blackburn (Brant):** It says: and that cannot be effectively dealt with under any other law of Canada.
>
> Does that mean the government, when contemplating proclaiming an emergency, would have to make absolutely clear that the *Criminal Code*, for example, could not handle the situation; in other words, if we had a riot or a series of riots in a city and it was not felt that by "reading the Riot Act" and imposing or using the *Criminal Code*, the regular law enforcement agencies could cope with that situation?
>
> **Mr. Snarr:** That is exactly right.

THE LAST RESORT CLAUSE WAS NOT MET IN THIS CASE

By defining a "national emergency" as a situation that cannot be dealt with effectively under any other law of Canada, the "last resort clause" creates a straightforward and stringent requirement. This standard was not met in the case of the Freedom Convoy protests, as existing law was sufficient to deal with them. The *Criminal Code* gave the police the power to arrest and charge protesters for a host of illegal behaviours. Ultimately, when protesters were charged it was under the *Criminal Code*. The border blockades were cleared or in the process of being cleared before the prime minister announced the invocation of the Act. There is no evidence that a single criminal charge was laid under the newly created offences under the *Emergencies Act*.

Police could also have used tools under provincial law, such as the Ontario *Emergency Management and Civil Protection Act*. Ontario had confirmed a state of emergency under that legislation on February 12, and made it illegal to block and impede the movement of goods, people, and services along critical infrastructure. And, of course, there were municipal bylaws available to police. Police could have enforced bylaws relating to noise, fireworks, fire, and vehicles.

As we explored in Chapter 3 there were significant failures in policing during the protests. But even according to multiple law-enforcement officers who testified at the Public Order Emergency Commission, the *Emergencies Act* was not necessary. There is extensive policing and government testimony from the Commission that existing legal tools had not been exhausted and that while perhaps the *Emergencies Act* was helpful, it was not absolutely necessary. While the *Emergencies Act* gave police some special tools that were helpful, being "helpful" is not part of the high threshold that the law requires. What is more, the police ultimately used the same policing plan that had been developed and approved in advance of the invocation of the *Emergencies Act* in order to clear protests.[28] So on this front as well, the *Emergencies Act* was unnecessary.

Former OPP Superintendent Carson Pardy testified at the Public Order Emergency Commission "in my humble opinion, we would have reached the same solution with the plan that we had," which had been approved on February 13.[29] A top Ontario government official, Deputy Solicitor General Mario Di Tommaso, said that the legislation was helpful but "not necessary." Superintendent Robert Bernier, who oversaw a command centre responding to the protests, also said that the emergency powers to compel towing was helpful and beneficial, but not necessary.[30]

Ottawa Interim Police Chief Steve Bell said that the legislation helped create an exclusion zone, but that regardless of the use of the *Emergencies Act* police already had a plan to clear protests. And Ottawa Acting Deputy Chief Trish Ferguson said the legislation "greased the wheels" on the existing police plan, again signalling the same message: helpful, but not necessary. The OPP has stated that "the *Emergencies Act* was not required to formulate an effective police response to this situation," and OPP Commissioner Tom Carrique has said that while the Act was "extremely helpful" for indemnifying tow truck drivers to remove the big rigs on Wellington Street, he felt that police hadn't exhausted all existing powers before the *Emergencies Act* was invoked.

Perhaps the most shocking admission in this regard came from former RCMP Commissioner Brenda Lucki, who testified that she did not believe the existing legal tools had been exhausted. However, despite this being a part of the legal threshold to invoke the *Emergencies Act*, Lucki did not inform cabinet of her opinion. While she had given her opinion in writing to Public Safety Minister Marco Mendicino's chief of staff, this view was not passed on to cabinet. Nor did Lucki raise it verbally during the cabinet meetings.[31] She failed to inform a special cabinet group, called the Incident Response Group, that a police plan to clear the protests had already been approved on February 13—the day before the Act was invoked.[32]

A lot of discussion has flowed around the need for tow trucks to clear the Ottawa protests. The *Emergencies Act* gave police the power to commandeer heavy tow vehicles. However, even that power already existed under the *Criminal Code* and the Ontario *Emergency Management and Civil Protection Act*. And in any event, tow trucks were already arriving in Ottawa before the *Emergencies Act* was invoked.[33] Superintendent Robert Bernier, an Ottawa Event Commander, said that the police had a full fleet of tow trucks ready the day before the *Emergencies Act* was invoked.

As well, American officials had privately offered the Prime Minister's Office tow trucks, but this offer was never publicly disclosed or followed up on.[34] Finally, one of the key sticking points in the plan turned out to be not the availability of tow trucks, but the compensation and indemnification for those tow trucks—a cost issue that could have been resolved with existing legal tools and without recourse to the *Emergencies Act*.

It should also go without saying that in a serious country and a liberal democracy, the lack of available tow trucks should not constitute a national crisis. The weight that this issue of tow trucks has been given should be viewed in context. The *Emergencies Act* was invoked, in part, to deal with a lack of tow trucks, and the law allowed for the new creation of criminal law by executive order. This issue is clearly small compared with the massive hammer that is the *Emergencies Act*.

Another apparently retrospective justification for the *Emergencies Act* was that the Act streamlined police response and cooperation by allowing police officers who came to Ottawa from other jurisdictions to bypass being sworn in. But the public subsequently learned that officers continued to be sworn in even after the *Emergencies Act* was invoked. And further, there is debate over how much time this would have even saved in streamlining. There was lack of agreement among policing witnesses who testified at the Public Order Emergencies Commission over how much time was saved by not needing to swear in officers, with some witnesses saying that cumulatively this streamlining may have saved a few hours at best.[35]

The *Emergencies Act* cannot be invoked if it is just helpful or expedient. Police disorganization and bureaucratic incompetence is not a part of the threshold of this powerful law. The law is only available to be used in cases of absolute necessity because existing laws cannot effectively address a situation. Here, that was manifestly not the case. The border blockades were cleared or being cleared before the *Emergencies Act* was invoked. No one was ever even charged under the new criminal provisions of the *Emergencies Act*.

THE THRESHOLD OF "THREAT TO THE SECURITY OF CANADA" WAS NOT MET

In addition to the last resort clause, the *Emergencies Act* has another internal threshold for "threats to the security of Canada" that must be met if the law is to be legally invoked. This threshold issue became one of the central topics in the POEC Inquiry into the use of the *Emergencies Act.*

The prime minister had declared a "public order" emergency in response to the Freedom Convoy, which is defined in the Act as "an emergency that arises from threats to the security of Canada [. . .] so serious as to be a national emergency."[36] The legislation also provides that the phrase "threats to the security of Canada" has the "meaning assigned to it by section 2 of the *Canadian Security Intelligence Service Act.*"[37] The *CSIS Act* defines threats to include things like espionage and sabotage, foreign-influenced activities, the use of or threats of serious violence for political, ideological, or religious goals, and covert unlawful acts directed to overthrow the government.

Strikingly, CSIS did not believe that the Freedom Convoy posed any threat to the security of Canada. Parliament's decision to incorporate the *CSIS Act*'s definition of "threats to the security of Canada" in the *Emergencies Act* was a deliberate choice to rely on a definition that had been exhaustively scrutinized by parliament in the recent past. Therefore, CSIS's view on whether a threat to the security of Canada existed is weighty. Yet cabinet departed from the CSIS assessment.

The shocking revelation that CSIS had concluded there was no threat to the security of Canada was made public through the POEC. David Vigneault, director of CSIS, gave both oral and written testimony that he "at no time" believed that the Convoy protests posed a national security threat, and that there were no signs of foreign interference. Vigneault communicated the CSIS assessment to the Incident Response Group—that small group within the cabinet tasked with responding to the protests. This was a shocking revelation because until that point, the public was under the impression that the *Emergencies Act* was necessary to protect national security.

CSIS's opinion appeared not to weigh on the government. Janice Charette (the Clerk of the Privy Council and Canada's top civil servant) testified that the government took a "wider" interpretation of the definition of "threats to the security of Canada." Consequently, the government's novel interpretation included things like threats to Canada's economic security. An internal memo from the Privy Council Office explained that the government could apply a wider definition than the one clearly outlined in the statute. "PCO notes that the disturbance and the public unrest being felt across the country and beyond the Canadian borders, which may provide further momentum to the movement and lead to irremediable harms—including to social cohesion, national unity, and Canada's international reputation. In PCO's view, this fits with the statutory parameters defining threats to the security of Canada, though this conclusion may be vulnerable to challenge."[38]

This definition, despite its risks, was accepted by the prime minister and the Incident Response Group. Cabinet's adoption of the novel interpretation was strange. For one thing, it clearly departed from the text of the legislation. For another, this novel interpretation was both counter-intuitive and went against the legislative history of the *Emergencies Act*.

CSIS Director Vignault was even persuaded to accept that the identical text of the two statutes had different meanings and agreed to support the invocation of the *Emergencies Act*. This is odd, because Vignault is not a lawyer and works regularly with the *CSIS Act*, and because the government's novel proposed approach was counterintuitive. One would expect that a plain reading of the text would lead someone with Vignault's training and background to reach the opposite conclusion. It was during Mr. Vignault's cross-examination at the inquiry that we learned how he reached this surprising conclusion. The Canadian Civil Liberties Association asked Mr. Vignault directly, "Where did you get this understanding that the *Emergencies Act* definition is 'broader' than the CSIS definition?" He responded that he had asked for a legal opinion from the Department of Justice.[39] Canadians will never have access to this opinion, as the government has claimed privilege over it.

THE TESTIMONY OF PRIME MINISTER TRUDEAU

The last day of hearings in the POEC Inquiry was the blockbuster day: the testimony of sitting Prime Minister Justin Trudeau. By 9:00

a.m. there was a line out the door of the National Archives, where the Inquiry was taking place. Members of the public were waiting in the cold November wind and rain to get inside. Unsurprisingly, the security was heightened from the previous days of the Inquiry, and it looked quite different: a new group of security had appeared—huge linebacker types wearing suits and earpieces.

Commissioner Rouleau entered the hearing room and Prime Minister Trudeau was introduced, but there was a long pause, and nothing happened. Usually the witnesses come up through the aisle in the middle of the room, which would have meant that the prime minister would walk straight through the crowd—that day, a largely (but not entirely) unfriendly crowd. Everyone from the lawyers to the Commission staff to the public looked around the room trying to figure out where Prime Minister Trudeau was, and if he was coming after all. After a long and awkward pause, Commissioner Rouleau announced that the Commission would take a break. But, just as the break was called, suddenly the Prime Minister was in the room, having come in through a side door.

Prime Minister Trudeau was well prepared for his testimony. He displayed a great deal of familiarity with the evidence the Inquiry had already heard, and at certain points even asked for different pieces of evidence to be pulled up on the screen, showing his command of the evidence before the Commission. Prime Minister Trudeau was clearly well rehearsed, with many of his answers already at his fingertips.

Trudeau's cross-examination by the Canadian Constitution Foundation

It is an incredible thing to cross-examine a sitting prime minister. This type of radical transparency and accountability is rare in Canada. The CCF's lawyer, Sujit Choudhry, commented on the significance of this level of accountability in an interview on the national broadcast television program *Canadian Justice*:[40]

> It is a testament to the strength of our institutions
> that a sitting prime minister would be cross-examined

live on national television in full view of the Canadian public, and under oath. It is quite extraordinary, and it speaks to the foresight of the drafters of the *Emergencies Act* that they would have entrenched in the statute a requirement for an inquiry.

Behind his round glasses Choudhry has piercing eyes. A former professor at the University of Toronto Faculty of Law and former Dean of the University of California, Berkeley, School of Law, Choudhry now has a highly specialized legal practice in complex and high-profile constitutional litigation. He is a respected and seasoned senior member of the bar, well qualified to take up the challenge of cross-examining the prime minister in the limited time that was granted to the CCF.

When asked about the experience, Mr. Choudhry said "he was very well prepared as a witness, he communicated well, and he had a couple of goals. One was to give evidence in this proceeding, and the other was to communicate to the broader Canadian public [. . .] On the evidence, I think he wasn't as successful. [. . .] I felt he made admissions or refused to give answers that supported the government's case."[41]

Choudhry used his limited time expertly to focus on the question of whether cabinet was fully informed of the legal opinion from the Ministry of Justice that showed the strange and novel thinking behind the notion that the threshold for national security threat is different under the *Emergencies Act* than under the *CSIS Act*. The prime minister is the chair of the cabinet, an important and serious responsibility. The unusual theory offered by Justice about the existence of a sudden difference between the definitions of "threat to the security of Canada" in the two statutes required vigorous debate within the cabinet.

Prime Minister Trudeau testified that cabinet was briefed orally on the opinion by Justice Minister Lametti, but they did not have the written legal opinion itself. This is significant because legal opinions generally lay out the gaps and risks of various approaches. Without access to the written opinion, cabinet did not have full knowledge of those risks. As a result, we at the CCF are of the view that in failing to provide this legal opinion to cabinet and allowing for vigorous debate, the prime minister failed in his duty as chair of cabinet.

We also learned through Choudhry's cross-examination of the prime minister that cabinet did not receive a copy of the CSIS threat assessment that denied the existence of a national security threat, and they did not receive even a high-level copy of the operational plan being developed by the police. Choudhry also asked the prime minister to waive privilege on all these documents, but the prime minister refused to do so on the advice of his counsel.

Trudeau's examination-in-chief

Some important revelations were also made during the prime minister's examination-in-chief, which was his testimony at the POEC when questioned by the commission lawyers. Commission counsel pulled up a transcript of a phone call between the prime minister and Premier Ford in which Prime Minister Trudeau said to Ford "you shouldn't need more legal tools" and asked him to explain what he meant by this. His statement obviously begs the question of why the prime minister would invoke the *Emergencies Act* to get more legal tools if he didn't think they were necessary, and speaks to the last resort clause, suggesting that the requirement was not met. Before answering, the prime minister took a long pause and then said he meant that the federal government could give Ontario more resources to enable it to use existing laws on the books, adding that at that point there was a sense that more things could be done.

The prime minister went on to say that they were probably the first government to lean into the possibility of using the *Emergencies Act*, which had never before been used. This, he said, was because of the pandemic. Trudeau testified that during the pandemic the government had "dusted off the *Emergencies Act* and got briefed on it" and were given what he called a "crash course" on the law. His government thought about using it early on during the pandemic and consulted the provinces on the possibility, but never decided to use the Act. Then, seeing the situation in Ottawa with the Convoy, the prime minister testified, his government began to entertain the real possibility of invoking the *Emergencies Act.*

This was an interesting revelation for two reasons. First, Trudeau could be using this anecdote as a foil to create a public perception that the Act was invoked carefully and gave the example of the pandemic to suggest that they had previously held back on invocation. Second, this may indicate a fascination with a new powerful tool. Trudeau's evidence was that the government really was not familiar with this legislation until the pandemic. Then they "dusted it off" and learned all about this fascinating and powerful instrument. They were given this new giant hammer, and perhaps jumped too eagerly at the opportunity to use this exciting new toy they had just been briefed on. When you have a hammer, everything looks like a nail, and the government had just been briefed on a giant new hammer. Perhaps the Convoy looked like the perfect nail.

Some of the prime minister's most important testimony concerned the legal threshold for the national security threat—which had been the focus of the Commission's inquiry that week. Recall that to declare a national security threat the *Emergencies Act* must satisfy the definition of "national security threat" according to the *CSIS Act*; that CSIS had said there was no national security threat; and that the government had departed from the text of the legislation and introduced a wider definition of "national security threat."

The prime minister was very well rehearsed to discuss this point, and excitedly defended his interpretation of the legal threshold under the *Emergencies Act*. He asked for the legislation to be pulled up. He clearly had his whole script ready and was eager to share it. Once the *Emergencies Act* was on the screen in front of Commissioner Rouleau, counsel, and the audience, Trudeau walked through the text. He said that the definition of "national security threat" under the *Emergencies Act* is about cabinet—not CSIS—finding reasonable grounds sufficient to invoke a public order emergency. He testified that the context and purpose of the two laws are different, and so are the people making the decision. The context, he said, is different because CSIS is using a narrow framework, to do things like obtain a wiretap or begin an investigation. Trudeau said every input he received indicated that things were getting worse: "There was a sense that things were spreading. And while there had been no serious violence up to that point, there was the potential."

On February 14, Trudeau received a memo from the Clerk of the Privy Council Office—the chief civil servant in Canada—recommending the invocation of the *Emergencies Act*. Trudeau described it as "a big thing" for the public service to recommend this. However, the memo also stated that since CSIS had not found any threat to the security of Canada, the government would prepare an additional threat assessment. None was ever prepared. As will be discussed later in this chapter, we believe that the decision by Cabinet and the prime minister to depart from the CSIS assessment of the threat level without that promised secondary threat assessment renders that decision unreasonable.

When asked at the end of the examination-in-chief whether using this law had "unleashed the kraken" that could potentially be used to quell protests in the future—like Black Lives Matter protests and Indigenous protests that have also blockaded infrastructure—the prime minister was unconcerned. Trudeau replied that Canada had never seen a protest like the Convoy, so it had never before occurred to the government to use this law. He was asked, now that this seal is broken, might it be used again? Trudeau replied that he has greater faith in Canadians and in our institutions and does not believe that Canadians would "shrug aside our fundamental freedoms so easily." This statement is especially troubling and shameless, given that this is exactly what civil liberties groups like the Canadian Constitution Foundation, the Canadian Civil Liberties Association, and the Justice Centre for Constitutional Freedoms have argued the prime minister did in this case. Prime Minister Trudeau concluded his remarks about reaching his decision to invoke by saying he is "absolutely serene" and confident he made the right decision.

After six weeks of testimony in Ottawa at the POEC, many observers, including the CCF, concluded that the federal government had failed to justify its invocation of the extraordinary *Emergencies Act*.

Unfortunately, Commissioner Rouleau found the use of the *Emergencies Act* was justified. But he also conceded that "reasonable and informed people could reach a different conclusion."[42] This is exactly what the CCF hoped for in bringing a legal challenge to the *Emergencies Act* by way of judicial review in Federal Court.

THE EMERGENCIES ACT AT FEDERAL COURT[43]

Inside a spectacular courtroom at the Supreme Court of Canada in April of 2023, Justice Mosley of the Federal Court heard arguments from a group of national civil liberties organizations about why the Trudeau government's use of the *Emergencies Act* was illegal and unconstitutional. The judicial review was separate from the POEC, and unlike the POEC, the decision from Federal Court becomes binding precedent.

The Federal Court had become the last guardrail of accountability for the Trudeau government's use of this extraordinary and powerful legislation. The report by Commissioner Rouleau for the POEC was a massive and disappointing exercise of deference to the government. There are inherent procedural and political limits to the effectiveness of the parliamentary Committees investigating the use of the *Emergencies Act*. And Canada's fourth estate, the mainstream media, has shown a disturbing level of spoon-fed acceptance of the government's rationale for invoking the successor to the *War Measures Act*.

Justice Mosley heard the case in a grand courtroom inside the Supreme Court of Canada, a massive grey structure perched on a cliff overlooking the Ottawa River. There were fourteen counsel present, as well as members of the public. The courtroom is two-and-a-half stories tall, with detailed wood panelling, two-story gold curtains, and lush red carpeting. The ceiling is coffered with rosettes. The wooden benches for the public are tortuous. We would know—we sat on them for three days.

Freezing rain pummelled the leaded windows on the last day of the hearing. During the break, counsel lamented their cancelled flights out of Ottawa amid claps of thunder and flashing lightning, perhaps an ominous portent, although no one was quite sure of what. Justice Mosley surprised the court on the second day of the hearings by telling those present, and the hundreds observing online via livestream, that he has a Class A trucker's licence. For a period as a young man, he told those listening, he had worked as a commercial trucker in southern Alberta. The irony, he said, was that he was probably the only one in the hearing room, in a case about the trucker convoy, who had ever actually worked as a trucker.

The applicants in the judicial review included the Canadian Constitution Foundation (CCF) and the Canadian Civil Liberties Association (CCLA). There was also a group of individuals who had been directly involved in the protests, including some who had their bank accounts frozen by the financial measures enacted under the *Emergencies Act*. Another group called the Canadian Frontline Nurses was also represented.

Three major themes emerged out of our two days of arguments. First, that the threshold to invoke the *Emergencies Act* was not met because existing legal tools had not been exhausted. Second, the Trudeau cabinet did not have reasonable grounds to believe a threat to the security of Canada existed—especially given that CSIS did not believe such a threat existed. Moreover, cabinet lacked any alternative threat assessment to support their departure from CSIS's assessment. And finally, the special regulations created under the *Emergencies Act* were unconstitutional. These regulations included a national prohibition on assemblies that "could lead to a breach of the peace" as well as the regulations that required banks to freeze accounts and share banking information with police without a warrant.

The Attorney General's response to arguments by these groups was breathtaking.

The government tried to stop this hearing from happening

The four lawyers representing the Attorney General began by arguing that the case should not be heard at all because they claimed the case was moot, which means there is no longer a live issue before the courts. To accept such a line of argument would make a government's use of this powerful legislation, which acts as a *de facto* amendment to the Canadian

Constitution, evasive of any review. Justice Mosley told the parties he would reserve a decision on mootness, and so the court proceeded with the three days of hearings on the merits. But it is breathtaking that the first two hours of the hearing on a powerful and never-before-used law were spent by the government saying, in effect, "nothing to see here."

It was not reasonable for cabinet to invoke a public order emergency

This was not where the government's requests for deference ended. On the merits, the Attorney General was tasked with responding to a mountain of evidence by the civil liberties groups about the legislative history of the enacting of the *Emergencies Act* as well as the events leading up to the invocation of this extraordinary legislation in response to a largely peaceful and non-violent (though highly disruptive) protest.

The Attorney General's response to this mountain of evidence was to assert that cabinet deserves a special and heightened level of deference. The Attorney General argued that cabinet is an apex decision-maker; accordingly, its authority is almost unlimited and mostly unconstrained by the language of the *Emergencies Act*. The mere assertion by cabinet that it believes itself to be acting reasonably is itself all that is required. The Attorney General argued that the decision to invoke the *Emergencies Act* was "quintessentially executive in nature, unconstrained" and that its decisions should be considered "very difficult to set aside."

Canada's system of parliamentary democracy already grants enormous power to the executive. Author and journalist Jeffrey Simpson famously called Canada's system of government a "friendly dictatorship" that places more power in the hands of the prime minister than any other democracy. The Attorney General's position that courts owe deference to cabinet for the mere fact that the decision was made at the "apex" of government is a shocking claim that would create a dangerous precedent and erase one of the few guardrails of accountability that exists in our system; judicial review by the courts. It cannot be that just because the decision-maker is cabinet, it is automatically deserving of more deference. It is not the nature or identity of the decision-maker that determines the level of deference owed when assessing if that decision was reasonable. It is the statutory language that determines the level of deference. Cabinet is not automatically entitled to greater deference just because it is cabinet.

Representing the CCF, lawyer Sujit Choudhry pressed on the government's lack of evidence to justify the invocation of the Act. For one thing, it seemed apparent that the government did initially believe more was necessary to justify departing from CSIS's assessment and invoking a public order emergency. In a previously described memo from the Clerk of the Privy Council to Prime Minister Trudeau, the Clerk gave him advice about invocation, relying on various inputs from different government departments. In that memo, the Clerk wrote that the government would prepare an additional threat assessment given that CSIS said there was no threat to the security of Canada. But no additional threat assessment was ever prepared. If a government is going to depart from CSIS's assessment it must show why that departure is reasonable. The government's failure to produce this assessment makes cabinet's decision to invoke the *Emergencies Act* against the truckers' protest in Ottawa unreasonable. The evidence shows the Clerk of the Privy Council—Canada's top bureaucrat—initially believed this additional assessment was necessary, yet cabinet proceeded to make the decision to invoke the *Emergencies Act* without it.

The Attorney General also doubled down on the disturbing claim made by Minister Chrystia Freeland in the POEC that threats of economic harm constitute a "threat to the security of Canada." During her testimony at the Inquiry, Minister Freeland took the position that Canada's security is built on economic security, both as a country and for individuals. Minister Freeland's claim was challenged on cross-examination by lawyers for the CCF and the CCLA. For the CCLA, lawyer Ewa Krajewska forced Minister Freelend to recon with her inconsistent views supporting labour strikes, and in particular the historic example of port strikes in Poland, all deisgned to cause economic harm, and the notion that the Convoy was a national security threat solely because it caused economic harm. Minister Freeland's inadequate response prompted the CCLA to follow her testimony with a press release stating that "'economic harm' is not grounds for the invocation of the *Emergencies Act*. The *Emergencies Act* and the *CSIS Act* do not contemplate economic harm as a national emergency."[44]

Yet during the hearing, the Attorney General pressed on this claim, arguing that cutting off crucial supply lines could also lead to serious unrest and violence as well as counter protests. The Attorney General argued that blocking borders causes the same kind of harm as physical damage to infrastructure. They cause shortages of food and medicine and harm Canada's international reputation.

Frankly, it is dangerous reasoning to maintain that economic harm is a form or threat of "violence" that justifies invoking a public order emergency. The reality is that protests cause economic harm. Consider how this might be applied in other protests: causing economic harm to a relevant party, for instance, is the explicit purpose of labour protests like strikes. This was the exact point Krajewska had made to Freeland.

Charter *arguments*

Criminal defence lawyer Janani Shanmuganathan represented the CCF on the *Charter* arguments in the Federal Court judicial review. A petite young woman with a cloud of dark curls and a new infant at home, Shanmuganathan fearlessly represented the CCF in the best tradition of the criminal defence bar.

Shamuganathan argued that various *Charter* rights had been violated by the restrictions on assemblies and the financial measures, and that these violations could not be justified under section 1 of the *Charter*. She further argued that the gathering restrictions violated the right to freedom of assembly (s. 2(c)) and freedom of expression (s 2(b)), and the *Economic Measures* violated the right to be free from an unreasonable search and seizure (s. 8). Both measures also violated section 7 of the *Charter*, the right to life, liberty, and security of person, because they came with a term of imprisonment of up to five years.

The *Emergency Measures* and the *Economic Measures* were both too broadly drafted and violated *Charter* rights. The *Emergency Measures* prohibited gatherings that may reasonably lead to a breach of the peace, as well as travelling to or materially supporting those gatherings. They were drafted so broadly that they captured people who did not create any blockades, had no intention to create a blockade, and might not even support blockades. They covered people bringing food or water to a protest, or walking to a protest that hadn't even yet begun. And that peaceful protester could risk five years' imprisonment.

The *Economic Measures*, which required the sharing of banking information about "designated persons" among the RCMP, CSIS, and banks violated the *Charter*-protected right to be free from unreasonable search and seizure. The *Economic Measures* were not limited to those participating in blockades but covered any "designated person": like the *Emergency Measures,* these regulations would permit the disclosure of banking information to police about people just standing on Parliament Hill holding a sign, or walking to the area to hold a sign. Banking information is deeply personal. Imagine how you would feel if a friend or neighbour could look through your bank statements—let alone the police and the government, all without a warrant.

Federal Court decision

The result of this case will be studied by law students and politicians for generations to come. Prime Minister Trudeau's invocation of the *Emergencies Act* will have long-standing impacts, just as his father's invocation of the *War Measures Act* did. The decision from the Federal Court will not come soon. The case involves an unprecedented piece of legislation. It is what lawyers call *sui generis*—it is of its own class. The decision will require a careful study of the parliamentary intent around the legislation, as well as extensive case law in statutory interpretation, the standard of review, and *Charter* jurisprudence. Not only that, but the decision will need to be translated into French before it can be released. But this decision is worth waiting for. It will guide courts and politicians in future emergencies, both real and—perhaps even more importantly—imagined.

CHAPTER 5
FREEDOM OF MOVEMENT

When Kim Taylor's mother passed away at her home in Kilbride, Newfoundland, on May 5, 2020 at the height of the first COVID-19 lockdown, Kim immediately began self-isolating in Nova Scotia, where she was living at the time. She also devised a plan that included staying in her parents' basement, which had a separate back-door entry, to isolate upon her intended arrival in Newfoundland to enable her to safely attend her mother's funeral. Kim even arranged with the funeral home director to schedule the funeral in the days after she had completed her fourteen-day quarantine.

Kim submitted an exemption form online requesting to enter Newfoundland and sent another follow-up later that day to ensure the request was received. She was determined to get to her mother's funeral safely. However, on the 8th of May, the government denied her request.

"When someone dies, there are certain things of a time-sensitive nature, and my goal was to get to the province as soon as possible to get into isolation," Kim told a CBC reporter at the time.[1] To her astonishment, the next business day, Kim was denied entry into the province. Her mother would have to be buried by her father alone and she would not be able to bid farewell to her mother, who she spoke to every day of her life.

On April 29, 2020, Newfoundland's Chief Medical Officer invoked the *Public Health Protection and Promotion Act* (PHPPA) to limit entry to Newfoundland and Labrador to residents, asymptomatic workers, and those in extenuating circumstances. The restrictions came into effect on May 4, 2020.[2] There had already been a fourteen-day quarantine requirement in place, but the government deemed it necessary to go further and ban all outsiders from entry, despite there being no evidence that individuals were not adhering to quarantine requirements. At the time, there were seventeen active cases of COVID-19 in the province, and this number was declining every day.

With the support of the Canadian Civil Liberties Association (CCLA), Kim launched a legal challenge against section 28(1)(h) of the PHPPA, asking the courts to declare it outside the legislative authority of the province or alternatively of no force and effect under section 6 of the *Charter*, which protects freedom of movement.[3]

Kim's first argument dealt with whether the province had the proper authority under the *Constitution Act, 1867* to regulate inter-provincial travel as it had. Traditionally, any matters—such as trade and cross-provincial travel routes—that transcend provincial borders fall within federal jurisdiction.

However, this argument was swiftly rejected by the court.[4] The court held that although the travel restrictions may have had a potential impact on federal undertakings, "any such effect is incidental to the purpose of s. 28(1)(h), which is directed to public health, not interprovincial travel. Such an effect does not change the essential character of s. 28(1)(h)."[5]

This wasn't a particularly compelling argument—although the intended outcome of the travel restrictions was clearly directed at public health, it seems undeniable that the means of targeting public health was, in pith and substance, the regulation of provincial border crossings. The entire upshot of the measure was to restrict movement between provinces. Moreover, concluding that the measures were aimed at public health ends—i.e., curbing the spread of COVID-19—in a sense presumes that the answer to the question was in issue. Was closing provincial borders in all cases strictly necessary to prevent viral spread when less-intrusive measures such as fourteen-day quarantines were available, and when all non-Maritime provinces declined to go so far as to prevent families from attending their own parents' funerals?

Kim Taylor's stronger arguments were about freedom of movement, guaranteed by section 6 of the *Charter*. After a lengthy analysis, the court concluded that Taylor's mobility rights under section 6(1) were engaged by the travel restrictions, but not her rights under section 6(2). The two subsections provide different protections. Section 6(1) guarantees the right to "remain in Canada" while section 6(2) is a right to move to and take up residence anywhere in Canada. The judge interpreted section 6(1)'s guarantee of the right to "remain in" Canada as "the right of Canadian citizens to travel in Canada for lawful purposes across provincial and territorial boundaries."[6] The court found that section 6(2), by contrast, specifically protects moving about the country for that purpose.[7] Since Kim wished to enter Newfoundland to grieve with her family rather than relocate, her section 6(2) rights were not engaged; however her section 6(1) right to remain in Canada was engaged.

Justice Burrage concluded that, "While restrictions on personal travel may cause mental anguish to some, and certainly did so in the case of Ms. Taylor, the collective benefit to the population as a whole must prevail. COVID-19 is a virulent and potentially fatal disease. In the circumstances of this case Ms. Taylor's Charter right to mobility must give way to the common good."[8] As we have seen, the amorphous appeal to what was necessary for the public interest not only allowed judges to neatly sidestep *Charter* rights, but also to avoid engaging with the actual potential risks of the conduct in question: in this case, given Kim's quarantine plan, her risk of spreading COVID-19 would seem to be negligible.

It's important to note that the judge found that the border restrictions were justified under section 1 of the *Charter*, although other provinces were able to weather the first wave without such draconian measures, and less-intrusive options such as mandatory fourteen-day quarantines were available and workable.

Kim also made the argument that her right to life, liberty, and security of the person—protected under section 7—was impacted by the restrictions. The section 7 case law refers to "fundamental personal choices" which the state cannot interfere with without violating section 7. The judge also rejected this argument, writing "with the greatest respect to Ms. Taylor, and while not discounting the importance to her of attending her mother's funeral, her decision to do so does not rise to the level of a 'fundamental personal choice,' as defined in the case law, so as to attract constitutional protection."[9] This rings untrue to lived experience: surely most people would consider attending their parent's funeral to be a fundamental personal choice.

Mobility rights are generally construed expansively. Section 6 is not subject to the section 33 notwithstanding clause. In the Supreme Court of Canada's decision in United *States v. Cotroni*,[10] Justice Bertha Wilson (in dissent), described the scope of section 6(1) as "designed to protect a Canadian citizen's freedom of movement in and out of the country according to his own choice. He may come and go as he pleases." However, as we'll see, the pandemic would take a wrecking ball to this right's construction.

In this chapter, we will examine the different ways government responses impacted the right to freedom of movement, including:

- interprovincial travel restrictions;
- the quarantine hotel nightmare;
- the legal challenge to quarantine hotels; and
- federal travel restrictions.

INTERPROVINCIAL TRAVEL RESTRICTIONS

In February 2020, then-federal Health Minister Patty Hajdu delivered an earnest lecture explaining Canada's circumspect approach to border closures in the face of horrific news from Italy and Wuhan.[11] Parroting the orthodoxies of the World Health Organization, Hajdu explained why, unlike Australia and the United States, Canada did not intend to shut down the border with China despite the increasingly grim news from Wuhan:[12]

It's much easier to support a traveller from a region experiencing an outbreak if you know where they're coming from . . . and when you shut down a border like that, it gets much harder to detect where they're coming from . . . and shutting down borders isn't very effective in controlling disease.

A year later, Hajdu struck a notably different tone at a House of Commons Public Safety Committee hearing. Canada's borders had been closed to all non-citizens for more than a year. Additionally, Trudeau's Liberal government had mandated a draconian practice of quarantining all arriving passengers in government-approved hotels to the tune of $2,000 for a three-day stay.[13]

Conservative health critic Michelle Rempel Garner recounted a harrowing sexual assault that had allegedly occurred at the government's newly mandated hotel quarantine facilities in Montreal, demanding to know what data justified forcibly confining Canadian citizens to monitored hotel rooms.[14]

This time, Hajdu's response was different. "Every woman deserves to be free of violence and a life of dignity,"[15] she noted. "But, these border measures are in place to protect Canadians, and they will remain in place until science and evidence indicate that it is safe to release them."

Throughout the pandemic, governments sought to control the movement of individuals between provinces as well as in and out of Canada, with mandatory quarantines, testing, and even outright bans on entering certain provinces. The Atlantic provinces were especially jingoistic. At the beginning of the pandemic, this reflected some logic, as there was perhaps an already vanishing hope that if we could establish a fortress against the virus we would be spared a full-blown outbreak. But once there was obvious and widespread community infection, that logic diminished.

Moreover, some of the measures had particularly cruel repercussions. Bans on interprovincial travel kept Canadian families apart even at their funerals and deathbeds. Quarantine hotels kettled travellers together in tight spaces and, in the name of social distancing, put individuals under the shoddy custody of overwhelmed hotels that could scarcely protect or feed them—that is, if travellers were wealthy enough or willing enough to pay the hefty fees.

The Atlantic bubble

Kim Taylor's saga wasn't the only story of an individual who was seriously impacted by provincial border closures. In the spring of 2020, Ottawa resident Jacqui Delaney was denied entry into New Brunswick. Her father, Roy Budden, had undergone emergency surgery on May 19, after being diagnosed with colon cancer less than a week before. His condition steadily declined, and on May 31, he died. Due to hospital restrictions, there was no one at the hospital to hold his hand in his last days in the ICU. Even his wife of twenty-five years was not allowed to be there until the last thirty minutes of his life. Delaney attempted to fly to New Brunswick to comfort her grieving family and attend the funeral. She was willing to self-quarantine upon her arrival. The province, however, did not respond to her reasonable request to enter in time. On June 3, she attended her father's funeral over Skype.

As in Newfoundland, it seemed plausible that a majority of New Brunswickers were firmly in agreement with the province's restrictions: Premier Blaine Higgs enjoyed one of the highest approval ratings in the country. In May 2020 this book's author, Joanna Baron, was quoted by the CBC discussing the view of the Canadian Constitution Foundation (CCF) that these border restrictions constituted unjustified violations of our constitutional liberties. Shortly after, she received more threats and hate mail than ever before in her career, with an onslaught of ominous emails from New Brunswickers. One memorable e-mail noted:

> You're farting in the wind. If more Canadians thought as you do we'd be just like Donald Trumpers who tout freedom over all else. You are free to do what you will until you endanger others. In this case the right to refuse a vaccine or decide where and when to amble

should be fully suspended until the coast is clear. It ain't clear. Nor are you.

To add insult to injury, the New Brunswick government, for a period, elected to outsource decisions regarding who was allowed to grieve for their dead family members to a non-governmental organization. From what we know, the government functionally delegated to the Red Cross not just the processing of requests to enter the province, but also the decision-making itself, without putting in place any means of oversight or appeal.[16] In other words, New Brunswick delegated the function of a government power that directly infringed the rights of Canadians to a private non-governmental organization. And it did so with no mechanism to appeal or review those decisions. Did this state of affairs really bear any proportionality to the actual nature of the threat?

While the Red Cross is a well-established and respectable charity, delegating this authority to it lacked democratic accountability. New Brunswick's Office of the Chief Medical Officer of Health, which is granted statutory authority to determine exemptions to the travel ban in section 9 of the province's *Emergency Management Order*, cannot delegate its authority to another actor, much less a private NGO. This is based on the administrative law principle of *delegatus non potest delegare*: the beneficiary of a statutory power cannot delegate its exercise.

The Atlantic provinces—Nova Scotia, Prince Edward Island, New Brunswick and Newfoundland and Labrador—decided in July 2020 to establish a "bubble" that allowed unrestricted travel among residents of those provinces and restricted travel to those from outside of Canada. Anyone who wished to visit those provinces was subject to screening, with non-essential travel forbidden, and a mandatory two-week quarantine for those permitted to enter. The bubble was paused during COVID-19's second wave in fall 2020 and resumed briefly in summer 2021.

Although the Atlantic provinces were the most early and aggressive in implementing movement restrictions, their actions were arguably not the most egregious or irrational among government measures related to travel. That honour goes to the federal government and its disastrous quarantine hotel program of early 2021.

THE QUARANTINE PRISON NIGHTMARE[17]

Towards the end of 2020, as the second wave of the virus crested over much of Canada, the national mood grew tense. Cases were surging, vaccines were still firmly out of reach thanks to a botched national procurement strategy, and the country settled into a particularly bleak winter.

Perhaps as a diversion from the frigid misery at home, the national media took up a public witch hunt for politicians who deigned to fly south and escape from the bitter winter. No exaggeration: over December and January each day brought a new headline confirming that a minister, member of parliament, or political staffer had been caught escaping to St. Barts,[18] Mexico,[19] Hawaii,[20] or California.[21]

In the most notorious case, Ontario Finance Minister Rod Phillips was chastised for spending three weeks with his family in St. Barts. The most inflammatory part was that Phillips (or his staffer) pre-scheduled and posted short videos with holiday greetings and a warning to continue to follow pandemic protocols filmed at his home in a Toronto suburb to be posted while he was later revealed to be enjoying aquamarine ocean and sun on one of the world's most expensive islands. He flew home early and was confronted by a full coterie of reporters at the Toronto airport. A few days later, Phillips resigned his role as finance minister.[22]

In the face of this national witch hunt and given the lack of ability to domestically manufacture vaccines, in early 2021 the federal government began to tighten the screws on its border measures. First, in early January the government announced that before their arrival in Canada, travellers would need to show negative results for approved COVID-19 PCR tests, in addition to existing rules requiring them to quarantine at home for fourteen days once they returned to Canada.[23] A few weeks later, Prime Minister Trudeau went further and threw down a major gauntlet, announcing that arriving Canadians would soon be required to book and pay for "approved quarantine hotels." Travellers would be responsible for the cost of a three-day stay, to the tune of about $2,000, including meals, as well as a second PCR test upon arriving in Canada.[24] This announcement was made when many travellers were already abroad, creating mad chaos. The CCF was inundated with phone calls from people outside Canada at the time in desperate search of advice.

The direct justification for the hotel quarantine was puzzling from the get-go. For one, it was a three-day stay, unlike the brutal but at least logical fourteen-day hotel quarantines adopted in Australia and New Zealand.[25]

Travellers to Canada were instructed to wait in a government hotel for the results of their PCR test taken immediately upon arrival; with a negative result in hand, they were free to leave and complete a fourteen-day home quarantine. To add to the irrationality, individuals who tested positive would be permitted to leave the hotel to isolate at home if they had a satisfactory quarantine plan. Which begged the question, what was the point?

Given that travellers already required a negative test taken within seventy-two hours to board the plane in the first place, testing positive upon arrival would occur too rarely to justify being detained for three days at the cost of a few thousand dollars, and odd in light of the fact that Canada's Chief Public Health Officer had outlined her view that transmission on airplanes is rare.[26] In any event, the virus would not replicate enough to show up on a test immediately upon arrival.

The rollout of the policy was an unmitigated disaster. Social media platforms were immediately flooded with videos showing the pandemonium in the government-approved hotels: crowded lobbies with hapless staff scrambling to accommodate individuals, some without masks, crumpled and tired from transcontinental flights. Many had reported waiting on backed-up government phone lines for up to twelve hours to book their hotels before departing for Canada.[27]

When the state takes its citizens into custody, it has an overarching duty not to endanger them and to provide them with the necessities of life. However, this baseline of a liberal democracy's responsibility was breached within a few weeks of the rollout of the quarantine policy, which was uniformly reported as causing mad chaos.

To wit: one woman reported being sexually assaulted at a hotel near the Montreal airport by another hotel guest, who entered her room and refused to leave until she threatened to scream. The guest faced one count of sexual assault, one count of breaking and entering, and one count of criminal harassment. It was reported that the locks at the quarantine hotel were inexplicably removed from the hotel room doors, leaving the occupants inside vulnerable.[28]

Another woman, Cristina Teixeira, and her family returning from her father's funeral in Portugal were forced into a government quarantine hotel and billed $3,500[29] for a single night. Despite receiving negative COVID-19 test results within twelve hours, travellers were billed for the cost of the entire three-day stay. Ms. Teixeira later received a partial refund, but only after her story was trumpeted widely in the media.[30]

A diabetic traveller named Ray Truesdale was left in a quarantine hotel without food for nearly twenty-four hours. "I got some food the first morning and went to reorder in the afternoon [. . .] the app didn't work. The front desk wouldn't answer the phone. I decided to go down to the lobby and it was pure pandemonium. A lot of other travellers hadn't eaten in hours. There were vegetarians being offered ham and cheese sandwiches [. . .] One day I went 23 hours before I got food."[31]

In the face of this widely noted incompetence, many Canadians decided to simply skip out on the mandatory hotel quarantine, rolling their luggage out to an Uber defiant in the face of possible fines Because, really, can a government that didn't manage to hire enough phone operators—or even put up a booking website—credibly threaten to follow up with fines for all of the hotel-dodgers?

LEGAL CHALLENGE TO THE QUARANTINE HOTEL PROGRAM

The quarantine hotel policy faced several constitutional challenges, one brought by the CCF, and four separate challenges at the federal level, with fourteen applicants, that were heard together.[32]

The CCF, along with five individual applicants, filed an urgent application on March 2, 2021 in the Ontario Superior Court seeking to have the quarantine hotel regulations struck down.[33] The CCF was represented by lawyer Jonathan Roth. Known as Yoni to his friends, Roth is a soft-spoken and cerebral young lawyer with retro glasses, a thick head of dark hair, and an incredibly deliberative manner.

For the CCF, Roth argued that the regulations were unconstitutional, based on their violation of the rights to liberty, the rights against arbitrary detention and against cruel and unusual punishment, and mobility rights guaranteed in the *Charter*. The stories of the individual applicants in the case were compelling.

All five individual applicants were seeking to travel outside Canada for compassionate reasons: one, T.J. Radonjic, needed to travel from Vancouver to Washington state to assist his wife recovering from shoulder surgery, as she was unable to shower or cook on her own. Another, Yann Le Héritte, was seeking to travel to France to make end-of-life arrangements for her ninety-one-year-old mother with dementia.

The hearing was held in June 2021 and was attended by more than six hundred members of the public via Zoom—at one point, the virtual hearing was so full that the judge himself couldn't get in to conduct the hearings. The CCF argued that the quarantine hotel rules violated the rights to movement (section 6), liberty and security of the person (section 7), and to be free from cruel and unusual punishment (section 12) and could not be saved under the reasonable limits clause, section 1. By June 2021, when the case was heard, the federal government's own expert panel had recommended discontinuing the hotel program.[34]

The government failed to proffer any concrete evidence on the justification for a three-day hotel quarantine, in addition to existing requirements for a negative test and a suitable home quarantine plan. The Minister of Health could only say that "the data was incomplete in terms of what combination of measures are needed" but that they hoped the hotel quarantine would provide "an extra layer of security for Canadians." Less than 2 per cent of cases in the country were connected to international travel at the time the measures were implemented.

There was a partial victory because of the litigation: on May 27, 2021, the federal government amended the rules to permit compassionate exemptions.[35] The Attorney General communicated this amendment to the CCF, requesting that we discontinue our litigation. We were eager, however, to make the constitutional arguments against the hotels on the merits and refused the government demand to discontinue.

At the hearing, the government's lawyers emphasized what they described as the severe threat of new variants—particularly those from Britain, South Africa, and Brazil. But by the time of the first hearing, these new variants were already spreading in communities across Canada. The government also claimed that internationally procured tests were liable to fraud.[36]

Ultimately, a judge of the Ontario Superior Court dismissed both the CCF's motion for urgent relief against the quarantine hotel regulations[37] and the substantive challenge.[38] He found that "the applicants' wish to choose to quarantine at home, and their spending priorities when they travel abroad during the pandemic, are decidedly first world, economic problems . . . that barely raise any discernible constitutional concern." In doing so, the judge adopted the reasons of a Federal Court judge in a separate challenge to the hotel quarantine rules.

The judge dismissed the opinion of the federal government's own expert panel, opining that "the expert panel did not provide scientific truth to the government. Nor are its recommendations of constitutional force. They are important input for the government in making policy choices to formulate laws."[39] In other words, while the expert panel's opinion was part of the basis of the government's decisions, it was not binding in any way. The judge concluded that while the quarantine hotel program was "not perfect," it was a "choice among a range of possible and rational choices."[40] The quarantine hotel program was not required to be demonstrably effective, but just to have a "rational connection" to a stated governmental objective. Given the severity of the impact on mobility rights, this represented a fairly astonishing level of deference to the government's ability to craft a regime that severely limited rights and mobility.

The judge even pointed out that the applicants had not presented evidence of "comparative risk between home and hotel quarantine"[41]—

a strangely onerous burden to place on individual citizens who bear rights against governmental overreach, and an odd precedent to set. Retaining scientific experts in litigation is extremely costly and a high bar for holding governments accountable for violations of constitutionally guaranteed rights.

The judge concluded by commenting that "Even if there were [a comparative analysis of the risks], the applicants have to show that the government's choices are arbitrary or not rationally related to its goal of harm reduction."[42] Such an analysis made it clear that the judge was willing to exercise a posture of complete deference to government policy. On the opposite side, the judge minimized the plaintiffs' real and concrete evidence of suffering.

In his injunction decision, the judge also deferred to the government's submissions of data, which were, by their own assessment, "incomplete internationally."[43] Despite this concession, the judge found the government's submissions were "deeply-rooted in science and comprehensive public policy development."[44] He also dismissed the applicants' claims that quarantine constitutes arbitrary detention or cruel and unusual punishment (even when a diabetic was deprived of meals for twenty-four hours, which is effectively life-threatening) as frivolous.

In retrospect, what did the quarantine hotels afford Canada? According to the government's stated rationale of protecting the country from variants, not much. The U.K. B117 variant spread rapidly across the country in early 2021.[45] British Columbia played host to the world's worst outbreak of the Brazilian P1 variant, with over seven hundred confirmed cases (including the majority of the Vancouver Canucks hockey team).[46] The multiple layers of what was essentially pandemic theatre, unsurprisingly, did not prove effective against seeding the variant.

The economic impact of the hotels, however, was well documented and staggering. In February of 2023, Public Health Canada reported spending in the amount of just under $389 million in less than three years on its designated quarantine facilities across the country. In one instance, documents showed that the government spent $6.8 million on one quarantine hotel in Calgary alone—which, it turned out, had housed and fed a total of fifteen people, amounting to an outlay of $450,000 per person, as highlighted by Calgary MP Michelle Rempel Garner. More than a year after the quarantine hotel program was discontinued, the contract with the Westin Calgary Hotel continued until October 30, 2022.[47] And in fall 2023, a lawsuit was filed alleging that one of the quarantine hotel operators misappropriated $15.7 million in funds from the Public Health Agency of Canada meant to be used for hotel rooms but pocketed for personal use.[48] The whole affair, needless to say, was ignominious.

FEDERAL VACCINE TRAVEL MANDATES

In August 2021, with a federal election on the horizon and an established tactic of making vaccination status a wedge issue, the Trudeau government announced a move that no other liberal democracy resorted to. Effective January 15, 2022, by an Order in Council issued under the *Aeronautics Act*, Canadians who could not show they were fully vaccinated were barred from travelling by airplane, train, or commercial ship, both domestically and internationally.

It's important to recall some pertinent context: by early 2022, while the approved COVID-19 vaccines had been shown to perform well in preventing severe disease and hospitalization, their effect on reducing transmission appeared fairly negligible, particularly in the face of the Omicron variant. In Ontario, where public health reported infections and vaccination status every day, within a week of the Omicron outbreak there ceased to be any link between the infection rate and vaccination status.[49] The only basis, then, upon which the government could reasonably justify the mandates was that it served the public interest to encourage vaccination to reduce the number of COVID-19-related hospitalizations.

But even this logic looks shaky when you consider that, in the aggregate, an unvaccinated person under forty is far less likely to be hospitalized than a vaccinated and boosted eighty-five-year-old.[50] Since elderly people are at markedly higher risk of hospitalization and death from COVID-19 than younger people, the logic of restricting travel to reduce hospitalizations would seem to imply that if the objective of the measures was preventing hospitalizations, older people, or those with pre-existing conditions, even if vaccinated, should also be forbidden from travelling, rather than all unvaccinated people, irrespective of age or heath. This is an obviously odious suggestion.

A coalition of applicants, led by former Newfoundland Premier Brian Peckford and assembled by the Justice Centre for Constitutional Freedoms (JCCF), challenged the federal travel Order as a violation of their section 2(a) rights to freedom of religion and conscience, section 6(1) rights of mobility, section 7 rights to life, liberty and security of the person, as well as rights to privacy and equality.[51] At the same time, the coalition alleged that the Order exceeded the authority of the *Aeronautics Act*. The Act allows a Minister to issue orders related to a "significant risk, direct or indirect, to aviation safety or the safety of the public."

This wording would seem to accord the Minister of Transport broad ambit to act—"public safety" is an extremely broad term—but calls into question whether a rule that is, in substance, directed at public health was ever intended to be subsumed within the *Aeronautics Act*. The applicants also challenged the fact that the Order was brought as a directive of the Minister of Transport, and thus did not receive parliamentary scrutiny and debate.

The mandatory vaccine requirement was suspended as of June 2022, although at the time the language used by Health Minister Yves Duclos was highly ambiguous, referring to a "transition in policies," and strongly hinting that the two-shot mandate would be converted into a rule extending to mandatory boosters during the fall respiratory virus season.

In October 2022, in the lead-up to the hearing of the Peckford challenge, the Federal Court held that the matter was moot, as the Order had been suspended.[52] In her reasons, Associate Chief Justice Jocelyne Gagne found that the use of judicial resources for a five-day hearing, when the travel mandate had already been lifted, outweighed the public interest in having the case heard on the merits. The applicants have appealed the finding of mootness.[53]

CHAPTER 6

THE RIGHT TO PRIVACY AND THE GOVERNMENT'S RESPONSE TO COVID-19

Just before midnight on New Year's Eve of 2020, police showed up at the door of a home in Gatineau, Quebec. Inside were six adults, celebrating the end of what had been a horrible year for pretty much every Canadian. What happened next was an intense confrontation with police.

In early December, the Quebec government had abruptly backtracked after saying family gatherings would be permitted over Christmas, citing the rising number of COVID-19 cases. As a result of this about-face, indoor and outdoor private gatherings were prohibited in Quebec.[1]

The police were called to this private home in Gatineau as a result of a neighbour's complaint, and the confrontation was recorded by the people inside on their cellphones. The video shows police stepping over the threshold of the home, then pulling a man outside as he screams. A tug-of-war ensues as a woman and an elderly man inside the home try to pull him back into the house. A Christmas wreath is knocked off the door and becomes trapped between the group where it is crushed and then trampled. The man in the centre of the confrontation is slowly pulled outside the house as police rip the hands of his friends and family off him. As he is led away struggling, a police officer comes back to close the door, and the family yells at him to get out. The officer yells at the family to get back inside. As the video ends, a woman outside can be heard screaming.

The video understandably went viral[2] and received significant media attention.

Gatineau police later confirmed that two people were arrested and fines were handed out. A police spokesperson told CTV News that the individual seen in the video was charged with assault and obstructing an officer. "The individuals were recalcitrant and refused to cooperate. The individual arrested in the video had assaulted a police officer, hitting him in the face a few times," said police, in French. The owner of the home was also arrested and charged with refusing to provide personal information. Both were later released at the scene, and fines were issued to those in attendance, $1,546 each.

Mathieu Tessier was one of the men in the video, and he said the confrontation was because an officer had allegedly grabbed his mother's arm and pulled her outside.[3] "At some point, they had no judgement at all. You can't treat people like this," said Tessier. "The truth is . . . they aggressed us."

For civil libertarians, this was an example of an unnecessary police escalation and the predictable and inevitable clash between the existence of highly restrictive public health measures and police enforcement. While the video is only one moment in time that doesn't show the full lead-up to or the aftermath of the altercation, there are serious civil liberties concerns. The video appears to show police entering a home without a warrant, aggressive police conduct towards a family, including elderly individuals, and the culture that led neighbours to call the police to report on a private six-person New Year's Eve celebration.

This chapter will consider how incidents like this one implicate our privacy rights. Privacy is core to who we are as human beings, and how we guard our autonomy against intrusions from the outside world, including intrusions by other citizens and by government. It is at the heart of what lets us live freely and with dignity, without the fear of being constantly observed by outside forces, either malicious or benign. Privacy rights protect us from the unjustified and arbitrary use of government power by controlling what can be known about us and done to us. Unreasonable interference with our privacy often provides the gateway to the violation of our other fundamental rights. For example, unreasonable detention can often begin with an invasion of privacy.

Privacy rights are protected in Canada by our *Charter*. Section 8 protects against unreasonable searches and seizure. This includes an unreasonable search of information. Federal and provincial privacy legislation provides protection against the disclosure of personal information. Section 9 of the *Charter* protects against arbitrary detention or imprisonment.

Of particular concern was government experimentation with giving police and government officials special powers to enforce extraordinary social distancing and lockdown measures. As this chapter will outline, these measures represent an unprecedented expansion of the range of circumstances under which people could be stopped by government authorities. Circumstances which, in normal times, would be beyond the scope of government authority to pry into people's private activities.

Governments even relied on private citizens to act as enforcers of these policies through COVID-19 "snitch lines," where neighbours called police or public health to report each other's social distancing failures, creating a culture of fear and distrust, undermining community cohesion, and exacerbating division along lines of socio-economic class and even race.

Several federal and provincial COVID-19 policies violated both sections 8 and 9 *Charter* rights. In this chapter, we will consider the ways that privacy rights were (or were not) impacted by:

- the COVID Alert app;
- proof of vaccination requirements and vaccine passports;
- the expansion of police powers to enforce COVID-19 restrictions;
- COVID-19 "snitch" lines and the culture of civil liberties; and
- the government tracking and storing of cellphone data.

TESTING AND TRACING: THE COVID ALERT AND ARRIVECAN APPS

Manual contact tracing

Testing and tracing had different iterations during the pandemic. There was manual contact tracing, where various public health regions across the country required public and commercial spaces to record the names and contact information of visitors. For example, restaurants in some regions required patrons to provide their name, phone number, and email address in the event that a positive case was reported in the restaurant. This outsourcing of contact-tracing requirements to private businesses raises concerns around data storage and retention.

COVID Alert app

The manual contact-tracing system was gradually supplemented by a digital system that encouraged people to disclose positive COVID-19 test results on a voluntary phone app released by the federal government, called the "COVID Alert" app. This was intended to make informing close contacts easier and more instantaneous, and to better protect privacy. The COVID Alert app was announced by Prime Minister Trudeau on June 18, 2020.[4] The app would eventually go on to be adopted by all provinces except Alberta[5] and British Columbia,[6] which both opted for their own test-and-trace systems.

However, the app would turn out to be an expensive failure. It cost a fortune and was barely used by the public. The app cost the federal government $20 million: of that, $15.9 million went into promotion and advertising, and another $3.5 million was spent on development and maintenance.[7] Despite the massive amounts spent promoting the app, it had low uptake. According to COVID Alert Impact Data compiled and released by the government of Ontario, as of June 12, 2021, the app had been downloaded 6,957,252 times in Canada and as of June 13, had only recorded 49,967 positive COVID-19 codes.[8] For comparison, Ontario had recorded 1,314,447 COVID-19 cases alone as of June 14 of the same year,[9] and Canada nationally recorded 3,897,879 cases as of June 17.[10] The app was discontinued shortly thereafter.

Overall, while a failure from a policy and cost perspective, the COVID Alert app did a good job guarding the privacy of Canadians. The app used Bluetooth technology to identify other phones that had been in close contact with a positive patient who had voluntarily uploaded a unique code they received from a health care provider when they tested positive. Those phones would then receive an alert over the app. Infected individuals could respond by self-isolating or testing themselves. The app would not store any personal information or track the user's name, address, or location, and all instances of positive COVID-19 contact would be recorded anonymously.

The Ontario Information and Privacy Commissioner applauded the app for "not compelling individuals to use the app or to disclose information about the use of the app."[11] The Privacy Commissioner further committed to monitoring the app to make sure it was used only for its intended purpose.

Overall, the privacy implications of the COVID Alert app were minimal because of a highly principled approach to the implementation of these measures. The privacy commissioners of the federal, provincial, and territorial governments jointly issued statements urging the government and others to avoid making such apps mandatory and to avoid collecting personal information. As a result, the COVID Alert app, which largely respected Canadians' privacy, proved nonetheless to be an expensive failure due to high costs and low uptake.[12]

ArriveCAN app

The fact that the COVID Alert app was discontinued is a positive development to be applauded. Governments abandoning policies that allow them to increase citizen surveillance is not the norm. Often during a crisis, governments will make changes enabling them to increase surveillance and intrude more deeply into the privacy rights of citizens, and those intrusions become permanent. In this sense, it is noteworthy that although the COVID Alert app was discontinued, the ArriveCAN app remained in place, although it is no longer mandatory.

The border-security app ArriveCAN was initially developed so that Canadians could upload negative COVID-19 tests and proof of vaccination when those were requirements to enter the country. However, the app remains in place as of this writing as an advance customs declaration feature. The use of ArriveCAN for this purpose is currently voluntary, and the government says it is in place to "give travellers a more modern and faster experience."[13]

ArriveCAN has not been without controversy. In July 2022, travellers reported that the ArriveCAN app was incorrectly notifying them to quarantine. A spokesperson from the Canada Border Services Agency confirmed that they had "identified a technical glitch with the app" that "can produce an erroneous notification instructing people to quarantine." The case of the ArriveCAN app demonstrates the lack of accountability around these apps—and the disruptive effects that false predictions can have on people's lives. For example, *CBC News* reported the story of Don and Karin Bennett of Burlington, Ontario. After returning home from a trip to Chicago in July 2022, Karin discovered several emails in her junk mail folder from ArriveCAN instructing her to quarantine. Karin was vaccinated against COVID-19, which ought to have made her exempt from quarantine during that time. Fearful of fines for travellers who break the rules, Karin decided to quarantine. "There's the threatening language of fines of $5,000, plus sending police to your house," said Don.[14] When apps produce false positives, this can result in confusion and mistrust in public authorities.[15]

Like the COVID Alert app, the cost of the ArriveCAN app was also controversial. In response to a question from a Conservative MP, the Canada Border Services Agency reported to parliament on June 1, 2022, that it had spent $19.7 million developing the app and $4.9 million on app maintenance.[16] But *The Globe and Mail* has contested this figure, citing a taxpayer cost of $54 million. This is more than double the initially disclosed amount.[17] What required such high costs is unclear. *CTV News* reported that Sheetal Jaitly, chief executive officer of the

Toronto-based digital innovation firm TribalScale, said it would have cost his company less than $1 million to build the app. In October of 2022 some of Jaitly's colleagues launched a voluntary hackathon with the goal of cloning the app and showing the public how fast and cheap it would be to build. "By Saturday mid-day, we had the majority of it complete," Jaitly said.[18]

CELLPHONE LOCATION MONITORING BY GOVERNMENT

In December 2021, the independent investigative journalism outlet *Blacklock's Reporter* was digging deep into federal government contracts and uncovered a bombshell.[19] The Public Health Agency of Canada (PHAC) had quietly put out a request for proposals (RFP) for a contract that would allow them to continue to track the mobility data of Canadians.

This was how it became known that PHAC had already been monitoring cellphone location data for thirty-three million mobile devices through a sole-source contract with TELUS for the previous eight months. The new data-collection RFP that PHAC was seeking would track cell location data from 2019 until 2023, and potentially beyond.

The issue became a national media story. "Due to the urgency of the pandemic, (PHAC) collected and used mobility data, such as cell-tower location data, throughout the COVID-19 response," a PHAC spokesperson told the *National Post*.[20] PHAC claims to have used the location data to evaluate the effectiveness of public lockdown measures and allow the agency to "understand possible links between movement of populations within Canada and spread of COVID-19," the spokesperson said.

The government says this data collection was necessary to understand movement patterns during the pandemic and emphasized that the request said that the data must ensure privacy for Canadians and be stripped of identifying information.

The government also claimed that they had in fact disclosed that this monitoring would be taking place. This is a dubious suggestion. The government claims that this disclosure was made in a March 23, 2020, news release. But the news release reveals nothing of the sort. In the release, the Prime Minister's Office announced that the government would provide support to BlueDot, a software company specializing in the spread of infectious diseases, and through PHAC, would use the company's disease analytics platform to support modelling and monitoring of the spread of COVID-19, and to inform government decision-making as the situation evolved.[21] This brief, nondescript mention of the use of modelling and monitoring data is not a reasonable demonstration of transparency or accountability,[22] and it is hardly a disclosure that the government would be tracking the cellphone location data of citizens.

Concerned by these revelations, the House of Commons called on the government in early February 2022 to suspend PHAC's plans for expanded surveillance. The vote by Members of Parliament followed the passing of a motion by the House of Commons Ethics Committee to halt the collection of data until privacy concerns were addressed. The committee motion was unanimously backed by MPs on the committee from all parties, including Liberals. However, when the motion came before the whole House, the governing Liberals voted against it.[23] Instead of addressing this hot political issue head-on, the government allowed it to quietly die when the tender expired on February 18, 2022.

The Ethics Committee conducted an investigation into PHAC's cellphone location surveillance and released a report in May 2022.[24] The report made twenty-two recommendations, including that the federal government stipulate in all future RFPs for collecting the data of Canadians that Canadians could choose to opt out of the data collection and that instructions for the opting-out method be easily understood, widely communicated, and remain publicly available.

The Ethics Committee report also concluded that when the government engages in data collection it should meaningfully consult with the Privacy Commissioner. In this case, the Privacy Commissioner came to the committee and said he was informed of the program but wasn't consulted. That is concerning, given that the *de facto* purpose of his office is protecting the privacy of Canadians.

In the end, privacy laws may not have technically been violated by this surveillance program, but that is due in part to the inadequacy of the laws themselves. The Privacy Commissioner has said Canada's current privacy laws are outdated for the digital age. The federal privacy legislation was drafted in the 2000s and Ontario's privacy legislation in the 1980s. Privacy expert Dr. Ann Cavoukian has called on government "to update privacy laws dramatically so they apply to all data, including anonymized data."[25] In an interview with this book's author, Christine Van Geyn, on *Canadian Justice*, Dr. Cavoukian went on to express concerns about mission creep with regard to data surveillance. "I'd be concerned within the government's other departments wanting to gain access to this information. It's an easy sell: PHAC may be approached by other groups like law enforcement. The concerns are real and that kind of third-party external authorization is lacking. People are going to want access to the data beyond those using it for its original purpose."

The technology-transparency advocacy group OpenMedia has also been harshly critical. In a statement about the PHAC surveillance OpenMedia said "While what was done isn't illegal, it surely falls short of how we'd want our government to behave. Ultimately the mobility data tracking used by PHAC took advantage of the flaws in our badly outdated privacy legislation—that the federal government has repeatedly promised and failed to update."[26]

This failure to update the *Privacy Act*, combined with the government's arguable exploitation of the gaps in that law to monitor the movements of Canadians during the pandemic, should be concerning for civil libertarians. While strictly speaking the conduct of PHAC may have been legal, it was certainly not respectful of the privacy of Canadian citizens and not reasonable as a political choice in a liberal democracy.

EXPANSIONS OF POLICE POWERS TO ENFORCE COVID-19 REGULATIONS

Some of the most troubling, and likely unconstitutional, violations of Canadians' privacy rights came in the form of expanded enforcement powers for police and government officials. The exceptional powers given to police and officials enforcing social distancing may themselves have been unconstitutional. And, in some instances, police went beyond even the exceptional powers they had been granted.

Ontario's stay-at-home carding enforcement order: O. Reg. 8/21

One of the most shocking privacy violations was an Ontario regulation enacted on short notice that gave police the exceptional power to stop and question people outside their homes. The regulation was enacted at the same time as the province enacted a strict "stay-at-home" order that prohibited citizens from even taking children to local playgrounds.[27]

On April 16th, 2021, Ontario Premier Doug Ford announced by press release that "effective Saturday, April 17, at 12:01 a.m., police officers and other provincial offences officers will have the authority to require any individual to provide their home address and purpose for not being at their residence. In addition, police officers, special constables, and First Nation [*sic*] Constables will have the authority to stop vehicles to inquire about an individual's reasons for leaving their home."[28]

The enforcement power given to police to back up this stay-at-home order was shocking. As laid out in O. Reg. 8/21: Enforcement of COVID-19 Measures, a regulation made under the *Emergency Management and Civil Protection Act*, Ontario police were to be given the discretion to demand any person found outside of their home provide their address and their reason for not being at home. The regulation was extreme and is worthy of reproducing in its entirety. Section 2.1(2) of the regulation said:[29]

(2) A police officer or other provincial offences officer may require any individual who is not in a place of residence to,

    (a) provide the address of the residence at which they are currently residing; and

    (b) provide their purpose for not being at their residence, unless the individual is in an outdoor or common area of their residence.

The regulation is a violation of the *Charter*'s guarantee against arbitrary detention. Random stops have been considered in other cases,[30] but Ford's regulation was different and far broader in scope.

Indeed, the Ford government's enforcement measures in O. Reg. 8/21 were basically unlimited in scope, allowing police the power not just to stop drivers, but to stop anyone found outside a place of residence. It is worth noting that Ontario Attorney General Doug Downey, appeared to have raised concerns at cabinet about the constitutionality of this measure. *CBC News* reported that sources confirmed to them that during a cabinet meeting Downey had raised concerns about the unconstitutionality of the police powers.[31] These concerns were shot down, and the controversial provision was passed even though Ford's cabinet included several other lawyers, including Christine Elliott, Caroline Mulroney, Ross Romano, and Prabmeet Sarkaria. The convention of collective cabinet responsibility means that decisions by cabinet must be publicly supported by all members of cabinet, even if they do not privately agree with them. If a member of cabinet wishes to openly object to a cabinet decision, then they are obligated to resign from cabinet. It is galling that the province's top lawyer and a group of other lawyers trained in constitutional law would have agreed to publicly support such a clearly unconstitutional regulation despite being well aware of its unconstitutionality.[32]

Several groups immediately responded to the Ford regulation by announcing they would challenge its constitutionality, and first among them was the Canadian Constitution Foundation (CCF). "Ontarians are essentially living under a 24-hour curfew and police will now be able to randomly stop people and vehicles and demand an explanation of why people are out living their lives," said CCF Executive Director and author of this book, Joanna Baron. "With these new police powers, Ontario is one step closer to becoming a police state."[33]

Both the CCF and the Canadian Civil Liberties Association (CCLA)[34] put out statements that they were preparing litigation. To assist members of the public who were frightened of the new regulations, the CCF also issued a "know your rights" guide with information about interacting with police and outlining how the new regulation interacted with Canadians' *Charter* rights.[35]

Many police departments announced that they would not be conducting random stops despite the new powers.[36] Of Ontario's forty-five provincially mandated police forces, all but three posted statements against random and unwarranted stops using the new power. Two services did not comment, and only the OPP came out in favour.[37] This was good news. Police need to interact with the community and have spent years trying to build community trust. Randomly stopping and harassing families walking outside would erode this trust. And, of course, police also need to abide by the *Charter*. It was sensible for police to announce they would not enforce an almost certainly unconstitutional regulation.

The Ford government quickly walked back the sweeping new police powers just one day later. "But we moved too fast," Ford said, "Simply put, we got it wrong. We made a mistake. These decisions, they left a lot of people really concerned. For that I am sorry, and I sincerely apologize."[38] *CBC News* journalist Mike Crawley reported that a source disclosed to him that "Ford was especially rattled by the way police force after police force announced they would not use the powers the government gave them."[39] Under the new amended regulations, which lasted from April 17 to June 1, in order for the police to require information of a person they needed a "reason to suspect" that a person was participating in a prohibited gathering. And they would need to believe that "it would be in the public interest to determine whether the individual is in compliance" with the "stay-at-home" order.[40]

But even the amended regulation remained a problem. The Ontario Human Rights Commission continued to criticize the Ford government's expansion of police powers to enforce COVID-19 rules, saying that even the new amended regulation continued to grant police "broad, vague, and highly discretionary authority to stop and question members of the public. Such discretionary powers are very problematic because they create confusion about the rights and obligations of people interacting with the police."[41]

Quebec's experiences with extreme police powers

The government of Quebec was perhaps one of the harshest enforcers of COVID-19 lockdowns throughout the pandemic and was the only province with a curfew.

In September 2020, Quebec public health director Dr. Horacio Arruda stated that public health was in discussions with the ministries of Justice and Public Security about allowing police to enter residences to enforce COVID-19 gathering restrictions. Arruda backtracked just a few minutes later, but the result was confusion.[42] Quebec Public Security Minister Geneviève Guilbault sought to clarify the government's message around the enforcement of COVID-19 restrictions, saying police wouldn't be allowed to enter a private residence without consent or a warrant. However, she added that if the epidemiological situation were to worsen "dramatically," the government would consider giving that power to police.[43] Instead of clarifying, this statement sowed even more confusion.

Examples of high-conflict policing incidents

In addition to the Gatineau arrests described at the beginning of this chapter, there were a number of high-conflict and troubling interactions between the public and police reported in Quebec. This was likely a result of Quebec having very restrictive COVID-19 measures combined with tough enforcement powers.

For example, another viral video taken on Christmas morning of 2020 showed a confrontation between police and people inside a home on Île d'Orléans. Gatherings for Christmas were prohibited in Quebec at the time. A Sûreté du Québec officer said police were dispatched to the house after they received a call reporting an illegal gathering. The officer could not say exactly how many people were in the home but that the number was in violation of public health measures. They said a fine of up to $1,546 was given out.[44]

In a May 2021 report, the CCLA summarized Quebec's strategy for dealing with the COVID-19 pandemic through police enforcement measures. Of particular concern was the Quebec curfew. The curfew that was imposed in the name of curbing the spread of COVID-19 prohibited people from being outside between 8:00 p.m. and 5:00a.m. The CCLA wrote that although the curfew was originally intended as a temporary shock treatment, it remained in place for three months with no plan to rescind it on the horizon. The CCLA wrote that:[45]

> The enactment of broad, complicated, and strict laws invites arbitrary and unfair enforcement. These consequences were evident in Quebec during the first wave of COVID-19. Throughout April, May and June many Quebeckers got in touch with CCLA to report instances of unfair, arbitrary ticketing. One person described being ticketed when the stranger walking behind them in the park stepped too close. One woman who works at a Montreal social service organization was ticketed for stopping to offer support services to a street-involved Indigenous client.

It is especially disturbing that the curfew did not include an exemption for people experiencing homelessness who may have had no place to go. Even Ontario's unconstitutional stay-at-home order included a homelessness exemption. This lack of an exemption led to tragic results.

In one incident, a homeless man living outside Montreal died overnight, and speculation was that he appeared to have died hiding from police who were enforcing the province's curfew. The body of Raphaël

André, originally from the Innu community of Matimekush-Lac John, was found in a portable toilet on January 17, 2021.[46] Mr. André was forced to leave a nearby shelter, the Open Door, which has been ordered closed for overnight stays ever since a COVID-19 outbreak there in December of 2020. He was facing the risk of a $1,550 ticket if caught by police outside.[47]

Federal Indigenous Services Minister Marc Miller said Mr. André's death could have been avoided. Montreal Mayor Valérie Plante had also asked Quebec to be more lenient with the city's homeless population. However, Legault rebuffed such demands. He justified his position by saying that exempting homeless people from the curfew rules would encourage others to "pretend" to be homeless,[48] a frankly cruel response.

Ultimately, a legal clinic obtained a court order that exempted the homeless from the curfew. Quebec Superior Court Justice Chantal Masse ruled that although the curfew was introduced in the public interest, its current application imperilled the lives, safety, and health of the homeless.[49] She also noted that the Crown did not challenge evidence presented to court showing tickets, which carried fines from $1,000 to $6,000, had already been given to homeless people for breaking the curfew.[50]

The CCLA report "COVID-19 and Law Enforcement in Canada: The Second Wave," also detailed a particularly egregious police interaction in December 2020, as recounted by a man named Mike from Quebec City:[51]

> I was walking with my partner, Alex, in downtown Quebec City when she began to have a shooting pain in her feet. She suffers from Acrocyanosis, a condition involving poor circulation, pain, and numbness. She needed to soak her feet in hot water to help with circulation so we went to the closest place we could think of—the apartment of an extended family member. I had to help her up the stairs, she was in a lot of pain. When we got inside we put her feet in hot water, and Alex's relatives made tea for us.

While we were there the Quebec City Police stormed in, 12 officers in all.

They entered without consent, no search warrant, and no "Telewarrant" issued by a Judge or Court. We asked them who let them in, how did they get in, and if they had a warrant. The officers admitted they didn't have a warrant but said the Ministry of Health had given them the authority to enter homes. They demanded to see our IDs and laughed at Alex when she said she had a medical condition. They told us we would go to jail if we didn't do what they said. We were all scared, and Alex was crying. At one point she had trouble breathing and fell to the floor.

The police searched the entire apartment—roaming through personal belongings, wardrobes and closets. They said they believed we were hiding more people. They even demanded to have access to Alex's Facebook account.

In the police report, they said that we were being hostile and non-compliant. That's simply not true. They also said they had our consent to enter the apartment. That is also not true.

I understand that due to COVID, laws and bylaws, especially in Quebec, have become extremely strict. However this seems to violate our basic constitutional rights as Canadians. Quebec or elsewhere.

We were all given fines of $1550.00.

In the words of sociologist Christopher Schneider, "the pandemic has seemingly augmented the ability of police to act as front-line moral entrepreneurs who occupy a unique position as rule enforcers with strict attention to risk management."[52] As a result of the expanding rules regarding "social distancing," curfews, and increased police discretion to enforce those measures, police abuses were bound to occur.

COVID-19 "SNITCH LINES" AND CANADA'S CIVIL LIBERTIES CULTURE

In George Orwell's dystopian novel *1984*, Winston, the protagonist, reflects on how the totalitarian state under which he lives uses people as informers in order to enforce the state's strict political and sexual ideology[53]:

> The family could not actually be abolished, and, indeed, people were encouraged to be fond of their children, in almost the old-fashioned way. The children, on the other hand, were systematically turned against their parents and taught to spy on them and report their deviations. The family had become in effect an extension of the Thought Police. It was a device by means of which everyone could be surrounded night and day by informers who knew him intimately.

In the novel, the totalitarian state of Oceania recognizes it cannot completely destroy familial relationships, so it instead uses those relationships as a tool to spy on its citizens. In the process, it devalues the relationships and breeds guilt and paranoia in the book's protagonist, Winston, because he knows he cannot trust anyone.

In Canada during the pandemic, COVID-19 "snitch lines" turned neighbours against neighbours, causing people to wonder whether they should turn their community members in for violations of "social distancing" rules. In an article in *The Signal*, Simon Smith relayed the story of Jenn Kidson and her mother's sixtieth birthday in Nova Scotia:[54] On a Sunday afternoon in 2020, Ms. Kidson watched in confusion as a police cruiser pulled into her son's driveway in West Chezzetcook, a rural community outside Halifax. Ms. Kidson and her family were celebrating her mother's sixtieth birthday party. They had just finished having some birthday cake and watching a video they'd made. There were nine of them present, within COVID-19 gathering restrictions at the time. The RCMP officer knocked on the door and informed the family that a neighbour had called the police to report a large gathering in the home. The officer apologized and left, as the gathering was not an infraction. "We laughed at the ridiculousness of it but, yeah, it was an uneasy feeling that a complete stranger took it upon themselves to police us," Kidson wrote in a text message to *The Signal*.

The thought that neighbours could be monitoring you for potential violations of often ambiguous "social-distancing" requirements leaves many Canadians uneasy. There was a potential for snitch lines to be abused by those out for revenge on neighbours they do not like, and the resulting atmosphere diminishes trust and respect between people who ought to be able to get along.

The author of this book, Christine Van Geyn, has a personal experience with this type of "revenge" reporting. A friend of Christine's was celebrating her young child's first birthday in Ontario by hosting an outdoor party in her driveway. It's no easy feat to host a birthday party for infants in Ontario in December, but at the time, Ontario had a strict gathering limit in place of ten people outdoors. In total this gathering had five masked moms and five infants. But the addition of a children's music instructor put them over the gathering limit. Later that week, the host mom received a knock on her door from two police officers. Apparently, a neighbour who had a pre-existing grudge against the party hostess had witnessed the outdoor baby birthday party and called the police. The neighbour had weaponized gathering limits and used it as a pretext to use police to punish a someone she disliked.

According to Alexander McClelland and Alex Luscombe, most reports of COVID-19 snitch lines came from southern Ontario although lines also existed in Newfoundland, Quebec, British Columbia, Alberta, and Saskatchewan.[55] They go on to offer the following criticism of snitch lines:[56]

> While there are many reasons to be critical of the current emphasis on COVID-19 snitching practices, one major concern pertains to how these calls may simply amplify and further entrench pre-existing inequalities

in policing enforcement. Who chooses to report and who gets reported on is not likely to be a random or equal opportunity phenomenon. By virtue of being more visibly alone, those who are homeless or who spend much of their time working in public spaces (e.g., food delivery drivers) are going to face a higher likelihood of being snitched on.

Eric Mykhalovskiy et al. echo that concern in their article on human rights concerns and COVID-19 policy, warning that snitch lines "can promote overzealous moralism, social division, and demonization of those who allegedly do not comply with public health requirements." As an alternative, they write "Rather than encouraging people to surveil one another, at considerable risk of unfounded complaints, overfocus on marginalized people, and discriminatory enforcement by police and by-law officers, we encourage more 'prosocial' responses—such as space for self-isolation and peer mental health support for homeless people—that align with established public health social justice traditions."[57]

In an article entitled, "COVID-19 pandemic is turning Canada into a nation of snitches," Christopher Nardi reports that, "According to a Leger Marketing poll published on Tuesday, no less than 40.7 % of Canadians said they intended to report any behaviour that goes against measures put in place to fight COVID-19. While only 22.8% said they weren't snitches, the remaining 36.5% said they didn't know or refused to answer."[58]

PRIVACY IMPLICATIONS OF VACCINE PASSPORTS AND MANDATES

While we will deal with the civil liberties and other implications of vaccine passports in Chapter 10, it is worth briefly discussing the implications of vaccine passports for privacy.

To be clear, we use the terms "vaccine passport" and "proof of vaccine policy" to refer to a government-imposed mandatory proof of vaccination that is required to access a public space or service. We are not referring to policies created by private businesses. This book only deals in passing with the voluntary decision by a business to require its employees to be vaccinated (see Chapter 10). While such requirements do raise privacy concerns, they are employment and human rights law issues, and do not engage constitutional rights.

Vaccine passports were adopted by the federal government and by every provincial and territorial government in Canada.

The use of vaccine passports raises privacy concerns as a matter of principle. The CCLA succinctly summarized the privacy concerns raised by vaccine passports:[59]

> Allowing private entities to collect and use personal health information about us is invasive. Tying the ability to participate in public life with a ubiquitous or persistent form of surveillance ("show us proof you have made a socially acceptable choice about your health") is a diminishment of the level of freedom we expect in a democracy that must be carefully examined for proportionality in the pandemic context. If the passport is digital or has a digital version, additional issues of technical privacy, security, and access arise.

When it became clear in mid-2021 that vaccine passports were going to be brought into force in provinces across Canada, the federal, provincial, and territorial privacy commissioners once again issued a joint statement, this time on the topic of vaccine passports. The commissioners stated that "The necessity, effectiveness and proportionality of vaccine passports must be continually monitored to ensure that they continue to be justified. Vaccine passports must be decommissioned if, at any time, it is determined that they are not a necessary, effective or proportionate response to address their public health purposes."[60]

For civil libertarians, the case justifying the use of vaccine passports was questionable from the start. But as the pandemic progressed it became obvious that new variants were evading vaccines. Vaccinated and boosted individuals were contracting and transmitting the virus. In that factual context, it is our view that the privacy commissioners' requirement that these tools be necessary, effective, and proportionate could not be met.

In addition to stipulating necessity, effectiveness, and proportionality requirements, the privacy commissioners also stressed that meaningful consent is needed to provide authority for the checking of vaccine status by public and private service providers. Additionally, there must also be a solid relationship of trust between providers and receivers. On the issue of consent to vaccine passports, the privacy commissioners also made a particularly interesting comment: "Individuals must have a true choice: consent must not be required as a condition of service." This requirement seems ultimately to have fallen by the wayside once vaccine passports became mandatory to access many places and services throughout Canada.

Beyond the principled question of whether vaccine passports were a justified intrusion into individuals' private health information, there were privacy concerns about the practical implementation of these tools.

Vaccine passports and the apps used by provinces and businesses to verify them were not always secure against leaks of sensitive personal information. The Alberta proof of vaccination app Portpass was the subject of several CBC reports regarding the app's failures to properly secure the personal information of users. On September 28, 2021, *CBC News* reported that "the user profiles on the app's website could be accessed by members of the public".[61] Then again, one month later the CBC reported, "Personal information belonging to more than 17,000 users of the private proof-of-vaccination app Portpass is still unsecured and visible online—including, in some cases, photos of drivers' licences and passports—despite assurances from the company that its data-security problems have been fixed."[62] Saskatchewan also had minor problems with its proof-of-vaccination services when up to nineteen residents of the province were erroneously provided with the QR code of another person, allowing them to receive that person's information.[63]

Fiascos like these go directly against the trust privacy commissioners had asked for during the consideration of vaccine passports a few months earlier. By haphazardly pursuing COVID-19 proof-of-vaccination requirements, the governments of Alberta and Saskatchewan exposed Canadians to grave privacy violations, allowing other individuals to access their intimate personal information. When the government fails to take these measures seriously enough to maintain their integrity, they diminish Canadians' trust that government measures are properly protecting their privacy.

CHAPTER 7
COVID-19 AND EQUALITY RIGHTS

Sascha King lives in Kitchener, Ontario, and is a personal trainer, disability advocate, and owner of the small business NorthXFit. NorthXFit is a special place. It is an accessible gym intended to make physical fitness available for the entire community, including the disability community. When Sascha founded the gym, she wanted to build a unique place where everyone would feel welcome and included, including individuals with special needs.

The gym has invested in special (and expensive) adaptive equipment that can be used safely by individuals with physical disabilities. The personal trainers at the gym have specific qualifications that help them train individuals with physical and mental disabilities. Among the gym's clients are individuals with brain injuries, special Olympians, individuals with Down syndrome, people with visual impairments, and many others. Many of Sascha's clients use the gym as a way of managing their disabilities.

The Ontario province-wide lockdown that came into effect on December 26, 2020, meant Sascha had to close her gym. She didn't want to do it, but it was the law.

Many of the clients at NorthXFit are unable to work out at home. They either lack the appropriate adaptive equipment or need professional assistance and supervision to work out. Telling a visually impaired client to watch a YouTube video at home to stay fit would be ignorant and insensitive. Yet that is what the provincial government seemed to be expecting NorthXFit clients to do. Even for the few clients Sascha had who wanted to stay connected virtually, the stay-at-home order in place meant she couldn't even drive to the gym to run an online class.

Physical fitness is important for everyone's well-being and especially for those with special needs. And it is even more important to stay healthy and active during a pandemic. But the lockdown made it incredibly hard for many people to stay fit and healthy because gyms were ordered closed. And for individuals who have certain special or adaptive needs, it is virtually impossible. The impact of closing the gym on these individuals who could not adapt to home workouts because of a disability was far different than it was on able-bodied people.

Of course, the lockdown didn't impact everyone equally. Although gyms were shut for ordinary citizens—including individuals with special needs—they remained open for the elite classes. High-performance athletes, like the Toronto Maple Leafs, were permitted to train in their exclusive and elite gyms. Millionaire twenty-year-olds were given special privileges, while disabled Ontarians were denied the right to maintain their health through fitness programs like the one offered at NorthXFit. If gyms could be open for the Maple Leafs, they ought to have been open for Sascha's clients, who needed them to manage their disabilities.

The Canadian *Charter* guarantees in section 15 that every individual is equal before and under the law and has the right to the equal protection and benefit of the law without discrimination. Sascha King challenged the Ontario order that closed her gym on the basis of the *Charter*'s section 15 guarantee of equality. She was represented by lawyer Ryan O'Connor, a bearded civil litigator with a penchant for craft beer and scarves and who also has a massive Twitter following.

O'Connor brought an application in Ontario Superior Court in January 2021.[1] The case did not get to a hearing, but it was a rare example of a successful challenge to COVID-19 restrictions because the legal challenge resulted in a policy change.[2] O'Connor tweeted an update about the case: "PARTIAL VICTORY: Ontario has amended the lockdown rules following the court challenge of our client [. . .]

to gym and fitness class closures which argues, in part that banning disabled Ontarians from the gym violates their Charter rights."

O'Connor was right. In response to Sascha's case, Ontario had amended the lockdown rules to allow gyms to open when they cater to clients with a disability who had a medical note requiring physical therapy that they could not receive elsewhere. Such gyms also needed to abide by specific health protocols. The change resulted in many gyms across Ontario being able to reopen under the disability exemption and demonstrated the benefit of going to court to challenge the constitutionality of excessive and unjust COVID-19 restrictions. While not technically a court victory, this was an important policy victory that affected the lives of many people.

This chapter will consider a series of cases like Sascha King's, including cases brought by the Canadian Constitution Foundation (CCF), and the legal issues they raised. The chapter will consider:

- what the right to equality means in Canadian law;
- the CCF's challenge to vaccine passports in British Columbia;
- equality concerns around vaccine passports generally;
- the inconsistent application of arguments around substantive equality; and
- masking requirements.

WHAT DOES EQUALITY MEAN IN CANADA?

Section 15 of the *Charter* establishes equality as a fundamental legal right of all Canadians. The language of section 15(1) guarantees that "every individual is equal before and under the law and has the right to the equal protection and equal benefit of the law without discrimination and, in particular, without discrimination based on race, national or ethnic origin, colour, religion, sex, age or mental or physical disability."

In addition to the specifically listed grounds in section 15(1) on which discrimination is prohibited, the Canadian courts have adopted what are known as "analogous" grounds. For example, sexual orientation, marital status, and citizenship have been found to be analogous to the listed characteristics in section 15(1), and discrimination on these grounds is also prohibited.

The Supreme Court of Canada has always emphasized that section 15 is concerned with "substantive equality" as opposed to formal equality. Formal equality is concerned with laws that are discriminatory on their face. For example, historic Canadian laws that subjected Japanese Canadians to internment, or laws that prohibited women from voting are "facially discriminatory."[3] Those laws directly gave different legal rights to individuals based on race and sex. Under the *Charter* it is easy to see how they would violate the section 15 protection to equal treatment under the law.

In contrast, "substantive equality" is concerned with laws that may be neutral on their face but are discriminatory in their effect. "Substantive equality" has been a part of Canadian equality jurisprudence since the first Supreme Court decision under section 15(1), a case called *Andrews*.[4] In that case, Justice McIntyre accepted that facially neutral laws may be discriminatory, stating "It must be recognized [. . .] that every difference in treatment between individuals under the law will not necessarily result in inequality and, as well, that identical treatment may frequently produce serious inequality."[5]

While substantive equality has always been a part of *Charter* jurisprudence, its scope has expanded quite dramatically and has been the subject of great debate.

By 2020, the Supreme Court had held that a concept called "adverse impact" discrimination violates the notion of substantive equality.[6] In the landmark section 15 case *Fraser v. Canada*[7] Justice Abella for the majority of the Supreme Court stated that whether or not the lawmaker *intended* to create a disparate impact is irrelevant.[8] As well, the Court emphasized that differential treatment can be discriminatory even if it is "based on choices" made by the claimant.

But the *Fraser* case has been subject to some criticism. The dissenting judges disagreed with Justice Abella's relaxation of the causation requirement between the impugned law and the alleged disadvantage, stating it is dangerous in lowering the claimant's evidentiary burden to the point of potential insignificance.[9] According to the dissent, "Substantive equality has become almost infinitely malleable, allowing judges to invoke it as rhetorical cover for their own policy preferences in deciding a given case. This discretion does not accord with, but rather departs from, the rule of law."[10]

Some scholars have criticized the *Fraser* decision and section 15 jurisprudence for lack of clarity and constant flux. Certain scholars who hold this view acknowledge that the *Fraser* dissent is right to criticise the confusing standards and constant shifting of legal tests, even if they ultimately disagree with the dissent and celebrate the outcome in *Fraser*, albeit cautiously.[11] Yet others have criticized the notion of substantive equality from a philosophical perspective, describing it as little more than an argument for equality of outcome.[12]

The reality is that some level of substantive equality is now an established part of section 15(1) jurisprudence. However, the contextual nature of substantive equality can make it hard to predict how a court will apply its interpretation of section 15.

This debate aside, in the context of COVID-19 policy in Canada, it is interesting to note that many (but not all) of the advocates of substantive equality appear to have all but abandoned their position when it comes to the differential impact COVID-19 restrictions have had on groups that are members of section 15 protected classes. If the position has not been abandoned by the advocates of substantive equality, the potential discriminatory impacts of these policies have certainly been ignored by many of them. This incongruity will be discussed in detail later in this chapter.

This book is not intended to resolve the dispute over the scope of substantive equality. This is a complex issue that courts are still wrestling with.[13] While as an organization the Canadian Constitution Foundation has a perspective on this issue, our purpose in raising the debate here is merely to point out the inconsistent (and perhaps even self-serving) manner in which concern for substantive equality is raised (or conveniently ignored) by its usual proponents.

VACCINE PASSPORTS GENERALLY[14]

Vaccine passports are a facially neutral policy. The provinces and territories did not set up vaccine passports in a manner which explicitly discriminated against the kinds of groups listed in section 15(1) nor did they explicitly discriminate along analogous grounds. Nonetheless, when governments were considering implementing vaccine passports, some groups expressed concern regarding the equality implications of their implementation.

The CCF repeatedly expressed broad civil liberties concerns about vaccine passports, which have certain negative impacts on personal medical decision making and autonomy. The Canadian Civil Liberties Association (CCLA) also expressed broad concern around vaccine passports, stating that "Socially sorting people based on personal decisions about their health, which they are legally entitled to make, runs the risk of creating different levels of freedom for different 'categories' of people, a risk that is likely to intersect with other systemic inequalities and affect some groups more than others."[15]

Chapter 10 of this book includes a detailed discussion of the civil liberties implications of vaccine passports. This section is dedicated to the equality concerns arising from this type of policy, which was adopted by every Canadian province and by the federal government. The equality concerns were largely related to medical exemptions, religious exemptions, and race-based substantive-equality concerns.

VACCINE PASSPORTS AND MEDICAL EXEMPTIONS

The troubling political rhetoric around medical exemptions

It's hard to fathom why Canadian governments would enact regulations like vaccine passports that would restrict access to public spaces and services that have no accommodations for people with disabilities. It is well recognized that it is unsafe for people with certain medical conditions to be vaccinated. One of the most widely known contraindications of the

COVID-19 vaccine is for people who have had an adverse reaction to the first dose. It seems common sense that governments would exempt such individuals from the vaccine passport requirement.

When vaccine passports first became a part of the policy debate in Canada, the CCF expressed scepticism about the legality and effectiveness of such measures broadly, but expressed immediate and urgent concern for people who could not be vaccinated for a medical reason or because of a sincerely held religious belief. For such individuals, blanket vaccine passport policies without exemptions were an urgent concern.

The CCLA also expressed concerns for people who might have been medically contraindicated for COVID-19 vaccination, stating:

> There are some people with pre-existing medical conditions or disabilities where vaccination would be counter-indicated, and it is unclear how many people that affects because the vaccines were generally (or primarily) only tested for emergency authorization on healthy adults. People who live with persistent illness or disability are among those who most need human rights protections to ensure equal treatment. Even if the passport simply indicates "medically exempt," that categorization may affect how individuals are treated (even if such differential treatment is technically prohibited).

But in late 2021, public policy on vaccination had fully shifted to black-and-white thinking, with no room for nuance or difference. The public health zeitgeist had become "vaccinate at any cost," and became so extreme that some governments would not even accommodate people who could not be vaccinated for medical reasons.

Some of those who asserted a right to a medical exemption were treated with contempt and suspicion, even when their medical conditions were well documented and their fears well founded. For example, a Toronto restaurant[16] self-righteously proclaimed that it wouldn't accept medical exemptions because of their own suspicion that such accommodation would result in "abuse."

The result of the desire by the government and the public to push vaccination rates higher and higher began bulldozing over vulnerable people.

When announcing new federal rules requiring proof of vaccination to travel on planes and trains, Prime Minister Trudeau stated[17] that medical exemptions "will be exceedingly narrow, specific, and to be honest, somewhat onerous to obtain." This is bizarre. If a treating physician recommends against vaccination, why shouldn't that be enough to obtain an exemption? Why would the prime minister seek to make a process "onerous" for people whose doctors contraindicated vaccination for them?

The answer is, of course, politics. And the politics on this issue shifted very quickly.

In British Columbia, Provincial Health Officer Dr. Bonnie Henry announced the province's vaccine passport policy just three months after saying that such a policy was discriminatory. At a May 26, 2021, press conference, Dr. Henry said "there is no way that we will recommend inequities be increased or use vaccine passports for services for public access here in British Columbia."[18] Yet on August 23, Dr. Henry announced that B.C. would be implementing this exact policy. The contradictory statements were so jarring they were turned into a popular video mashup on Twitter.[19]

None of this happened because the policy suddenly became more equitable and less discriminatory. It happened because the politics in B.C. changed.

This was the case across the country. In Ontario, NDP leader Andrea Horwath expressed suspicion[20] around medical exemptions for two Progressive Conservative members of provincial parliament, calling their exemptions "statistically curious." In Manitoba, the vaccine passport policy was in place for weeks without any accommodation for medical exemptions until there was a threat of litigation by the CCF.[21]

It should be startling to hear politicians and health leaders speak this way, and it should be especially startling to hear it from physicians themselves. The relationship between patient and physician is sacrosanct, but in 2021 we entered an era where the political goal of increasing vaccination rates inserted itself between the patient and his or her physician.

While it is not unreasonable to vet claims of medical exemptions, making the standard exceedingly narrow, specific, and "onerous," to quote the prime minister, had serious negative consequences.

Manitoba immunization cards and medical exemptions

In the summer of 2021, the Manitoba Chief Provincial Public Health Officer, Dr. Brent Roussin, enacted two orders related to vaccine passports. The orders, made on June 30 and August 3, excluded unvaccinated people from entering certain public spaces and provided no exemptions for individuals who could not be vaccinated for medical reasons or for reasons of faith or conscience.

In response to these orders, the CCF wrote to the Manitoba government to express concern that the orders were discriminatory and a violation of section 15 of the *Charter*. The CCF was not alone: the Manitoba government also received a letter from the CCLA about the concerns that organization had around the province's plan for a vaccine passport.[22]

In our letter to the Manitoba government, the CCF described the story of Sarah, a woman who had developed pericarditis and pericardial effusion following her first dose of a COVID-19 vaccine. Sarah experienced heart palpitations within fifteen minutes of receiving her first dose of the vaccine. The palpitations eventually subsided, but in the days following her vaccination she experienced increasing and unfamiliar pain in her chest as well as shortness of breath. The pain became more intense and frequent, so on the fourth day following her vaccination she went to the hospital, where she was diagnosed with pericarditis and pericardial effusion. These specific heart conditions are rare adverse reactions to the COVID-19 vaccine. Sarah was advised by her physician not to get a second dose of any COVID-19 vaccine as it would not be safe for her.

The Manitoba government amended the June 30, 2021 Order, which would have prevented Sarah from eating in restaurants as a person who is considered "unvaccinated." The August 3, 2021 Order made it possible for Sarah to participate in more parts of public life than the June 30 Order did. For example, under the August 5 Order, individuals who were not fully vaccinated could now eat with friends at restaurants if the restaurant ensured a two-metre separation between tables.

However, many restaurants began requiring patrons to show the government-issued Manitoba Immunization Card to enter their premises, a card Sarah was not eligible for. The government had created a process for proving immunization, but it had not created any process for individuals like Sarah whose particular disability made them ineligible for the Immunization Card which was being relied upon by businesses.

In our letter to the Manitoba government, the CCF stated that we were prepared to litigate if the government failed to create an accommodation for people like Sarah. The advocacy work of the CCF for medical exemptions from COVID-19 vaccine passports and an interview with Sarah were featured on the front page of *The Globe and Mail*.[23]

Sixteen days after we at the CCF sent our letter, the Manitoba government announced that they would create a process for obtaining medical exemptions.[24] To be sure, the process to receive exemption was imperfect: it required approval by public health and the exemption was not transferrable across provinces. But it was a step in the right direction and an acknowledgment that preventing people from entering public spaces because they have a medical condition is discriminatory, something that is, frankly, common sense.

In response to the decision by the Manitoba government to create a process for obtaining medical exemptions from the vaccine passport policy, CCF Litigation Director and author of this book, Christine Van Geyn, said "We are pleased that the Manitoba government has decided to create medical exemptions for the vaccine passport policy. This is exactly what we asked for in our letter to the Manitoba government and we are happy the government is listening to our concerns."[25]

Christine went on to compare the Manitoba shift in policy to the extremely restrictive vaccine passport regime in place in British Columbia. "Manitoba's willingness to make this accommodation for medical exemptions shows how callous and discriminatory the BC vaccine passport policy is. The BC vaccine passport policy contains no obvious medical exemptions, other than a difficult procedural reconsideration through public health that is difficult to access."[26]

British Columbia had what the CCF called "the worst vaccine passports in Canada,"[27] and this policy became the focus of a major piece of litigation for the legal charity.

British Columbia vaccine passports and medical exemptions

Dr. Bonnie Henry announced the British Columbia vaccine passport policy on August 23, 2021. This was just three months after saying that such a policy would exacerbate inequities.[28] As Dr. Henry herself warned, the B.C. policy did increase inequities. It was in the end far more discriminatory than similar policies in other parts of Canada. Unlike other provinces, however, including Quebec and Ontario, the B.C. government early on said repeatedly that there would be no medical or religious exemptions.[29]

For all practical purposes, Dr. Henry's repeated statements that there would be no medical exemptions were accurate. While the September 10, 2021, public health orders establishing the vaccine passport policy did create a route to obtain medical exemptions, the exemption application was difficult to access because it was bureaucratic and so overly restrictive that it was out of reach of most of the patients who should have been able to receive them.

This is how the B.C. "exemption" system worked: an individual who had a medical contraindication against vaccination could request what was called a "reconsideration" of the September 10 public health orders, pursuant to section 43 of the *Public Health Act*. These reconsiderations were to be made by emailing the Provincial Health Officer with a signed and dated statement from a medical practitioner, based on a current assessment, that the health of that person would be "seriously jeopardized" if the person were to receive a first or second dose of a COVID-19 vaccine. The person seeking the reconsideration was to include a signed and dated copy of each relevant portion of the person's health record. But the government continued to amend this process, narrowing it to become more and more restrictive.

Later on,[30] the government amended the process further, so that patients were required to fill in a government form with a check box of "acceptable" reasons to seek a medical exemption. Those reasons were limited to anaphylaxis, pericarditis, or myocarditis, or certain cancer treatments. If a patient had a medical condition not listed on the check box, they were not even able to apply for an exemption.[31] The government then later amended the order so that even if a patient was granted an exemption, it would be on an "activity by activity basis." A patient could be granted an exemption to regularly attend a weekly activity, but if the patient wanted to go out for dinner with friends, they would need to submit a separate request. Not only was such a request unlikely to be processed within any reasonable time, but the process infantilized patients, requiring them to seek government permission to go about their daily lives.

More broadly, this process put the government in between a patient and his or her physician and created a burdensome and time-consuming bureaucracy with uncertain outcomes. Obtaining a correct diagnosis can take months in complex cases, as can collecting medical records and writing a persuasive argument to public health. This can be especially challenging for patients who may be dealing with the physical and emotional trauma of an adverse reaction to a first dose or another serious medical condition. The patient then had to await a decision from the government, and during this entire lengthy period was excluded from access to public spaces. For a period, the government even announced they were no longer considering exemptions and scrapped every application that had been submitted and created a whole new system.[32] This type of procedural unfairness is damaging to the rule of law and the public's trust in the system.

The CCF's legal challenge to the B.C. vaccine passport regime

The CCF argued from the start that this dog's breakfast of a system created by the British Columbia government was unconstitutional. The CCF challenged the law and worked with three individuals who were directly harmed by the restrictive and bureaucratic B.C. regime. The CCF was represented by Vancouver lawyer Geoffrey Trotter.

The first applicant was Erica, a teenage girl who got her first dose of Pfizer in May 2021, shortly after it became available for her age group. Four days later, Erica woke up with sharp, stabbing pain in her chest, which got progressively worse. Erica underwent heart and blood tests, and after several hospital visits over the course of several weeks, was ultimately diagnosed with heart inflammation (pericarditis). Her physicians concluded that this was likely an adverse reaction to the vaccine.

Erica's case is similar to Sarah's from Manitoba and should be a clear-cut case for an exemption. Heart inflammation is a recognized adverse reaction to the Pfizer COVID-19 vaccine, especially among teenagers. Erica should have been eligible for a medical exemption from the vaccine passport. Without an exemption, Erica would not be able to go to the types of public places teenagers go to hang out, such as movie theatres or restaurants. Throughout the pandemic kids were already highly isolated. Without a medical exemption, Erica would continue to be more isolated than most of her peers.

If obtaining a medical exemption is a challenge for the most clear-cut cases like Erica's, consider how challenging it is for patients who have more complex medical histories or more difficult-to-diagnose adverse medical reactions. This was the case with Sharon, the second individual the CCF worked with.

Sharon is a woman in her thirties who developed nerve damage, including partial paralysis of her arm following her first dose of a COVID-19 vaccine. Neurological problems can be complicated and difficult to diagnose, and obtaining a correct diagnosis often involves consultation with multiple doctors and specialists. A complete diagnosis can take months, and that's after a specialist referral is completed, which itself can take months.

Sharon had repeated appointments with specialists following her adverse reaction, and while her case was complex, her doctors suspected she has a condition called brachial neuritis. They also believed it was an adverse reaction to her first dose of the COVID-19 vaccine.

Sharon was getting physical therapy to regain movement in her arm, but the progress was slow, difficult, and frustrating. She was especially concerned because after developing brachial neuritis following her vaccine, she got pregnant. Sharon worried that she would not even be able to hold her baby once she was born because of her arm paralysis. But even more importantly, she worried that a second dose of the vaccine could cause further nerve damage, including nerve damage that could hurt her unborn baby. Her physician and neurologist shared these concerns.

Yet Sharon was unable to receive an exemption from the vaccine passport under the B.C. regulations. B.C. public health officers told Sharon that she should get the second dose because they said it was possible her condition might resolve with treatment and was not life threatening. The effect of denying Sharon a vaccine passport exemption would be to isolate a new mom with a disability and to ignore the fears she and her doctors had about injuring her unborn child, all because bureaucrats deemed her injury to be "not serious enough."

This is outrageous and shows the dangers of painting everyone with one brush and trying to use a "check box" for diagnosis and medical exemptions.

Consider now cases involving Bell's Palsy, which is also a rare condition but more common than Sharon's condition of brachial neuritis. In August 2021 Health Canada added a warning of Bell's Palsy to Pfizer vaccines.[33] Ontario had reported three hundred and thirty-eight incidents[34] of vaccine-related Bell's Palsy between December 2020 and December 2022. Bell's Palsy causes partial paralysis of the face that can last for months. It is an emotionally and psychologically difficult condition to live with, even if it is temporary for most people. But because this is usually not permanent or life threatening, it is not considered by public health a contraindication against a second dose. However, it is perfectly reasonable for a person who developed Bell's Palsy to decline a second dose, and it is wholly unreasonable that public health will not accommodate exemptions for such patients. Yet Bell's Palsy was not one of the "check box" conditions for exemptions in B.C., or an eligible condition for exemption in other provinces, including Ontario.[35]

Physicians were also apprehensive about an additional problem: the "soft warning" regulators in many provinces gave to physicians about granting such exemptions. For example, in British Columbia the College of Physicians and Surgeons sent a letter[36] to doctors on September 15, 2021—two days after the vaccine passport PHO order went into effect—to ensure that any exemption opinion letter was supported by "objective clinical information about the patient and not simply a repetition of the patient's self-diagnosis."

While it may sound reasonable to create a vetting process, the practical result was a chilling effect on doctors. Patients like Sharon found it difficult to find a doctor who would support a medical exemption when their adverse reaction to the first dose was neurological in nature or otherwise difficult to diagnose, other than in reliance on the patient's self-report. No doctor wants to risk a professional misconduct investigation, and given the 2021 political climate around vaccines, many were unwilling to take the professional risk, even if they were convinced their patient had an adverse reaction to a first dose. Patients like Sharon found that their physicians would write a letter to support a workplace exemption, but not a letter that would be sent to public health for an exemption from the government system. This suggests that the regulator's soft warning worked.

The CCF heard from many patients who had medically complex health conditions or who had an adverse reaction to the first dose, and whose doctors had told them "off the record" that they should not get vaccinated or fully vaccinated. However, due to pressure from the regulator, in particular in British Columbia, these physicians would not publicly support claims for medical exemptions from the government vaccine passports, which needed to be approved by public health.

Take Veronica, for example. Veronica is another B.C. resident who worked with the CCF to obtain a medical exemption, but she faced serious obstacles. She has a very complex medical history, is mobility-impaired, and has a genetic disability and contraindications for many medications. Although she is a young woman, she has already undergone around fifteen surgeries with difficult recoveries. Veronica does not react well to medical interventions and has had sufficient drug reactions to warrant serious concerns about how her body would react to the COVID-19 vaccine. The vaccine was simply a higher-risk choice for her than it was for a perfectly healthy person.

However, because of the extremely restrictive nature of B.C. Public Health's list of contraindications, patients like Veronica faced challenges finding physicians who would even consider listening to their concerns, likely due in part to that "soft warning" doctors received from their regulator. The result was that patients with complex disabilities like Veronica, who can already face social isolation, were denied access to public spaces. In Veronica's case this was especially traumatic because she used a public pool on a daily basis to manage her disability, and it was her main source of daily mobility. Without a vaccine, Veronica was denied access to the pool and her health deteriorated. Without access to the pool, Veronica required an increase in the number of nerve-blocking injections she took. The "adverse impact" of the vaccine passport system on a person with a disability like Veronica's was greater than it would be on a perfectly able-bodied person.

It's important to remember that what these patients sought was a reasonable exemption based on genuine health concerns. They are not opposed to vaccination. In fact, they even worried that their stories might be used to further polarize people and feed into anti-vaccination narratives. The patients in the CCF just wanted to be treated fairly by their government. For most people the COVID-19 vaccines are safe, and the chance of an adverse reaction is low. In our view, the government will not make headway in persuading the hesitant to take up vaccination if they deny the reality that adverse reactions occur, and if they refuse to show any compassion for people who have experienced them.

These individuals were not trying to find a loophole or lie about a disability order to obtain an exemption. They were sick, and they were frightened. Their cases should be a slam dunk. But these patients all needed to work with lawyers to do something as simple as eat inside a restaurant or go to the movies.

The B.C. government's conduct was frankly cruel. The medical exemption process was unworkable for most people, even if they had a supportive physician. And limiting the number of medical exemptions to very few closed "check box" categories made it harder for individual patients to find supportive physicians. The B.C. policy was too hardline and unyielding in a free society, and it violated the *Charter*'s guarantees of equality.

The decision in the CCF's B.C. vaccine passport case

The CCF's litigation in British Columbia is still in progress and is now at the appeal stage. The lower court decision was disappointing and, like many COVID-19 cases about constitutional rights, was not decided on the merits of the case but rather on procedural grounds.

On September 12, 2022, Chief Justice Hinkson of the B.C. Supreme Court issued his decision[37] dismissing the case as premature, finding that the three individuals who brought the case around medical exemptions had not exhausted their opportunity to apply to the Public Health Office (PHO) for a medical exemption. As a result of that finding, Justice Hinkson did not resolve the three petitioners' arguments regarding *Charter* breaches.

The government evaded constitutional review in this case by filing evidence that they were secretly accepting medical exemption applications for conditions beyond those in the limited list in mandatory government application forms, and granting general exemptions despite the PHO orders, which stated that only activity-by-activity exemptions would be granted. But this only became known four months later, when the CCF's lawsuit forced the government to file evidence in the case.

Essentially, the government defended unconstitutional orders by saying they secretly didn't actually follow them, and then faulted the petitioners for not having known this.

The three women in the CCF's case were in an impossible situation. In the CCF's view, it is obvious that the B.C. vaccine passport regime as set out in the PHO orders and the mandatory "check box" forms did not have an open category for medical exemptions. Further, B.C. health care professionals were dissuaded by their regulator from writing letters in support of exemptions on the basis of the PHO's own statements that only listed conditions would qualify for an exemption. The result was that these patients could not find physicians who would support writing a letter for their medical exemptions, even when these same physicians would write supportive letters for other purposes, like employment exemptions.

On October 6, 2022, the CCF announced we would be appealing the decision. "We believe that there were errors in the lower court decision. Most significantly, there was an error in the finding that the three women who brought this case could have applied for a reconsideration for an exemption from the vaccine passport system, making their court challenge premature. On the face of the Provincial Health Officer's (PHO's) orders and their mandatory forms, these women were ineligible to apply," said CCF Litigation Director and author of this book, Christine Van Geyn. "The government cannot save a bad and unconstitutional law or order by secretly not applying it in practice, as the government argued it had done. By accepting the government's argument and declining to even consider the constitutional issues, the lower court decision sets a dangerous precedent which undermines the rule of law and the principle that the *Charter* is the supreme law of Canada."

The appeal is expected to be heard in October of 2023.

RACE-BASED CONCERNS AROUND COVID-19 RESTRICTIONS: WHITHER SUBSTANTIVE EQUALITY?

For advocates of the expansive view of substantive equality, discussed earlier in this chapter, COVID-19 policies like vaccine passports, stay-at-home orders, and curfews should have been a huge concern. These policies all have the potential for differential impacts that run along racial and other protected section 15(1) lines. But governments in Canada failed to initially even track racial disparities in vaccine uptake, and few groups usually concerned about substantive equality raised alarms about differential impact although, as we will see, some did.

Vaccine passports and racial inequity: failure to initially track data in Canada

Government bureaucracies typically concerned with the issue of racial equality in other policy areas did not even initially collect detailed demographic data on vaccine uptake so that the disparate impact of vaccine passports could be studied. This should be surprising, but it appears that the concern over substantive equality gave way to the ideological commitment to "vaccinate at any cost."

When it comes to non-Indigenous visible minority Canadians, the Canadian government failed to initially track or release data on vaccine and vaccine passport uptake. Some scholars and journalists raised the alarm that the lack of data could cause the government to be blind to potential harms caused by its policies. According to *CTV News*, Dr. Kwame McKenzie, CEO of the Wellesley Institute, was quoted as saying "but nobody's really doing anything about this because if you are not counted, you do not count. It's as simple as that."[38]

In the summer leading up to the implementation of vaccine passports across Canada, the CBC reported that "Black Canadian leaders say governments must do more to help overcome vaccine hesitancy in their communities."[39] The article quotes Toronto orthopaedic surgeon, Dr. Ato Sekyi-Otu, leader of the health care task force of the Black Opportunity Fund, as saying, "It's not surprising that if someone has a bad experience with one institution, for example, criminal justice, when he or she is nineteen years old, he or she may not want to take the vaccine in 2021 when he or she is forty-five years old." The article cited a survey by Innovative Research Group in partnership with the African Canadian Civic Engagement Council and the Black Opportunity Fund.

According to the survey they conducted shortly before the introduction of vaccine passports, between May 18 and June 4, 2021, vaccine hesitancy was highest in Canada among Black Canadians. Thirty-three per cent of Black Canadians expressed some degree of vaccine hesitancy compared to 25 per cent of non-Black visible minorities and 19 per cent of white Canadians.[40]

Further, their survey also showed that while 65 per cent of white Canadians had received a first dose at the time of the survey, only 45 per cent of Black Canadians had and only 43 per cent of non-Black visible minority Canadians. Some commentators in the *Canadian Medical Association Journal* have suggested that "vaccine hesitancy in Black communities is not merely because of misinformation or gaps in health literacy; it is linked to medical distrust and structural racism."[41]

Statistics Canada reported similar survey results, saying "among groups designated as visible minorities, willingness to get the COVID-19 vaccine ranged from 56.4% among the Black population to 82.5% among the South Asian population."[42] Also of note is that Arab Canadians and Latin American Canadians also showed markedly higher amounts of vaccine hesitancy over non-visible minority Canadians.

Later in 2021, Statistics Canada confirmed a gap in vaccine uptake between non-visible minority Canadians and visible minority Canadians. According to one of their reports, "one-third of adults belonging to groups designated as visible minorities (33.6%) were vaccinated compared with almost half of the non-visible minority adult population (49.5%)".[43] Interestingly, Indigenous Canadians were an exception to the general trend of vaccines taking longer to reach visible minority Canadians. According to the same report, "Survey results show that just over half of Indigenous adults (52.5%) had been vaccinated. While coverage rates were similar for Indigenous (78.4%) and non-Indigenous (80.4%) seniors (60 years of age or older), younger Indigenous adults (18 to 59 years old) had a significantly higher coverage rate (43.0%) than their non-Indigenous counterparts (29.4%)." At least as far as halfway through 2021, only a couple of months before vaccine passports were widely implemented throughout Canada, visible minority Canadians were significantly behind non-visible minority Canadians in vaccine uptake, a result which in itself would be concerning even had the government not chosen to restrict access to various goods and services on the basis of vaccination.

From April 12 to May 12, 2021, Statistics Canada conducted the COVID-19 Vaccination Coverage Survey, which again neglected to study any race-based differences in vaccination and vaccine hesitancy. The only relevant data from that study for these purposes was on vaccine hesitancy among immigrants compared to non-immigrant Canadians. Vaccine hesitancy seemed to largely disappear in Canada the longer the pandemic progressed.

By August 2021, Statistics Canada reported that vaccine hesitancy among both visible and non-visible minority Canadians had shrunk and actually reversed directions. According to a survey they conducted between June and August 2021, 6 per cent of non-visible minority Canadians expressed that they were unlikely to get vaccinated compared to just 3 per cent of visible minority Canadians.[44] Despite reporting on actual vaccine uptake based on age and education, the government failed to report on vaccine uptake by members of religious, racial, and disability communities, which section 15 protects.

Finally, in June of 2022, the government released the results of a survey on vaccine uptake based on ethnicity. By this point, vaccine passports had been in full swing across Canada for months. The survey of around 12,000 people found that the proportion of people having received at least one dose of a COVID-19 vaccine was lower among people who self-identify as off-reserve First Nation (81%), Black (82%) or Arab (85%), but higher among South Asian people (96%) than among individuals who are neither Indigenous nor part of visible minorities (93%).[45]

The government's early failure to track vaccination rates across demographics other than age or sex hid potential inequality implications of the vaccine rollout and the vaccine passports. At best, attempts to study vaccination inequality have had to focus on differences in vaccine hesitancy or other proxies, which do not directly prove vaccine inequalities along racial or ethnic lines. For example, one report by the

Wellesley Institute attempted to track vaccine inequality in Ontario by using neighbourhood-level statistics and comparing the racial makeup of those neighbourhoods. They found that "South Asian, Black, and Latin American[s] were associated with lower rates of vaccination."[46] Still this study was conducted before vaccine passports rolled out.

The call for this type of study did not sound from many of the typical advocates for substantive equality in Canada. In the view of the authors of this book, the failure of the traditional voices for substantive equality to question the collateral impacts of vaccine passports or even call for demographic study suggests that this equality concern fell to the wayside behind a single-minded focus on increasing vaccine uptake.

Where were the advocates for substantive equality?

Although few of the usual progressive voices for substantive equality raised alarms about how policies like vaccine passports would impact protected groups, such as racial minorities or Canadians with disabilities, there were some exceptions.

The CCLA wrote in a statement that "Not all members of our society are at equal risk or have equal means to navigate the pandemic while maintaining their health, safety, and income. Front line workers in service and retail are often women, newcomers, racialized, and/or financially insecure, and a vaccination passport regime that predicates participation in the workplace or other activities on proof of vaccination will disproportionately impact those individuals who have little social or political power to resist."[47]

Concerns were also raised by Professor Kristen Voigt in her paper on the ethics of COVID-19 vaccine passports:[48]

> Even if not directly discriminatory, at least two worries about discrimination and COVID passports remain. First, vaccine passports could facilitate discrimination because—as we know from other policies, including measures to curb COVID-19—enforcement and policing disproportionately focus on members of margin-

alized groups. [. . .] Second, a passport scheme could also be seen as an indirect form of discrimination when implemented in contexts where vaccination rates are lower among marginalized or disadvantaged groups.

As one American commentator noted, racial disparity in vaccine uptake when combined with vaccine passports "evokes an uncomfortable image: professional-class white people disproportionately allowed into shops, baseball games and restaurants, with people of color and members of the working classes disproportionately kept out."[49]

The substantive equality concern is that past and current disadvantages associated with some minority communities may make it more difficult for those communities to access vaccines and, therefore, to access community goods and services as equals after the implementation of vaccine passports. For example, some commentators suggested that historical mistreatment of Indigenous peoples by the Canadian government may be behind some vaccine hesitancy in indigenous communities. According to Ian Mosby and Jaris Swidrovich:[50]

After the arrival of 1200 doses of the Moderna vaccine in his home community, former Assembly of First Nations National Chief Matthew Coon Come articulated his concerns in a widely shared social media post, writing "Mistissini is [sic] now the experimental rats of this experimental vaccine. [. . .]

The fears and hesitancy articulated by Coon Come are, of course, not universal, and many Indigenous leaders have come out strongly in support of vaccines. However, the reality is that these concerns are nonetheless widely held by many First Nations, Inuit and Métis people. As former Manitoba Keewatinowi Okimakanak Grand Chief Sheila North explained: "Back in residential school days, [people], that are now elders, remember being used as guinea pigs or [having] vaccines tested on them when they were children without their permission or their family's permission.

The University of Toronto Centre for Ethics also hosted a lecture by Sophia Moreau from the University of Toronto Law School and Sabine Tsuruda of the Queen's University Law School about the moral and legal risks of vaccine passports.[51] Sabine Tsuruda explained that the passports raise "at least three serious social justice problems," including a "disproportionately large burden on society's least advantaged, most marginalized members." Second, they would "legally sanction an underclass of non-immunized [. . .] members of society," and third, because of all of this, Tsuruda argued "there is a good chance these policies would actually violate anti-discrimination laws."[52]

This book's author, Christine Van Geyn, called out the silence of many of the usual advocates for substantive equality, and how they conveniently ignored their own ideology when it served the popular majority calls for vaccine passports. In a debate she participated in as part of the Massey College Ethics Series,[53] Christine said "If you're concerned about disparate outcomes and things like equality of outcome, you should be concerned about vaccine passports. Things like rates of vaccination and likelihood of interacting with police can run along racial and economic lines. If you're concerned about increasing police interactions with those communities, or with terminating employment in lower income or racialized communities, you should be concerned about vaccine passports."

Christine emphasized the change in tone during the pandemic, and the progressive endorsement of base majoritarian instincts: "one of the things we do in a liberal democracy is accommodate people who are different from us. The desire to mistreat people who are different from us is a very primitive and deep-felt instinct that liberal democracies, with the ethic of tolerance, try to frustrate and temper. That instinct is now being given a nod to go ahead and condemn people who are different from us."[54]

Stay-at-home orders, lockdowns, curfews, and racial inequity

The Doug Ford Ontario stay-at-home order and sweeping police powers announced on April 16, 2021, had serious implications for racial equality. As explored at length in Chapter 3, Ford gave police the power to stop pedestrians and vehicles to demand people identify themselves.[55] This section will explore the section 15 *Charter* implications of these expanded police powers, as well as the implications of other enforcement measures related to COVID-19 restrictions generally.

The new Ontario police powers raised an important equality concern. It is quite similar to the practice of "carding," a type of random street check that the province had explicitly banned in 2017. The provincial government enacted a regulation that prohibited carding and outlined exactly when police can collect identifying information.[56] Carding was banned because of concerns that random street checks were being conducted in an arbitrary and discriminatory way, and had a disproportionate impact on minority communities, potentially in violation of our *Charter*-protected right to equal protection under the law.

The new police power was so similar to carding that the government and cabinet would have to have been aware of the risks for minority and low-income communities yet proceeded to enact the regulation anyway.

Ultimately the government repealed the enforcement powers less than twenty-four hours of them being enacted, before any legal challenge could commence.

The Quebec curfew raised similar concerns around enforcement and street stops. Minority communities tend to deal with more policing and, in particular, the original curfew order contained no exemptions for people experiencing homelessness. In an interview with the CBC, Jessica Quijano, co-ordinator of the Iskweu project at the Native Women's Shelter of Montreal, grew frustrated when talking about the curfew. "Police do not have a positive relationship with the homeless community," said Quijano. Quijano said Montreal's homeless population already deals with racial profiling on a regular basis, and the introduction of this curfew has only made matters worse.[57]

The CCLA also raised concerns about how the curfew would disproportionately impact racial minorities. "A curfew is particularly problematic because it purports to empower police officers to stop and question individuals simply for being outdoors at certain times of day," Cara Zwibel of the CCLA said in a statement. "The burden of these police stops is likely to fall disproportionately on racialized individuals and other marginalized groups."[58]

The Quebec government ultimately amended the curfew order to make exemptions for homelessness, but not until after the premier had doubled down on the measure, stating that such an exception could not work because people would "pretend to be homeless." Tragically, one person died, and it is suspected he died hiding from police because he had nowhere to go and the curfew had essentially criminalized homelessness. The government eventually did make that exemption, but tragically for that individual, it was already too late.[59]

MASK MANDATES AND ACCOMMODATION

Mask mandates were implemented across Canada during the COVID-19 pandemic. While masking was controversial among a small subset of people, more broadly there were open questions about exemptions, especially where disabilities and medical issues were potentially implicated. For example, masking can be a challenge for people on the autism spectrum who have sensory-processing difficulties, especially when they are children. This raises section 15 equality concerns.

In December 2021, *CTV News* did a province-by-province overview of masking guidelines and their exemptions.[60] Approaches appeared similar throughout the provinces, with exemptions being narrowly tailored towards genuine cases of physical or mental disabilities and legitimate medical conditions that would prevent the use of masking. Generally, children were not required to mask, and most places permitted mask exemptions to be claimed at face value without the requirement of any proof. Early on in the pandemic, the CCF had written to several municipalities to advocate for a policy, ultimately largely adopted, of accepting claims for exemptions at face value.[61]

However, unsettling incidents still arose. For example, there were reports across Canada of instances where children on the autism spectrum were forced to leave stores for being unmasked. In August 2020, for example,[62] six-year-old Ruby went to the Disney Store in London, Ontario with her mom. Ruby is on the autism spectrum, and when she was unable to properly wear her mask, the family was made to leave the store. In that case, the local public health rules at the time did not require children under twelve to wear a mask and allowed for exemptions for people with disabilities. However, local businesses did not always grant exemptions, resulting in unfortunate instances like this one.

There were some complaints made to human rights tribunals regarding masking. Often these complaints failed, either because their claim to have a religious exemption was found to be without merit, or because their claim to have a disability was either not credible or the service provider offered reasonable accommodation.[63]

CHAPTER 8
FREEDOM OF EXPRESSION

Plandemic is a 26-minute conspiracy video that claims that the COVID-19 virus was fake or human-made and the result of collusion between Bill Gates, Barack Obama, and Anthony Fauci. It features a discredited scientist, Judy Mikovitz, who claimed her vaccine research had been buried. The video was viewed 2.5 million times within days of its release on Facebook, Vimeo and YouTube on May 4, 2020, and eight million times within a week, effectively proving even more fast-spreading and infectious than the coronavirus itself (by contrast, another viral pandemic video from a popular TV sitcom, when the cast of *The Office* announced a Zoom wedding, garnered 618,000 interactions in a week.).[1] The title became a meme: many anti-vaxxers and conspiracy theorists still refer to the COVID-19 outbreak as the "plandemic," usually while decrying the evils of the World Economic Forum and its plans to create a new world order.

The fact that the coronavirus crisis entailed twin pandemics of a respiratory virus and viral misinformation became alarmingly apparent, and from the beginning, widespread and bizarre theories about the pandemic came into popular circulation, including that the true cause of the coronavirus outbreak was the adoption of 5G wireless networks, that mRNA vaccines contained microchips that would permanently alter human DNA, and that hydroxychloroquine was an effective treatment against a COVID-19 infection.

The impact of spreading misinformation over the course of an outbreak of a novel infectious virus was clear from the outset, and governments responded accordingly. The NGO Human Rights Watch estimated that at least eighty-three governments worldwide justified violating the exercise of free speech and peaceful assembly by the need to respond to alleged COVID-19 misinformation.

In some cases, the damage done by misinformation, particularly about vaccines, was substantial. One scholar noted that "as [many as] 12 million persons may have forgone COVID-19 vaccination in the United States because of misinformation, resulting in an estimated 1,200 excess hospitalizations and 300 deaths per day. If five fully loaded 747s crashed each week due to wrong information, regulators would be apoplectic."[2] Perhaps this is overstating the case, but there can be no doubt that a firehose of information, much of it false, flooded the internet about the "Operation Warp Speed" vaccines, and had huge consequences for individual medical decisions.

However, it turns out many "official" government narratives about the virus were later discredited themselves. Two notorious examples are illustrative. First, the lab-leak theory, that the COVID-19 virus escaped from the Wuhan Institute of Virology, was initially rejected as ignorant and even racist.[3] It is now a commonly accepted hypothesis that COVID-19 emerged from an accidental lab leak from the Wuhan Institute of Virology, located a few hundred metres away from the wet market connected to the first infections. This theory is highly credible and even thought to be "more likely than not" by the U.S. Department of Energy,[4] although due to obfuscation by the Chinese Communist Party will likely never be definitively proven.

And, of course, there were frantic early attempts on the part of health officials, most famously U.S. Surgeon General Jerome M. Adams, to discourage the general public from hoarding masks. In February 2020, Adams tweeted,[5] "Seriously people—STOP BUYING MASKS! They are NOT effective in preventing general public from catching #Coronavirus, but if health care providers can't get them to care for sick patients, it puts them and our communities at risk!"

Teresa Tam, Canada's chief medical officer, also discouraged wearing masks in public before reversing her stance.[6]

It was always difficult to make sense of these claims—if masks didn't reduce transmission, why was it important to preserve health care workers' access to them? However, in the confusion of the first few weeks of the pandemic, when bleach and toilet paper were impossible to find and we were all Cloroxing our groceries, somehow this passed muster.

The underlying point is that allowing governments to, in any way, monopolize the truth is a very bad idea, as truth can only emerge through open discourse and testing of hypotheses. Here, one of the trickiest quandaries of our current era presents itself. On the one hand, there was real evidence throughout the pandemic that individuals became taken in by misinformation and made decisions that led to harm both individually and collectively. For example, some vulnerable individuals refused to get vaccinated and ended up in ICUs or dying of COVID-19. Our brains didn't evolve to properly process the amount of opposing viewpoints circulating about vaccination and other public health measures.

On the other hand, we know from the above examples that there were many unsettled questions throughout the pandemic, including, for example, the efficiency of various public health interventions such as lockdowns, mask mandates, and school closures and the risk/benefit calculus of vaccines for different populations where open discourse was actively suppressed by various governments, judges, and regulators. This chapter will discuss some particularly egregious instances of clamping down on free expression and its sister right, freedom of assembly in Canada.

In this chapter, we will see how various government actions related to COVID-19 impacted all forms of free expression. Protesters opposing extended lockdowns and other public health measures were banned from organizing or even communicating online. A bombastic Calgary street pastor was slapped with a judicial order actually mandating a script to be affixed to any statements he made publicly about the virus. And doctors falling out of line with the mainstream consensus on lockdowns were threatened with disciplinary action by their regulatory colleges.

This chapter will consider:

- a judicial order that banned a group from protesting in advance, and even posting on social media about protesting;
- the "doublespeak" from public health officials about the safety of protesting, depending on the cause;
- a stunningly draconian judicial order requiring a sketchy pastor to preface his critiques with the verbal requirement of a surgeon-general's warning;
- the impact of professional regulators on policing the speech of its members; and
- the passing of a redundant law forbidding protests outside hospitals.

WHY FREEDOM OF EXPRESSION MATTERS

Section 2 of the *Charter* guarantees Canadians the freedom to peacefully assemble, and to express themselves politically, and specifically protects the right to political dissent. The guarantee is content-neutral. Nonetheless, governments, and other government-sanctioned bodies such as regulators and administrators, implemented policies that had a chilling effect on free expression throughout the pandemic and directly restricted the right of Canadians to peacefully assemble to express their grievances with COVID-19 policies.

Freedom of expression and peaceful assembly are fundamentally important to the functioning of Canada's liberal democracy. They guarantee that Canadians can peacefully organize and express themselves in matters relating to public policy. Without these rights governments would be free to act unopposed, and their policies, including unjust policies, would be uncontested. Without healthy questioning of authority, we can never be sure that the government is doing what is in our best interests and whether the evidence for their positions is sound. In the landmark Supreme Court of Canada case *R. v. Keegstra*, the Court emphasized the importance of freedom of expression, particularly in the political process. According to the Court:[7]

> Freedom of expression is a crucial aspect of the dem-ocratic commitment, not merely because it permits the best policies to be chosen from among a wide array of proffered options, but additionally because it helps to ensure that participation in the political process is open to all persons. Such open participation must involve to a substantial degree the notion that all persons are equally deserving of respect and dignity. The state therefore cannot act to hinder or condemn a political view without to some extent harming the openness of Canadian democracy and its associated tenet of equality for all.

Political expression is considered core expression, and as such can only be restricted for the most substantial and pressing government objectives, unlike other forms of expression such as pornography and advertising, which are marginal to the goals that underlie protecting free expression.

There are at least three reasons why freedom of expression mat-ters. First, it promotes truth-seeking: there can be no advancement of knowledge and testing of ideas without open discourse. Second, it is a condition necessary for the flourishing of democracy since there can be no political dissent and thus meaningful democracy without free expression. And third, free speech promotes individual autonomy since we develop as rational beings through unencumbered expression.

A PREVENTATIVE ORDER AGAINST PROTESTS: FREEDOM NOVA SCOTIA

In May 2021, an anti-lockdown group called Freedom Nova Scotia was planning several protests intended to criticize Nova Scotia public health orders and mask mandates. Following an *ex parte* application to the Nova Scotia Supreme Court (a hearing held in judges' chambers based only on the submissions of the government, without the input of Freedom Nova Scotia), the Court granted the government an injunction against the protests until the emergency orders put in place for the third wave of the pandemic were lifted. Notably, the injunction also contained an order forbidding protest organizers to post or communicate about potential future gatherings on social media platforms, making the order essentially a gag order. Because the application was heard *ex parte*, the protest's organizers were neither contacted about the court proceedings nor allowed to participate to defend their rights and contest the government's evidence.

At the time, Nova Scotia's chief medical officer, Dr. Robert Strang, said:[8]

> We're in a very serious situation. We're in the middle of a global pandemic [. . .] We cannot let a small group of individuals who willfully dismiss the science, willfully dismiss the evidence around how their actions could put other people at significant risk. We cannot allow that to happen and I'm very pleased with the judgment.

The government also quoted the premier of Nova Scotia, who claimed the protesters were anti-science and depicted them as a fringe group. These allegations were illustrative of a pattern that government officials generally followed when attempting to justify abridgements of freedom of expression and assembly during the COVID-19 pandemic. Critics of government policies were frequently depicted as political extremists and in ignorant denial of proven scientific facts, despite a lack of evidence that all protesters held such extreme views and the fact that many reputable scientists and intellectuals also opposed heavy-handed COVID-19 lockdowns.

The Nova Scotia Office of the Premier released a statement shortly after the government was granted the injunction. In the view of the government, preventing the protest was essential to protect people from

COVID-19.[9] In *Freedom Nova Scotia v. Nova Scotia*,[10] the judge went extraordinarily far in deferring to government claims of public health necessity to issue a ruling that went beyond banning protests to even forbid online communications about potential protests.

In his decision, Justice Norton explained that the injunction sought by the government was a *quia timet* injunction. This means that the government sought an injunction based on a potential harm that could occur in the absence of it, even though no harm has actually occurred yet. After discussing the relevant precedent for *quia timet* injunctions, the Court summarized the three-part test for granting such injunctions:[11]

1. There is a presence of harm that is about to occur imminently,
2. There is a high probability that the alleged harm will occur; and
3. That monetary damages would not be an adequate remedy.

Notably, the Nova Scotia Supreme Court considered that interlocutory (interim) injunctions relating to public health measures had been sought during the pandemic, but not by the government. A previous Alberta decision played an important role in the framing of the Nova Scotia decision. *Ingram v. Alberta (Chief Medical Officer of Health)*[12] was a case where an Alberta gym owner sought an interlocutory injunction against Alberta's public health orders and mask mandates on the grounds that they violated her rights under the *Charter* and the *Alberta Bill of Rights* and that they would damage her business and the value it had to shareholders. In Justice Norton's discussion of *Ingram*, he remarked that "it was not enough at irreparable harm stage for the applicants to simply say that *Charter* rights were being infringed; and to ask the court to presume."[13]

There's a clear double standard at play here, even considering that governments are presumed to be acting in good faith. The court in *Ingram* concluded that harm caused to Ingram by the mandatory closure of her business was too speculative to be made out, at least given the evidence she presented in that case. It is unclear whether the Court would have gone a different way had she presented more evidence than just her opinion that her business would be harmed.

Ultimately, the standard the Nova Scotia government was required to meet in order to obtain an interlocutory injunction forbidding the group from organizing or even communicating about a protest was staggeringly lower than the standard Ingram had to meet in order to succeed in thwarting the Alberta public health measures. The Nova Scotia government did not have to prove that by allowing the protests to proceed, there would be some imminent harm, such as people dying or becoming severely ill from COVID-19 due to the protesters. Instead, the Nova Scotia government only needed to prove that they were discharging their duty to promote or protect the public interest when they implemented the very public health orders the protesters wanted to challenge.

Having set up such a low standard for public authorities to succeed in seeking interlocutory injunctions, even when Canadians' *Charter* rights are implicated, the Court went on to have no difficulty in granting the injunction against the Nova Scotia protests based on an affidavit by the province's chief medical officer, Dr. Robert Strang. All Dr. Strang had to say was that if the protest continued, he believed the continued spread of COVID-19 would be imminent.[14] So for Ms. Ingram, who wanted the Alberta courts to accept her word that her business would suffer imminent harm if restrictions continued, her word was not enough. But for the government of Nova Scotia who wanted the Court to stop Canadians from protesting their public health measures, their word that the protests would cause imminent harm was all it took.

Justice Norton concluded his decision by praising Nova Scotia's "aggressive" public health measures, and reiterating criticism of the protesters as "wilfully blinded" and anti-science, chastising their "callous and shameful disregard for the health and safety of their fellow citizens."[15]

135

The judge went on to make several obiter dicta comments which contain no legal reasoning and instead are, remarkably, almost entirely policy observations:[16]

> The intensive care units at our hospitals are filling with COVID patients. The health care workers in this Province have been working tirelessly for more than 14 months to manage this crisis. Schools have had to close. Businesses have had to close. Many Nova Scotians are unemployed as a result. Yet, Nova Scotia has done better than many other provinces because its public health officials have taken an aggressive approach based on science, medicine and common sense. The vast majority of Nova Scotians have and continue to support and follow the public health recommendations with a view to returning to pre-COVID activity and enjoyment of life as quickly and as safely as possible.

Freedom Nova Scotia remains a highwater mark, among many such highwater marks, of court deference to government assertions of justified action even in the absence of supporting evidence. It was gratuitous for the Court to go so far as to use *ad hominem* attacks against protesters, especially when those protesters were not allowed to argue their interests and rights in front of the Court or to defend themselves against the government's criticism. Shockingly, the injunction granted by the Court even went so far as to restrict anyone from organizing, requesting, inciting, or inviting others to an "illegal public gathering" and promoting "illegal public gatherings" on social media.[17]

The CCLA also viewed the injunction as worrisome. The group sought standing after the injunction had expired to challenge the constitutionality of the order, arguing that it set a poor precedent. In its brief, the CCLA argued that "the COVID-19 pandemic is ongoing and at any time the Attorney General could return to this Court on an *ex parte* basis to again seek an order that would infringe upon the constitutionally protected rights of Nova Scotians."[18]

The CCLA continued, stating that "even if the case is moot, the interests of justice require that a re-hearing in open court proceeds."[19] It urged the use of judicial resources in the form of a hearing, given the far-reaching nature of the *ex parte* decision and even called the injunctive relief "illegal." Ultimately, however, the judge refused to exercise his discretion to allow the hearing to move forward, laconically musing that "The Injunction Order was granted in markedly different circumstances which existed six weeks ago. Who knows what another six weeks will bring. The mind contemplates anything from an extinguished pandemic to a raging variant fuelled fourth wave."

The case was met with swift scepticism from the legal community. One lawyer, in a case comment, aptly noted that "in COVID-court however, 'harm' is assumed. It is deemed to be the case that a handful of maskless people (vaccinated status unknown) congregating outside will spread COVID and do so at a higher rate, and with greater 'harm' than say, going to the supermarket, or having an election."[20]

Indeed, it is impossible not to recall the notorious public health doublespeak concerning the relative risk of the Black Lives Matter protests, which was on full display in the fever-dream period of summer 2020 where the first wave of COVID-19 and the horrifying murder of George Floyd coincided. At the time, a first smattering of anti-lockdown protests was starting across the United States (and, to a much more muted degree, in Canada), which were roundly condemned across the political spectrum. But when crowds across the United and Canada took to the streets to protest racial injustice following the shocking video of George Floyd's murder under the weight of Minneapolis police officer Derek Chauvin, the consensus among the media was the opposite: not only were the protests, which occasionally spilled into vigilantism and violence, permitted, but the case was made that they were actually salubrious.

At the time, the Ethics Committee of the Society of Internal Medicine in the Hastings Center blog arrived at this conclusion:[21]

Black people die at the hands of law enforcement more than others and are **disproportionately policed and incarcerated**. The resulting mass incarcerations have **significant health consequences** for inmates and their families. The pandemic has also disproportionately affected Blacks, who are more likely to be essential workers and live in crowded conditions and thus are at increased risk of contracting and dying from the virus. Black people also experience discrimination in the health care system, contributing to worse medical outcomes. Historically, civil rights movements have led to progress with a positive impact on public health.

Therefore, the Black Lives Matter protests against police killings and mass incarceration and for equal treatment are aligned with public health recommendations, with the exception that they are taking place during a pandemic. [emphasis added]

It's not hard to see how this logic was spurious and led to cynicism about the neutrality of public health officials. Anti-lockdown protests were forbidden because they contradicted medical guidelines while behaviour with identical risk (if not higher-risk profiles, given their size and scope) for viral spread, namely, BLM protests were not just permitted but actively encouraged due to their "alignment with public health recommendations."

COMPELLED SPEECH: ARTUR PAWLOWSKI

Artur Pawlowski is a pugilistic street pastor and the founder of Street Church Ministers based in Calgary. He has never exactly been a shrinking violet and has embraced some truly kooky views. In 2005, Pawlowski, along with other street evangelists, used the PA system of a truck to deliver sermons around downtown Calgary. An opponent of abortion and homosexuality, Pawlowski once claimed the 2013 southern Alberta floods were caused, in part, by God's unhappiness about homosexuality. Nobody would dispute that Pawlowski was out there. Perhaps because of this, his conduct was countered with one of the most brazenly unconstitutional instances of a judge proscribing compelled speech in any Western democracy.

When the pandemic hit, Pawlowski quickly became an outspoken critic of public health measures. As lockdowns and other public health measures dragged on, Pawlowski ramped up his incendiary actions. During Easter 2021, police visited his church following reports that it was flouting public health and social distancing orders. In a viral video,[22] Pawlowski shouted at the police, "Get out! Get out immediately! Gestapo is not welcome here! Do not come back, you Nazi psychopaths! Detaining people at the church during the Passover!" On that occasion, police left, and no tickets were issued, but Pawlowski was arrested in May 2021 for organizing an in-person gathering during a brutal third wave of the virus.

For months, Pawlowski, along with his brother Dawid and the owner of the Whistle Stop Cafe in Mirror, Alberta, named Christopher Scott, as well as fringe Calgary mayoral candidate Kevin J. Johnston, encouraged their followers to contravene public health restrictions and gather in large groups unmasked.[23]

Two judges issued orders aimed at controlling the Pawlowskis and Scott in May 2021. That month, health inspectors had locked the doors to the Whistle Stop Cafe in Mirror, Alberta, which Scott had been operating for months in open defiance of Alberta Health Services orders. One day after he was served with a judge's order to obey restrictions on public gatherings, Scott held a large anti-restriction rally that attracted hundreds.[24]

Throughout the pandemic, the Pawlowskis repeatedly hosted and promoted large, maskless gatherings for church services in Calgary and also denied health officials entry to their church in southeast Calgary.

In 2021, after being found in contempt of court for violating a court order "directed at mitigating the risk posed by the novel coronavirus (COVID-19)," the two brothers were given highly unusual sanctions by Justice Germain in the case of *Alberta Health Services v. Pawlowski*.[25] Justice Germain declined to sentence the brothers to jail time, despite the exhortations of the AHS, for fear it would make them into martyrs. He wrote that the Pawlowskis and others breaching health orders are "on the wrong side of science, history, and common sense on this issue."[26]

Shockingly, among the sanctions imposed on the two brothers by the Alberta Court of Queen's Bench was the condition that whenever either brother criticized Alberta Health Services orders or recommendations, they must recite the following disclaimer:[27]

> I am also aware that the views I am expressing to you on this occasion may not be views held by the majority of medical experts in Alberta. While I may disagree with them, I am obliged to inform you that the majority of medical experts favour social distancing, mask wearing, and avoiding large crowds to reduce the spread of COVID-19. Most medical experts also support participation in a vaccination program unless for a valid religious or medical reason you cannot be vaccinated. Vaccinations have been shown statistically to save lives and to reduce the severity of COVID-19 symptoms.

This unusual order quickly raised concerns about its validity under section 2 of the *Charter*, which protects freedom of thought, belief, opinion, and expression, including the right to be free from compelled speech. "I said, I will not obey this court order," Pawlowski told Fox News at the time, before the order was stayed upon appeal. "I refuse to obey a crooked judge's order. He's not a judge, he's a political activist."[28]

Sarah Miller of JSS Barristers, Pawloski's lawyer, said she had reached out to several criminal lawyers, and they had never heard of such a requirement in a probation order.[29] "If the Alberta government issued the compelled speech law tomorrow that said if you are going to express views contrary to a majority of people [you must also recite a disclaimer] there would be a *Charter* complaint automatically by civil liberties groups," she said. "And when a judge does it there may be a bit of a different analysis, but that doesn't mean we should ignore freedom of expression rights and I think it is pretty problematic that Justice Germain went down that road."[30] The Alberta Court of Appeal seemed to agree. In July 2022, the appeals court set aside the speech provisions imposed against the Pawlowskis.[31]

Compelled speech has attracted particular attention by constitutional scholars for a number of reasons. Professor Richard Moon has written that "compelled expression is wrong because an individual's communication (what she says or writes) is closely linked to her sense of self and to her place in the community. Our ideas, feelings and, more broadly, our identity, take shape in public expression, when we give them symbolic form and make them accessible to others, who respond or react to them in different ways."[32] The exchange of information and functioning of discourse depends on the basic premise that expression reflects something authentic to the individual. Once that perception is broken by an apparatus of the state prescribing words that we must say, we become fundamentally cut off from an important source of truth. Moreover, compelling speech appears to run dangerously close to compelling thought. Philosopher Charles Taylor wrote that language gives form to our feelings and ideas and brings them "to fuller and clearer consciousness."[33]

As for Pawlowski, his saga has continued. He is being prosecuted for two counts of criminal mischief and a charge under Alberta's *Critical Infrastructure Defence Act* related to the Coutts border blockade, at which he gave a 20-minute sermon encouraging protesters to "hold the line." A scandal briefly bubbled up when sources reported to the CBC that Alberta Premier Danielle Smith held meetings with the Justice Minister's office proposing that Pawlowski be granted amnesty, but in the end it didn't materialize.[34] Pawlowski was ultimately convicted of violating Alberta's *Critical Infrastructure Defence Act* in May 2023.[35]

DOCTORS AND COVID-19 CRITICISM

Dr. Kulvinder Kaur Gill is a physician practising in Brampton and Milton, Ontario with a medical background of research in virology. Her current practice is in an allergy, asthma, and clinical immunology clinic. During the pandemic, Dr. Kaur became a strident critic of Ontario's public health measures, tweeting that: "There is absolutely no medical or scientific reason for this prolonged, harmful and illogical lockdown." Another tweet read: "If you have not yet figured out that we don't need a vaccine, you are not paying attention."[36] Without a doubt some of Gill's other rhetoric was questionable, but these tweets seemed fair game.

Her regulatory body was watching. On the 30th of April, 2021, the College of Physicians and Surgeons of Ontario, the body legally charged with licensing and disciplinary authority over the medical profession in Ontario, issued a statement threatening disciplinary measures against doctors who communicate "anti-vaccine, anti-masking, anti-distancing and anti-lockdown statements and/or promoting unsupported, unproven treatments for COVID-19."[37]

These ominous warnings were not limited to Ontario. The College of Physicians and Surgeons of British Columbia issued a joint statement with the First Nations Health Authority that was similar to the Ontario warning. Their statement expressed concern that some B.C. physicians were "spreading information that contradicts public health orders and guidance" and that this included "misinformation that promotes anti-vaccine, anti-mask wearing, anti-physical distancing and anti-lockdown stances, as well as COVID-19 treatments that are not supported by widely accepted scientific evidence."[38]

Many Ontario physicians strongly disagreed with the CPSO's statements on COVID-19 "misinformation." In a petition called the "Declaration of Canadian Physicians for Science and Truth," more than seven hundred Ontario physicians and twenty thousand citizens criticized the CPSO's statement. They stated:[39]

> The CPSO statement orders physicians for example,
> not to discuss or communicate with the public about

"lockdown" measures. Lockdown measures are the subject of lively debate by world-renown[ed] and widely respected experts and there are widely divergent views on this subject. The explicitly anti-lockdown Great Barrington Declaration was written by experts from Harvard, Stanford and Oxford Universities and more than 40,000 physicians from all over the world have signed this declaration. Several international experts including Martin Kuldorf (Harvard), David Katz (Yale), Jay Bhattacharya (Stanford) and Sunetra Gupta (Oxford) continue to strongly oppose lockdowns.

The CPSO is ordering physicians to express only pro-lockdown views, or else face investigation and discipline. This tyrannical, anti-science CPSO directive is regarded by thousands of Canadian physicians and scientists as unsupported by science and as violating the first duty of care to our patients.

In the view of these physicians, the CPSO's statement was a denial of the scientific method, a violation of the physicians' pledge to use evidence-based medicine for their patients, and a violation of their duty of informed consent.

To return to the College's Inquiries, Complaints and Reports Committee's decision regarding Dr. Kaur's tweets, the committee professed to be committed to the principle of free speech: "The Committee accepts that there is a range of views about the effectiveness of using provincial lockdown[s] as a means of controlling the spread of [COVID-19]. The Committee has no interest in shutting down free speech or in preventing physicians from expressing criticism of public health policy." However, they went on to fault Kaur Gill for stating "unequivocally and without providing evidence that there is no benefit to the lockdown."[40]

The committee, somewhat bizarrely, pointed to lockdowns in China and South Korea that did appear to have a mitigating impact on the spread of the virus (an odd comment, because lockdowns had been imposed in Ontario as well since the outset of the pandemic). "For the respondent to state otherwise is misinformed and misleading and furthermore an irresponsible statement to make on social media during a pandemic,"[41] the Committee wrote.

It also evaluated her claim that a vaccine was not needed, noting that a herd immunity strategy "would involve a significant death rate"[42] and that Gill did not provide any evidence for her claim. It concluded that the tweet was "irresponsible" and a "potential risk to public health."[43]

We have seen that one of the primary strategies of governments when their emergency orders were challenged in courts was to cite medical experts. Government officials claimed that their policies were supported by science and that critics and protesters were wilfully blind and callous to the available evidence. At the same time, governments and other organizations were pressuring doctors and medical experts not to publicly disagree with government narratives about COVID-19. Not only is this antithetical to the scientific method, which involves subjecting claims to criticism and falsification, it also creates an environment in which the dice are loaded in favour of government policies.

The authors of this book spoke on the condition of anonymity to one physician who faced chill from his regulator. Following some public tweets about consent and autonomy as it related to vaccines, complaints were made by members of the public to the College of Physicians. We can't reveal the content of the tweets without revealing so much information that this physician could be identified, but take our word for it that the tweets were reasonable and respectful, while also raising concerns about the importance of consent to vaccination and the importance of avoiding coercion. The College investigated the tweets and issued the physician "advice." The advice related to how some members of the public could be "offended" by this physician's public statements.

Advice is not disciplinary action, but it must be disclosed by the physician when applying for hospital privileges. We also know, following the Divisional Court decision in the Dr. Jordan Peterson case,[44] that the existence of previous advice from a regulator can be used against the professional when weighing the reasonableness of subsequent administrative action. Although the entire notion of "advice" is that you can take it or leave it, apparently in the Ontario Divisional Court's view, failing to take it weighs against the professional. The physician we spoke with disclosed that he is taking the rare step of seeking an administrative appeal of that advice and is deeply concerned that public complaints against physicians created a chilling effect during the pandemic that could continue in the post-pandemic era.

In sum, a reasonable disagreement existed among scientific experts over how to respond to COVID-19 with public health measures. Because there was no clear consensus on how to best respond to the virus, forbidding debate was one-sided and could not be justified. And it is this policy implication of reasonable scientific disagreement that makes lockdowns and the like a political issue, and not merely a scientific one. What matters here is not just the (scientific) truth-seeking function of free expression but also the political dissent function of free expression: dissenting from one-sided, rashly made policy decisions.

CRACKDOWNS ON HOSPITAL PROTESTS

In fall 2021, and especially during the federal election campaign, a previously unseen brusqueness in public protests sprang up across Canada, with Prime Minister Justin Trudeau's campaign stops being regularly interrupted by chants of "Trudeau Must Go!"

The country felt unusually polarized, and in large part the prime minister himself was to blame. Trudeau, who has always possessed a unique ability to telegraph empathy, had made a strategic decision at the outset of the snap election to pursue vaccination and vaccine mandates and passports as a wedge issue,[45] scapegoating his Conservative Party opponent Erin O'Toole for O'Toole's alleged softness on mandates. Notoriously, Trudeau referred to unvaccinated Canadians as a "small fringe minority" with "unacceptable views."[46]

It was perhaps not surprising, then, that mass protests opposing vaccine mandates and ongoing lockdowns and school closures began to materialize, and in some cases protests around hospitals grew so large that health care workers were unable to safely get to their jobs.[47] In the weeks following the Liberal Party's re-election as a minority government, Trudeau followed up on the promise he made on the election hustings to address the growing trend of hospital protests. Trudeau had declared during the campaign that "it's not right that the people tasked with keeping us safe and alive during this pandemic should be exposed to hatred, violence, fear and intimidation."[48] He did so by criminalizing protests outside of hospitals, with a law that was redundant at best, and a blatant free speech violation at worst.

The Liberal government introduced a law which amended the *Criminal Code*[49] and made it an offence to block a member of the public from obtaining health care services with the intent to provoke a state of fear or impede a health professional in the performance of their duties. It would also become a crime to intentionally obstruct or interfere with another person's lawful access to a place where a health professional provides health services.

The problem, of course, is that this conduct—preventing hospital workers from getting to their jobs, tending to a patient or creating a public disturbance—was already illegal under the *Criminal Code*. The issue was not the lack of effective legal mechanisms, but the failure of the police to enforce existing laws (a theme that would be repeated, to disastrous effect, with the Freedom Convoy and explored in Chapter 4). The new law was thus a political convenience and a performative measure with very little substantive impact.

At the time, criminal lawyer Michael Spratt pointed out that the law might actually make it harder to prosecute protesters: "With the added intent element [. . .]—the requirement that the prohibited act be done with the intent to provoke a state of fear—it may be more difficult for prosecutors to prove their case under Trudeau's new law."[50]

MANAGING THE TWIN PANDEMICS WITH SANITY

The COVID-19 pandemic was the first in history that saw the conjunction of viral contagion and fast-moving social networks. Information spread even faster than a highly infectious virus, and even the most pro-free-speech countries resorted to measures that ordinarily they would reject as unconstitutional limitations on expression in a free society.

In selectively censoring narratives that were critical of the dominant government response to the virus, governments undermined their own appearance of partiality and potentially even reinforced scepticism about the authority of public health.

It's important to note that one area of speech regulation this chapter does not comment on is the restriction of speech relating to the virus, and especially vaccines, on social media platforms. Facebook, YouTube, and Twitter all quickly implemented algorithms that flagged content that ran counter to the mainstream scientific consensus on these topics.

On the one hand, it's clear that given the firehose of information that erupted early on in the pandemic, some streamlining of which facts could be relied upon, and which could not, was necessary. And the social media platforms are private companies, not governments. As civil libertarians, we tend to think that private companies, no matter how widespread their influence or how vital a role they play in society, ought to be able to make their own rules. Alternative social media platforms such as Rumble were available for those who did not wish to get their information on platforms that restricted content.

However, when a restriction on speech is ultimately backed by government coercion, as in the case of a judicial order forbidding individuals from protesting or even communicating about the possibility of protesting online, or of a regulatory college policing the social media content of its member physicians, it's different from a private actor's decision. You may have a right to delete your Facebook account if you don't like the platform's policy on posting about COVID-19, but you don't have a right to ignore a judicial order or law. Thus, only restrictions on speech that are both demonstrably necessary and sufficiently tailored should be acceptable under the *Charter*, particularly when the speech in question is political and thus at the core of the guarantee of free expression.

CHAPTER 9
FREEDOM OF RELIGION

The Toronto International Celebration Church (TICC) located in North York is a vast, impressive facility. Popular with first-generation Canadians, the church serves not just as a site of worship but also as a place for newcomers to gather and form a sense of community, helping to facilitate a smooth integration into Canadian society. As is typical of many religious institutions, the church is also an important community hub for senior life, with 35 per cent of its congregants over the age of sixty-five.

The church enjoys a capacity of one thousand people. Under Ontario's Stage 2 capacity restrictions in 2020, it was allowed to operate at 30 per cent of that capacity (three hundred people).[1] Unlike some other religious institutions we'll encounter in this chapter, the TICC took pandemic restrictions seriously. They provided sanitizing wipes, hand sanitizer, free gloves, and masks as needed. They installed a state-of-the-art HVAC air filter system. They designated a church employee to take the temperature of anyone entering the building. They even adopted a system of single-capsule servings of Holy Communion wine.[2] The government's own records indicate that not a single instance of transmission of the virus occurred at a religious house of worship in Ontario where social distancing and masking measures were adopted.[3]

The COVID-19 lockdown rules at the time were absurd in their inconsistency. Renting out TICC's building with its thousand-person capacity to a movie studio to film a scene of a five-hundred-person church service would have been permitted under the lockdown rules,[4] but masked, socially distanced religious services would not be. Furthermore, the church—on the border of the Toronto and Vaughan regions—would be permitted to operate if it were situated about a kilometre away, just to the north of Steeles Avenue.[5]

On November 23, 2020, the Greater Toronto Area entered "Stage 1" of Ontario's reopening plan. Contrary to how it might sound, this represented an increase in Toronto physical-distancing restrictions, not a decrease. At the time, the second wave of the COVID-19 pandemic was ramping up in the province. Under Stage 1, religious services were restricted to allowing no more than ten people to attend at once.[6] This represented a 99 per cent reduction in the number of worshippers who could attend in-person services at the TICC.

This left a cruelly small number of congregants able to attend in-person services. The TICC retained renowned criminal defence lawyer Michael Lacy and sought an interim injunction against the strict capacity restrictions of Stage 1, on the grounds that they violated religious freedom.[7] Instead, the TICC asked that they be permitted to hold church services at 30 per cent capacity.[8] "We are not COVID deniers," the affidavit said. "At the same time, we want to be able to exercise our religious freedoms and provide a forum for others to do so in a safe and meaningful way. We believe we were able to do so with the 30 per cent capacity limit."[9] The Canadian Constitution Foundation intervened to support the church and was represented by Toronto lawyer Ryan O'Connor.[10]

In his endorsement ordering the hearing of the emergency injunction about reopening the TICC at 30 per cent capacity, Justice Myers wrote "The Government says it is trying to prevent a super-spreader event at Christmas. The applicant says it is trying to preserve Christmas."[11]

As part of its case for an injunction allowing it to reopen, the TICC tendered evidence from its founding pastor, Peter Youngren, concerning the indispensability of in-person services. The pastor emphasized that in-person worship was an important part of the religious practices of the church. He noted that several passages in the Bible mandate members of the church congregation to regularly meet in person, including the admonition in Hebrews 10:25 to "not neglect the gathering of yourself together." Pastor Youngren believed, accordingly, that fellowship between believers is also mandated in the Bible. For him, that fellowship ranks in importance with prayer, scriptural teaching, and Holy Communion. Pastor Youngren said that the Bible emphasizes congregational prayer where the whole church comes together in prayer.[12]

Evidence submitted from the church's congregants painted a vivid, heart-breaking story of the impact of lockdowns on parishioners. For example, Betty Berzowski, a seventy-seven-year-old woman who had attended the TICC since 2002 lived alone and never missed church. She also enthusiastically volunteered when her health permitted. Betty did not have a computer and could not watch services online. With Christmas coming and Toronto in lockdown, and unable to meaningfully connect with her faith and community, Betty faced a lonely and isolated winter.[13]

Another TICC congregant affected by the lockdowns was Perzol Joan Descanzo, a twenty-five-year-old immigrant from Saudi Arabia. During the first lockdown, Perzol became anxious and depressed and would often lie awake all night and then sleep through the day. Perzol was introduced to the church through a friend when services resumed in the summer of 2020. Before this, she was not a member of a church and did not practise her faith. Perzol received spiritual help from her new church family, which allowed her to overcome her anxiety and panic attacks. She became active in the church, attending weekly services and joining one of the church's young-adult support groups. But Perzol testified that in the fall of 2020, once the government had locked down religious services, she was afraid she would slip back into depression if she did not interact with her new church family.[14]

In this chapter we will consider:

- restrictions on in-person worship;
- the case of *Beaudoin v. British Columbia;*

- Gateway Bible Church and the Great Barrington Declaration; and
- the Church of God firebrand.

RESTRICTIONS ON IN-PERSON WORSHIP

When the COVID-19 virus first appeared in March 2020, few religious institutions in Canada resisted lockdown orders that forbade or severely restricted worship activities. The nature of religious services, which tend to feature extended lingering, singing, and close contact between worshippers, made it clear that they could be high-risk centres of infection. And, like the public at large, religious leaders expected shutdowns to be extremely limited in duration. However, as provinces implemented reopening plans that seemingly favoured nonreligious gatherings, such as allowing attendance at restaurants, bars, and big box stores, over constitutionally protected religious ones, resistance to ongoing restrictions intensified. In Canada, restrictions on religious gatherings were extreme. In Ontario alone, religious gatherings were restricted to just five people from March to June 2020. From December 2020 until February 2021 and from April to June 2021, religious gatherings—even when they were conducted outdoors—were limited to just ten people.[15]

Part of the problem, as we will discuss in this chapter, is that although freedom of religion is a well-documented and protected right in Canadian constitutional traditions, the surrounding rights that allow believers to actually manifest their faith—such as freedom of thought, belief, and conscience—have received scant attention in the jurisprudence.

Government restrictions on in-person worship services during the COVID-19 pandemic represented the most serious infringement in recent history on one of the most fundamental aspects of religious practice: gathering as a congregation.

Throughout the pandemic, groups advocating for religious liberties argued that religious institutions were necessary safeguards of freedom and militate against excessive state authority by promoting pluralism, in the sense of granting sources of meaning, belonging, and moral order to individuals' lives. From the perspectives of these groups, religious groups limit the sphere of authority of state action. As the Association for Reformed Political Action (ARPA) put it, "Government shares 'constitutional space' with these other institutions which, like governments, also have responsibilities, duties, and a constitutionally protected public role during a time of crisis."[16] As a general principle, these groups thus advocated for "maximum feasible accommodation"[17]—i.e., granting religious and other institutions of civil society the maximum liberty to operate in their normal spheres of activity, subject only to core state functions.

For religious groups, gathering in worship is an activity that rightfully attracts special constitutional protection, as it fulfils purposes at the core of section 2(a), 2(b), and 2(c) *Charter* rights. Proponents of religious liberty argue that restrictions on religious gatherings ought to be significantly more difficult to justify, since religious institutions and their activities contribute to the benefits of a free society.

The upshot of this view? In order to justify substantial limitations on the right to gather in worship, merely pointing to evidence of the possibility of transmission at any gathering is not enough. Rather, given the strong protection our constitution grants to religious liberty rights, the government has a general onus of demonstrating, when imposing gathering limits or defending them in a court challenge, that the reduced transmission from such limitations would be sufficient to justify the severity of the intrusion into constitutional rights.

While governments must generally meet a high constitutional threshold to justifiably limit religious gatherings, they may be justified in limiting certain activities that carry demonstrably higher risk due to their nature, such as religious singing. Interestingly, ARPA also made specific arguments in the *Trinity Bible* case (also referred to as the *Church of God* case)[18] defending the constitutionally protected nature of congregational singing as guaranteed by freedom of expression, which "communicat[es] transcendent truths and acts as a means of express[ing] oneself."[19] Through communal singing, worshippers both praise God and uplift one another.

There is no doubt that congregational singing can be construed as a core activity protected by the rights to free expression and religious liberty. However, an activity like singing, where vocalization that causes one's voice to emit aerosols (i.e., droplets), would seem to present unique risks. Recall the notorious case of a choir in February 2020 in Skagit, Washington, where 87 per cent of those who attended two choir practices ultimately contracted COVID-19.[20] At the time, scientists surmised that the virus' exceptionally high attack rate in Skagit reflected two types of transmission, but in retrospect we know that COVID-19 spreads most easily through fine droplets emitted through talking, coughing, and singing. Thus, congregational singing, though undoubtedly a protected religious activity, might fall into the category of activities that can be specifically connected to a demonstrated risk of transmission and restricted accordingly.

Ultimately, Justice Davies of the Superior Court dismissed the TICC's application for an interim injunction against the lockdown measures.[21] In general, the bar for obtaining an injunction against a government action is extraordinarily high, since the law is presumed to produce a public good.[22] There are three prongs that must be met for an interim injunction to be granted: first, there must be a serious issue before the Court; second, the applicant must prove that they would suffer irreparable harm if the injunction is not granted; and third, the "balance of convenience"—weighing the harms and benefits to both sides—must favour the party seeking the injunction.[23]

Justice Davies in *TICC* agreed that there was a serious issue before the Court: namely, whether the government's physical-distancing restrictions were carefully tailored enough that they would not impair religious freedoms any more than was reasonably necessary to respond to the COVID-19 pandemic.[24] She also noted that Ontario had already conceded that the regulations infringed the TICC's religious freedoms by impairing the ability of people to attend their church services.[25] At the same time that the TICC, and all other religious bodies, were restricted to having only ten people attend religious services, Ontario regulations also allowed some businesses to remain open at up to 50 per cent capacity and others still to operate without enforcing the indoor mask mandate.[26] On the other hand, public health authorities and available evidence suggested that COVID-19 had been spread at some religious gatherings and that there was a very high probability that someone in a three-hundred-person crowd would be contagious with COVID-19.[27]

Justice Davies also ruled that the TICC's case met the second prong of the test for interim injunctions: the TICC and its followers would suffer irreparable harm to their religious freedoms if the injunction was not granted. The Justice noted here that Pastor Youngren had testified that attending religious services was mandated by the Bible, and that several members of the TICC said in-person prayer was an important part of their religious practice.[28] Because the TICC had more than 1,500 members, there was no way all their members could attend religious services under the ten-person maximum gathering restrictions. Their freedom of religion would be irreparably and immeasurably harmed by the government's decision to prevent them from attending their religious services.

It was at the third step of the test for concluding an injunction was appropriate that Justice Davies sided with Ontario, dooming the TICC's case for an interim injunction. The Justice noted that although the TICC was seeking an injunction against the gathering restrictions only for itself, the effect of a ruling in its favour would lead other churches to seek similar injunctions based on this precedent.[29]

While it was certainly correct that a ruling in the TICC's favour would have a significant precedent-setting impact, her decision was still a disappointing result. First, there was evidence before the court that the TICC's circumstances were exceptional, given the size of its facility. Second, the task of a judge on an application for an injunction for interim relief is to properly attend to the circumstances of those appearing before her who are currently suffering irreparable harm, not to consider the broader policy implications of an injunction.

BEAUDOIN V. BRITISH COLUMBIA AND THE IMPORTANCE OF THE STANDARD OF REVIEW

Beaudoin v. British Columbia[30] was a 2021 case involving Alain Beaudoin (an activist), Brent Smith (a pastor of the Riverside Calvary Chapel), John Van Muyen (the Chair of the Council of Immanuel Covenant Reformed Church), and the Free Reformed Church of Chilliwack. The parties jointly challenged the government of British Columbia's blanket prohibition on in-person worship. They alleged that the Gatherings and Events orders of the Provincial Health Officer, Bonnie Henry, violated their freedom of religion, expression, assembly, association, right to life, liberty and security of person, and their equality rights. This much was conceded by the government. The dispute in the case came down to whether the rights violations could be justified.

From the outset of the pandemic in spring 2020, B.C. Provincial Medical Officer Bonnie Henry issued several Gatherings and Events (G&E) orders restricting attendance numbers at religious institutions pursuant to her authority under the B.C. *Public Health Act*. In March 2020, she issued an order prohibiting public gatherings in excess of fifty people. In November of the same year, in response to the second wave of COVID-19, she imposed further restrictions through a G&E order banning *all* in-person gatherings, including religious services, although this did not apply to online services, drive-through services, or individual meetings with religious figures.

In January 2021, Dr. Henry issued another order that allowed for drive-in services provided there were no more than fifty vehicles present and provided for a maximum of ten people at weddings, funerals, and baptisms. When justifying her orders, Dr. Henry claimed that more restrictions were required for religious settings than for bars or restaurants because the social interactions entailed by religious environments were "fundamentally different than some of the transactional relationships we have if we're going to a store or even an individual working out in a gym, [or] an individual going to a restaurant with your small group of people."[31]

Unlike in previous cases we have seen, such as Kim Taylor's challenge to the Newfoundland travel restrictions, the petitioners in *Beaudoin* attempted to use their own expert evidence and brought evidence of inconsistencies in some of Dr. Henry's exemptions to her orders (she allowed synagogues exemptions but revoked them when other religious groups sought the same exemptions).

However, Chief Justice Hinkson ruled that he could not even consider much of this evidence, holding that, barring exceptional circumstances, he was limited to the record before the decision-maker—in this case, Dr. Henry—on an application for judicial review.[32] To do otherwise would be to second guess Dr. Henry's decisions based on information she could not have acted on because she could not have known it.

The Court next turned its attention to the standard of review applicable in this case. Chief Justice Hinkson decided that Dr. Henry's role when making G&E orders was "more akin to an administrative decision than a law of general application" and as a result, the test from a case called *Doré*, which afforded significant deference to the decision-maker, was the appropriate test in the case, not the more exacting *Oakes* test, which would apply to a law.

Essentially, the *Doré* test—so called for a 2012 Supreme Court of Canada decision—allows judges to review the decisions of administrators, including public health officials. The *Oakes* test, by contrast, sets the parameters for assessing the constitutionality of laws of general application and requires governments to show a pressing and substantial objective, as well as non-arbitrariness, minimal impairment, and proportionality. *Doré* sets a different standard. In the words of Chief Justice Hinkson, under *Doré*, "the issue is not whether the exercise of administrative discretion that limits a Charter right is correct (i.e., whether the court would come to the same result), but whether it is reasonable."[33] In other words, it is a much more deferential standard.

Ultimately, the Chief Justice concluded that Dr. Henry's orders were both reasonable and consistent with the statutory objectives under which she was operating. The Court found once again that although the petitioners' section 2(a), (b), (c), and (d) rights were infringed and the impacts of the G&E Orders on the religious petitioners' rights were substantial, the public health benefits of the gathering limits outweighed the impact on rights.

Interestingly, this case did contain one small victory for liberty. As discussed in Chapter 2, British Columbia conceded that to the extent that Dr. Henry's orders restricted the activist Beaudoin from holding outdoor public protests between November 19, 2020 and February 10, 2021, those orders were unconstitutional violations of Beaudoin's section 2(c) and (d) rights and therefore of no force or effect. The Chief Justice agreed and held as such in the decision.

GATEWAY BIBLE BAPTIST CHURCH AND THE GREAT BARRINGTON DECLARATION

Gateway Bible Baptist Church v. Manitoba[34] involved several Manitoba churches and individuals who jointly challenged the constitutionality of Manitoba's Public Health Orders (PHOs), issued from the outset of the pandemic in spring 2020 into summer 2021 that restricted in-person gatherings within the province, even at religious services. These PHOs prohibited public gatherings of more than five people, and included an order closing churches, mosques, temples, and synagogues to the public.[35] The order relating to religious institutions would eventually be amended to allow outdoor gatherings where everyone attending remained inside their cars.[36]

The *Gateway* case was one of the first instances where a judge was confronted with conflicting expert evidence from medical and public health experts on the efficacy of lockdowns and other public health interventions and, in particular, was forced to confront the Great Barrington Declaration, an influential and polarizing statement against the predominant approach to lockdowns signed by a coterie of influential medical and scientific experts. In the case, both the government and the applicants introduced extensive but conflicting expert scientific evidence to the Court and had it considered.

This was in stark contrast to earlier COVID-19 litigation, where government-driven narratives went unchallenged. In the *Taylor* case[37] concerning Newfoundland travel restrictions discussed in Chapter 5, Kim Taylor and the CCLA introduced no expert evidence challenging the government's narrative regarding COVID-19, while the government relied on the opinions of several experts. In *Beaudoin*, the Court gave little consideration to the expert evidence of the petitioners because it was outside of the record available to B.C.'s chief public health officer Dr. Henry as she made her various orders restricting gatherings. In *Gateway*, however, the Court did consider evidence that directly countered government narratives.

Nonetheless, the Manitoba Court of Queen's Bench framed the evidentiary question in *Gateway* as follows:[38]

> [. . .] after a review of any contrary scientific evidence and challenge, does there nonetheless remain a credible evidentiary record that supports Manitoba's position that any restrictions on the identified fundamental freedoms are rationally connected, minimally impairing and reasonable and proportionate public health policy choices vis-à-vis what are acknowledged and conceded to be, Manitoba's pressing and substantial public health objectives?

In other words, Chief Justice Joyal was not prepared to weigh in substantively on which side's experts were more credible or which side's understanding of the COVID-19 pandemic was more likely to be true. Instead, for the government's narrative to survive, it needed only maintain its own credibility in the face of contrary evidence, without doing anything close to conclusively defending its position—a very low burden of proof for restricting a very important constitutional right.

If the applicants failed to prove that the government's understanding of COVID-19 was not credible, the government could continue to rely on its own evidence to justify its measures. Indeed, this is exactly what happened. After a very detailed overview of all the expert opinion provided in the case, Chief Justice Joyal was not convinced "of any obvious or definitively faulty science being applied by Manitoba,"[39] and he also said, "Manitoba's own evidence convinces me that it is on solid ground in its section 1 justification of measures and restrictions, which I repeat, represent the public health consensus and approach followed across most of Canada and the world."[40]

When it came to applying the *Oakes* test, which asks whether a rights infringement may be "demonstrably justified in a free and democratic society,"[41] the Manitoba court differed from the British Columbia Supreme Court about how much deference to show to the government's decisions. It's important to note that the Manitoba court's application of the *Oakes* test was more stringent than that of the B.C. Supreme Court. Put simply, the Manitoba court departed from the B.C. court's decision in *Beaudoin,* discussed above,[42] to treat COVID-19 public health orders as akin to administrative decisions rather than laws and therefore governed by a more lenient framework, laid out in a case called *Doré.* Instead, the Manitoba court took the same view as the Newfoundland and Labrador court in *Taylor* and would apply the more stringent *Oakes* test if *Charter* infringements were found.

In the Manitoba *Gateway* case, the applicants alleged that the equality rights under *Charter* sections 2(a) freedom of religion, 2(b) freedom of expression, 2(c) freedom of peaceful assembly, section 7 right to life, liberty and security of person, and section 15 equality rights were all infringed. Manitoba conceded and the Court agreed that section 2(a), (b) and (c) were infringed, but as in *Beaudoin,* the Court did not agree that section 7 or 15 were engaged.[43] Having found a section 2(a) breach, the Court went on to conduct an Oakes analysis of Manitoba's religious gathering restrictions.

In order to pass the hurdle of the *Oakes* test, the government is required to show that their measures are minimally impairing of the rights in question. In *Gateway* for the first time, a controversial and prominent counterpoint to lockdown measures was presented to the court for consideration. This was the Great Barrington Declaration, an open letter authored by scientists from Oxford University, Harvard University, and Stanford University and other members of the medical and scientific communities in October 2020 in response to lockdowns. The Declaration advocated for "Focused Protection," which has several key elements, including the following: [44]

1. Prioritizing the protection of those who are most at risk, such as the elderly and those with underlying health conditions.
2. Implementing measures such as testing, tracing, and isolation to help protect those who are most vulnerable.
3. Allowing those who are at lower risk to continue their daily lives as normally as possible, including going to work and participating in other activities.
4. Ensuring that the economic and social costs of the pandemic are minimized, particularly for those who are most vulnerable.

Jay Bhattacharya, one of the authors of the Declaration, testified as an expert witness in *Gateway* and proposed "focused protection" to the Manitoba court. The Court rejected this approach summarily, concluding that: "the applicants' theory respecting focused protection (as a more minimally impairing approach) raises for the Court not only concerns about the practical effects flowing from the resigned acceptance of general community spread in the pursuit of an elusive herd immunity, it also raises significant ethical and moral questions." [45]

To summarize the Manitoba Court's view from *Gateway*, focused protection involves increased risks to the persons most vulnerable to COVID-19, and the applicant's experts failed to address how more widespread circulation of COVID-19 could be accommodated by Manitoba's health infrastructure. This was enough for Chief Justice Joyal to hold that there were no less-intrusive measures that could have been equally effective in flattening the curve. [46]

Effectively, the judge in *Gateway* allowed the government to disregard the constitutional weight of religious freedom on multiple levels. First, the judge allowed the government to ignore the applicants' claim that the government could be less restrictive on religious freedom while equally effective in preventing the spread of COVID-19. Second, the judge signalled that the government was automatically justified in limiting religious freedom more restrictively, as long as doing so prevented COVID-19 transmission. The elephant in the room, though, is how far this logic can be taken. In other words, when is the need to mitigate COVID-19 small enough that equivalent restrictions on constitutional freedoms would cease to be acceptable? No judge was willing to transparently weigh in on the actual threshold at which harm to rights could no longer be countenanced. Without this answer, it seems like the answer is that any degree of mitigation is acceptable as long as there are credible medical experts out there who are willing to justify it.

Returning to the court's *Oakes* analysis, the final step of the test asks if there was proportionality between the beneficial and harmful effects of the disputed law. Once again, the Court found that Manitoba's orders were proportionate in the circumstances: "Based on the evidence, it is not difficult to conclude that the PHOs do indeed achieve an important societal benefit: protecting the health and safety of others, especially the vulnerable."[47] The judge noted that the measures were temporary in duration, thus in his view reducing the severity of the infringement.

The court noted that, in applying the *Oakes* test, the court should not engage in a scientific inquiry into the costs and benefits of the policy in dispute but only needs to be satisfied that a reasonable person having seen all the evidence would be satisfied that the state was justified in infringing the right at stake to the degree it has. Having accepted the credibility of the government's experts, it was easy for the court to find that the gathering restrictions were a proportionate response to the harms and risks COVID-19 posed to vulnerable groups. As a result of the Court's *Oakes* analysis, Chief Justice Joyal held that the Manitoba PHOs were constitutional; saved by reasonable limits under section 1 of the *Charter*.[48]

THE CHURCH OF GOD FIREBRAND

Henry Hildebrandt's last name rhymes with "firebrand," and he certainly plays the part. He is the pastor at the Church of God's Aylmer, Ontario congregation, a church serving a largely rural community in the southwest of the province. Hildebrandt is fifty-eight and has a distinctive appearance, with a thick salt-and-pepper beard. He wears white dress shirts and black vests and previously came under scrutiny for allegedly advocating for corporal punishment of children using straps and sticks—resulting in the local Children's Aid Society taking children from his congregation into custody—as well as allegedly forbidding congregants from taking their sick children to medical doctors.[49]

During the pandemic, Hildebrandt became known as an outspoken anti-vaxxer who openly flouted pandemic restrictions even during the first wave of the virus, holding services in the church's parking lot (flanked by signs exhorting worshippers to stay in their cars) and eventually indoors, ignoring provincial gathering restrictions and resulting in fines and contempt of court orders. He was a regular figure at anti-lockdown rallies across Ontario,[50] as well as alongside the Freedom Convoy in Ottawa.[51] In May 2021, a Superior Court Justice ordered the doors of his church to be locked. The province issued fines of over $275,000. The congregation continued to worship on the church's front lawn.[52] Some of the police's conduct in investigating Hildebrandt was despicable, including hiding in the bushes and spying on his services while worshippers stayed dutifully in their cars.[53]

A *Toronto Life* feature story about Hildebrandt and his church describes him and his followers as strict adherents to a literalist interpretation of the Bible.[54] They also believe that the church must gather: in-person worshipping is the heart of their faith, and they were very clear that online services were a wholly unacceptable alternative. Many Church of God congregants do not use the internet, so Zoom services were not an option.[55] Hildebrandt has argued publicly[56] that by forbidding religious services, the government infringed upon his congregation's rights to freedom of religion and peaceful assembly. Why should their services be capped at ten churchgoers if big box stores and restaurants were permitted to serve thousands of customers a day? A cartoon sign on Church of God lawns depicted a shop and abortion clinic as open while a church was boarded up and flanked by a police officer in riot gear.[57]

A judge of the Ontario Superior Court issued a restraining order in February 2021 forbidding Hildebrandt and his assistant pastor Peter Wall from hosting services in violation of the *Reopening Ontario Act*. By April 2021, the Church of God was back to openly hosting services with unmasked congregants. The Church, Hildebrandt, and Wall were held in contempt of court for violating the order three times between May and June of 2021, for violating the order that restrained gatherings, and for actively participating in an additional gathering.[58]

At the sentencing hearing, the government sought fines of $10,000 against both Hildebrandt and Wall and a fine of $50,000 against the church, as well as an order locking the church building.[59] Reviewing the mitigating and aggravating factors, the judge quoted from one of Hildebrandt's sermons, streamed live on YouTube:[60]

> The gathering, the gathering on 751 John Street North in Aylmer Ontario this morning is just a fraction, is just a representation, of the 7000 of Canada that have not bowed their knee. And they aren't about to. And the number is growing. It's growing its growing, its growing.
>
> Is it alright with you if we just speak directly? It has nothing to do with a virus. It has nothing to do with a virus. Nothing! I will prove it to you. If it was a virus, the officers will wear gloves before they touch the dirty pastor. . . . It's not about a virus. It's—the attack on the church of God in Aylmer has nothing to do with a virus! Nothing! . . . It is a made-up thing. It is . . . It is righteousness versus evil. It is light versus darkness. It is Satan versus God. And right now, we are at war, folks! We are in Canada at war right now!

The judge concluded—accurately—that "Pastor Hildebrandt is not so much conducting a service of worship as he is promoting his role as leader of the resistance to these public health restrictions."[61] He concluded by granting the order for the church doors to be locked and ordered a $10,000 fine against Hildebrandt as the "directing mind" of the Church of God. Wall, on the other hand, was fined only $3,000 as the judge found he was merely taking orders from his superior.[62]

The Church of God ended up joining with another Ontario evangelical church, Trinity Bible, in a challenge to the COVID-19 gathering restrictions, discussed earlier in this chapter. As in the Manitoba *Gateway* case, in the *Trinity Bible/Church of God* case the Ontario Superior Court of Justice heard expert opinion on both sides of the issue regarding the efficacy of COVID-19 gathering restrictions in religious settings. Unlike in *Beaudoin* and *Gateway* however, in this case Ontario actively challenged whether the right to freedom of religion was infringed at all by the gathering restrictions being challenged.

In the *Trinity Bible/Church of God* case Ontario accepted that ten-person limits on gatherings, both indoors and out, did constitute an infringement on freedom of religion;[63] however, they also argued that when gatherings were allowed to be a little larger, such as 15 per cent, 25 per cent, or 30 per cent capacity, the restrictions were merely a cost and not an infringement.[64] The province argued that even though the whole congregations of churches might not be able to attend church at once, the churches could hold multiple services to ensure everyone could attend even if they could not all be there at once.[65]

The court, however, was unconvinced by these arguments. According to Justice Pomerance:[66] "Ontario has conceded the sincerity of the beliefs asserted by the claimants, though it takes issue with the notion that all congregants need to be together at the same time. I have no reason to doubt the sincerity of the claimants' beliefs. It is not for me to dictate to the claimants how they should observe the edicts of the faith." On their evidence, the religious ideal is one in which the entire congregation can join together in prayer."[67]

The court in *Trinity Bible/Church of God* was accordingly reluctant to engage in a theological evaluation of the churches' beliefs and practices. Instead, Justice Pomerance accepted that in-person, communal prayer and religious gatherings were a sincere and non-trivial aspect of the churches' religious beliefs and practices. The spirit of the *Charter's* section 2 guarantee of freedom of religion is to allow individuals to decide, either by themselves or as a part of their religious community, how they wish to practise their religious beliefs. Whether that involves religious services of whatever size is properly a matter left to religious individuals, not courts or the government. It is a fundamental aspect of freedom of religion.

Much like the Manitoba and Newfoundland courts, the Ontario court in *Trinity Bible/Church of God* turned to the *Oakes* test[68] to determine whether the government was justified in imposing a limit on freedom of religion. At the same time, however, the Ontario court also paid the government significant deference within the context of the pandemic, sounding a familiar note: "This case calls for even greater deference to government decision making. Public officials were faced with an unprecedented public health emergency that foretold of serious illness and death."[69]

Like the other provincial courts before it, the Ontario court in *Trinity Bible/Church of God* proved itself unwilling to interfere with the discretion of public officials. The COVID-19 pandemic was seen as unprecedented, and scientific and medical understandings were constantly evolving. Public officials, in the view of the court, were tasked with an extremely difficult process involving balancing serious competing harms under a state of incomplete and changing information.

It is with that deference in mind that the Ontario court conducted its *Oakes* analysis in *Trinity Bible/Church of God*. At the first stage, the court found that there was indeed a pressing and substantial objective: reducing COVID-19 transmission and thereby reducing hospitalization and death.[70] Next, the court also found a rational connection between the objective of reducing COVID-19 transmission and the means, restricting in-person gatherings: fewer gatherings means less person-to-person interaction and therefore fewer opportunities for COVID-19 to spread.[71]

The question of minimal impairment is where the issue became more complicated. First, Justice Pomerance noted that *Oakes* does not require the government "to choose the least ambitious means of protecting the public."[72] Instead, the government only needs to choose a means that falls within the range of reasonable alternatives. Further, the judge signalled that he would not be subjecting the province's decisions to rigorous scrutiny: "Ontario is not required to justify its choices on a standard of scientific certainty. That would set an impossible burden, particularly where, as here, the social problem defies scientific consensus."[73]

The churches in *Trinity Bible/Church of God* argued that the province's failure to set different gathering limits for indoor and outdoor gatherings showed the restrictions were unjustifiable since it is known that COVID-19 is far more transmissible in indoor settings. The court rejected this argument, saying Ontario's experts were nonetheless still concerned that COVID-19 could spread outdoors, especially if "high-risk activities like singing and loud prayer are taking place."[74]

Similarly, the court rejected the churches' argument that there was an inconsistency between the higher gathering limits set in retail settings and the lower gathering limits set in religious settings.[75] The court said these differences were justifiable since the nature of these two settings is different. In retail stores, the court reasoned, people come and go quickly, while employers and employees observe strict masking and sanitary requirements. In churches, on the other hand, people stay for long periods of time, and will be tempted to greet each other since it is a social and community environment. The court finally noted that Ontario gathering restrictions "were carefully tailored to reflect evolving circumstances, new scientific evidence, and changing levels of risk."[76] Rather than banning religious gatherings outright, the government changed limits according to the severity of the COVID-19 pandemic both geographically and temporally. All in all, the court found Ontario's gathering restrictions minimally intrusive.

The court emphasized that human life is sacred and not reducible to a value that can be compared against others.[77] However, this platitude conceals a far more complex reality: as a society, we are continuously forced to make risk-benefit calculations. For example, it is generally accepted that we could drastically reduce car-accident mortality by reducing the speed limit to, say, 30km/h, but the inconvenience and trade-offs from doing so are simply unacceptable.

Justice Pomerance adopted Ontario's section 2(a) argument to pass the proportionality stage of the *Oakes* test. He concluded that the harm done to the churches and their congregations was less than the harm that would be done to the public because the churches and their congregations could mitigate their losses by modifying their church services to comply with provincial orders.

Interestingly, both the Manitoba *Gateway* case and the *Trinity Bible/Church of God* case draw upon the American Supreme Court decision in the case of *South Bay United Pentecostal Church et al. v. Gavin Newsom, Governor of California*.[78] In that American case, Chief Justice Roberts denied an application for an injunction by a church against Californian gathering restrictions that affected religious services. The Canadian courts cited the opinion of Chief Justice Roberts with approval in both *Gateway* and *Church of God*.[79] In particular, they cited Roberts' exhortation to defer to the sound judgment of elected officials in public health matters: "The precise question of when restrictions on particular social activities should be lifted during the pandemic is a dynamic and fact-intensive matter subject to reasonable disagreement. Our Constitution principally entrusts '[t]he safety and the health of the people' to the politically accountable officials of the States "to guard and protect." The dynamic and nuanced particularities of public health policy was properly the domain of politicians, not cloistered judges.

This is particularly interesting because when the U.S. Supreme Court changed its tune, the Canadian courts did not follow, suggesting their regard for U.S. jurisprudence was highly conditional on said jurisprudence fitting their generally left-of-centre norms. After Justice

Ruth Bader Ginsburg passed away and Justice Amy Coney Barrett was appointed by President Trump to replace her, the U.S. Supreme Court took a notably more sceptical stance towards state COVID-19 restrictions on religious gatherings. In the case of *Roman Catholic Diocese of Brooklyn, New York v. Andrew M. Cuomo, Governor of New York*[80] the majority of the U.S. Supreme Court prevented New York state from imposing ten and twenty-five-person gathering limits on religious services while secular businesses nearby remained uncapped. Indeed, the majority criticized New York's restrictions for not being narrowly tailored, finding that "stemming the spread of COVID-19 is unquestionably a compelling interest, but it is hard to see how the challenged regulations can be regarded as "narrowly tailored." They are far more restrictive than any COVID-19-related regulations that have previously come before the Court, much tighter than those adopted by many other jurisdictions hard-hit by the pandemic, and far more severe than has been shown to be required to prevent the spread of the virus at the applicants' services."[81]

Justice Gorsuch wrote a memorably grumpy concurrence, criticizing the state for allowing secular businesses to operate without capacity restrictions while religious gatherings were capped:[82]

> At the same time, the Governor has chosen to impose no capacity restrictions on certain businesses he considers "essential." And it turns out the businesses the Governor considers essential include hardware stores, acupuncturists, and liquor stores. Bicycle repair shops, certain signage companies, accountants, lawyers, and insurance agents are all essential too. So, at least according to the Governor, it may be unsafe to go to church, but it is always fine to pick up another bottle of wine, shop for a new bike, or spend the afternoon exploring your distal points and meridians. Who knew public health would so perfectly align with secular convenience?

Although the Ontario court in *Trinity Bible/Church of God* had the benefit of witnessing the American Supreme Court's change of heart, it is perhaps not a surprise that it was not Justice Coney Barrett or Justice Gorsuch's opinion that was cited with approval by Justice Pomerance, but Justice Sonia Sotomayor's dissent, arguing that the caps on religious gatherings were justified.[83]

It is quite odd indeed that Canadian courts would draw on American religious liberty dissent jurisprudence to *deny* the requirement that laws that affect the exercise of religious practice must be tailored to be minimally impairing. The minimal impairment requirement has been at the heart of U.S. religious free exercise jurisprudence since the passage of the *Religious Freedom Restoration Act* in 1993.[84] This is why, in cases like *Roman Catholic Diocese v. Cuomo*, we see judges being forthright in scrutinizing the impairments on liberty in ways that Canadian judges definitively failed to, such as: were the restrictions appropriately tailored? Were other jurisdictions less restrictive? It would have been a pleasure to see such an honest grappling with the gravitas of the rights at stake. Unfortunately, as we will see in the next chapter on vaccine passports, by permitting serious intrusions into the most essential of everyday activities, a lack of serious grappling with rights impairments became a signature of the pandemic in Canada.

CHAPTER 10
CIVIL LIBERTIES AND VACCINE MANDATES AND PASSPORTS

On January 11, 2022, Quebec Premier François Legault made a shocking announcement: the province would be imposing a tax on its unvaccinated citizens. At the time, hospitals across Canada were facing a surge in the number of patients because of the more virulent Omicron strain of the COVID-19 virus. Just four days earlier, federal health minister Yves Duclos publicly mused about the likelihood of mandatory vaccination, offering an open-door invitation for policies like Legault's "unvax-tax." So, while shocking, it was unsurprising that Premier Legault took up the invitation, solidifying his reputation for being the most illiberal pandemic premier in Canada.

"We're looking for a health contribution for adults who refuse to be vaccinated for non-medical reasons," Legault said. "These people, they put a very important burden on our health-care network. I think it's reasonable a majority of the population is asking that there be consequences,"[1] said Legault.

Legault did not say when the "unvax-tax" would be implemented or how much it would cost, but he did say he wanted it to be significant enough to act as an incentive to get vaccinated—more than $50 or $100. He said the tax could be included in people's provincial tax filings.[2]

The revelation of the "unvax-tax" was made during a press conference announcing the new interim Quebec public health director, a replacement for Dr. Horacio Arruda. Dr. Arruda had been coming increasingly under fire for appearing more and more political and for his decision to reinstate an overnight curfew just before New Year's Eve. Some pundits have even speculated that the announcement of the "unvax-tax" was a form of distraction from the negative attention that had been aimed at Arruda.[3]

The reaction to the unvax-tax from civil liberties organizations, bioethicists, and taxpayer advocacy groups came fast and furious. Joanna Baron, the executive director of the Canadian Constitution Foundation and author of this book, argued that "Quebec's new proposed health tax on the unvaccinated is a terrible idea. It is likely contrary to the *Canada Health Act* and raises serious constitutional questions."[4] Baron stated that the unvax-tax "must be condemned outright," and that "Imposing a fine as a condition to accessing an essential service such as health care goes above and beyond other prerequisites to engage in certain activities in society [. . .] Access to health care is a fundamental need that arises from being a human being in a vulnerable body."

The Canadian Civil Liberties Association also condemned the unvax-tax, noting the *Charter* recognizes individual autonomy over our bodies and medical decisions. "Allowing the government to levy fines on those who do not agree with the government's recommended medical treatment is a deeply troubling proposition," said Cara Zwibel, director of the CCLA's fundamental freedoms program.[5]

Vardit Ravitsky, a professor of bioethics at the Université de Montréal, told *CTV News Channel* that the tax would further certain inequities created by the COVID-19 pandemic. "From an ethical perspective, we're trying to select public health interventions that are the most equitable and just possible. This . . . does not respect this principle," Ravitsky said.[6] According to a report by the Canadian Press, advocates working with Black and Indigenous communities said the "unvax-tax" "risks further entrenching inequities in Canada's pandemic response, and adding another burden to those who are marginalized."[7]

Even medical experts opposed the proposed tax. A group of five-hundred doctors and medical students called Médecins Québécois pour le Régime Publique" proposed six alternative measures for increasing vaccination rates in Quebec, many of which sought to make vaccines more available in various communities, and having phone-in or in-person appointments where vaccine-hesitant people could anonymously discuss their questions or concerns about the vaccines in a non-judgmental environment.[8]

Franco Terrazanno, federal director of the Canadian Taxpayers Federation, warned about the possible ramifications of taxing personal health care choices. "Today, politicians will say the unvaccinated should pay. What about tomorrow? Will you need to pay a tax every time you put butter on your popcorn? If you gain weight after Christmas, will you have to write a cheque? When your kid falls off their bike trying a new jump, will a tax bill come with their stitches? People do lots of things that land them in the hospital."

In a pluralistic society where people will have legitimate conscientious, cultural, religious, and even medical reasons not to get vaccinated it is unrealistic to expect a 100 per cent vaccination rate. At the time the unvax-tax was announced by Legault, 90 per cent of eligible adults in Quebec were already vaccinated.[9] Charging mandatory levies against the unvaccinated simply crosses the line of what may be permitted in a free society. Even in public health emergencies, provinces must respect the fundamental right to make free and informed decisions over one's own body.

Fortunately, the "unvax-tax" was not to be. On February 1, 2022, just as the Freedom Convoy protests in Ottawa were in full swing, the Legault government dropped the proposal to tax unvaccinated people following the controversy over this policy and increasing public frustration over COVID-19 generally.

Legault's extreme unvax-tax policy was an example of the natural extension of the reasoning behind vaccine passports, which were one of the most widely debated responses to the COVID-19 pandemic in Canada. Canada was certainly not alone in implementing vaccine passports; they were adopted in various European countries and in some major American cities. But Canada's vaccine passport policies were unique in how widespread they were, and in how severely they were applied and enforced in certain provinces. While vaccine passport policies were initially popular,[10] in hindsight they were unjustified—especially given the ineffectiveness of vaccines in curbing the transmission of COVID-19, Omicron in particular. And in any event, popularity is never a justification for a policy that violates constitutional and human rights in some cases. One of the purposes of rights dialogue is to restrain the majoritarian impulse to trample minority rights.

The key arguments for the vaccine passports were twofold. First, the vaccine would curb the further transmission of COVID-19 by vaccinated people. Second, the vaccine would limit the severity of the disease in vaccinated people, which could protect Canadian hospitals from being overwhelmed. With the benefit of hindsight, it has become increasingly apparent that the COVID-19 vaccines did not effectively curb transmission, especially with later strains of the virus.[11] Indeed, in October 2022 a Pfizer spokesperson told the European parliament that the vaccines had never even been tested for preventing transmission.[12] The second argument ignores the fact that Canadian hospitals teeter on the brink of being overwhelmed as standard operating procedure.[13]

It is not the role of a civil liberties organization like the Canadian Constitution Foundation to advise people on whether to be vaccinated. That is a personal choice for individuals to make and should be informed by consultation with their primary care physician. Individuals and their own doctors know their unique medical needs better than the government does, and better than a legal charity does.

Speaking personally, the authors of this book believe that getting vaccinated is a reasonable and indeed responsible choice for many people. Evidence suggests that the COVID-19 vaccine has been effective at reducing the severity of disease, especially for the early strains, and the chance of adverse reaction is low. For us, the trade-offs weighed in favour of vaccination. However, other individuals may have unique circumstances, different medical or health needs, life experiences, or conscientious beliefs that lead them to make a different choice than we did. Different choices among individuals is normal. Given that the rationales for vaccine passports have proven to be quite weak, the policy appears to have been wielded as a sledgehammer designed to pressure people into making a personal choice about their own body through punishment. Our Constitution and human rights laws are intended to prevent this type of abuse. In many cases, they failed.

In this chapter, we will consider:

- the difference between vaccine passports and employer mandates;
- provincial and federal experiences with vaccine passports;
- vaccine passports and the *Charter;*
- government vaccine mandates on specific industries; and
- the human rights implications of privately imposed vaccine mandates.

WHAT IS A VACCINE MANDATE OR VACCINE PASSPORT?

The terms vaccine mandates and vaccine passports are often used interchangeably and are somewhat imprecise. The simple fact is that pressure to get a COVID-19 vaccine could have come from anywhere. Your friends or family might not have wanted to meet with you in person unless you were vaccinated. You might have lost your job if you weren't vaccinated. You might not have been able to travel or visit cafes, restaurants, or bars. Or, in the bizarre scenario from Quebec at the introduction to this chapter had come to pass, you could have been fined or taxed. All these examples are illustrative of pressures to get vaccinated but, legally speaking, they all function very differently.

It is also important to remember that the Constitution of Canada, including the *Charter,* does not apply to private individuals. The *Charter* does not constrain your friends, your family, or your employers from asking or requiring you to get vaccinated. The *Charter* is only intended to protect you from specific kinds of abuses originating from the government.

GOVERNMENT-IMPOSED VACCINE PASSPORTS: FEDERAL AND PROVINCIAL EXPERIENCES

There are constitutional and other legal limits on government-imposed vaccine passports. By government-imposed vaccine passports, we are referring generally to situations when a government mandates a vaccine passport on members of the public or on certain industries. We are not referring to employer vaccine mandates.

Throughout the pandemic, every province and territory, with the exception of Nunavut, implemented some form of a vaccine passport system that denied unvaccinated individuals at least some level of access to public places. Different provinces took different approaches to vaccine mandates, and some provinces took vaccine passport measures more seriously than others. For instance, Nunavut was the only territory to refrain from implementing any vaccine passports,[14] and Alberta was the most lenient province with their vaccine requirements. Unlike every other province and territory, unvaccinated Albertans had the option of showing proof of a negative COVID-19 test result in the previous seventy-two hours in order to access the same public settings as those with vaccine passports.

In some ways, Quebec was one of most aggressive provinces with its vaccine passport regime and vaccine mandates. It was the first province in Canada to implement vaccine passports on September 1, 2021. Even with aggressive vaccine passport measures, the province maintained some of the strictest social-distancing requirements in the country. For example, Quebec was the only province that imposed a curfew. And unlike most other provinces, Quebec steadily tightened the access to public spaces for its unvaccinated citizens. On January 18, 2022, the province made vaccination mandatory to access the provincial liquor and cannabis stores.[15] The province further considered (but did not pursue) narrowing the definition of "fully vaccinated" to require Quebecers to receive a third dose if they wanted to maintain what freedoms they had left under Quebec restrictions. Quebec was also unique in that, in January 2022, it required big box retail stores like Walmart, Costco, and Canadian Tire to enforce vaccination requirements in order to access their stores.[16] Even funerals and places of worship in the province were required to check vaccine passports for a certain period.[17]

VACCINE PASSPORTS AND THE CHARTER

Government-imposed vaccine passports may engage and even violate rights guaranteed under the *Charter*, and there was some litigation alleging such violations. In earlier chapters we touched on the impact of vaccine passports on several rights: the federal government's vaccine passports impacted mobility rights for those travelling by planes and trains (Chapter 5); they had negative privacy implications (Chapter 6); for those who could not get vaccinated, their equality rights were violated (Chapter 7); and vaccine passports also undermined religious freedom (Chapter 9).

In addition to these rights, vaccine passports arguably also violated section 7 of the *Charter*, which guarantees the right to life, liberty and security of the person. Canadian case law on section 7 emphasizes the importance of bodily autonomy. Thus, as more and more areas of daily life became subject to vaccine passports, the choice to remain unvaccinated began to box individuals in. As more choices were removed, vaccination edged closer and closer to becoming mandatory. Any decision to get vaccinated must be voluntary. When all these policies act together, and when the government's stated purpose behind vaccine passports is to create an incentive for vaccination, serious questions arise around whether vaccination remains a real choice.

British Columbia litigation by the Canadian Constitution Foundation

A powerful example of this came from the CCF's legal challenge to the B.C. vaccine passports.[18] The CCF's Litigation Director and author of this book, Christine Van Geyn, met with a teenage girl named Erica in April 2022. Erica was one of the CCF's applicants in the B.C. challenge to provincial vaccine passports, and they met to attend the hearing of the challenge in downtown Vancouver at the B.C. Supreme Court. Erica had developed serious pericarditis following her first dose of the Pfizer vaccine. This is a rare form of heart inflammation that can be caused by the vaccine and is more likely to occur in the younger population. The B.C. government was refusing blanket exemptions from the vaccine passport for individuals like Erica who could not be vaccinated. Even though public health officials and Erica's own physician told her it was not safe for her to be vaccinated, the government would not give her a blanket exemption from the vaccine passport.

Christine asked Erica if she ever considered just going and getting her second dose anyway. Erica replied that she "thought about it a lot," and had even seriously considered it. Even though her doctors warned her it was unsafe, Erica had been growing increasingly hopeless from the isolation she was experiencing. She was unable to see friends and family members. She was fired from her job as a swim coach for being unvaccinated, even though she was medically unable to be fully vaccinated. As more and more choices were removed from her path, vaccination was slowly becoming the only path forward for Erica. Fortunately, the opportunity for Erica to participate in the CCF's legal challenge gave her another path. This example shows one of the ways that the *Charter*'s section 7 guarantee of security of person can be engaged and potentially violated through vaccine passports.

Ontario litigation by the Justice Centre for Constitutional Freedoms

B.C. was not the only province that faced a legal challenge for draconian vaccine policies. A legal advocacy group called the Justice Centre for Constitutional Freedoms (JCCF) brought a legal challenge against Ontario vaccine passports that was heard in July of 2022.[19] This case centred around eight Ontario residents who were denied public access to various places for being unvaccinated. One applicant, Sarah Lamb, received one dose of a COVID-19 vaccine but decided against a second after experiencing an adverse reaction she attributed to the first shot. Another, Jackie Ramnauth, had concerns about the vaccines due to an underlying blood clotting disorder she has had since 2007, especially after the AstraZeneca vaccine was suspended due to blood clotting issues. The JCCF argued the vaccine passport system violated Canadians' fundamental freedoms and undermines the medical principle of informed consent. However, the challenge was unsuccessful, and the application was dismissed.

INDUSTRY-SPECIFIC MANDATES

Both the federal and provincial governments created mandates for certain industries. These are different from employer mandates because they were mandates imposed by the government in its capacity as a regulator, not employer.

Federal government industry mandates

On August 13, 2021, the federal government announced its intention to implement a vaccine mandate for regulated air, rail, and marine transportation workers.[20] On December 7, 2021, the federal government announced that it would expand this mandate to all federally regulated workplaces. This would be achieved, they said, by proposed regulatory changes.[21] This expansion would have been massive, as many industries are federally regulated, including banks, courier services, radio and television broadcasting, and telecommunications companies.

By the time of the December announcement, the requirements for employees in the rail, air, and maritime transportation sectors were already in place. But the broader expansion was not to be. Although the December press release stated that the government intended to bring the regulations into force in early 2022, nothing emerged.

It is unclear why the federal government abandoned efforts to bring in a wider vaccine mandate for federally regulated workplaces. By early 2022 many large institutions had already adopted vaccine mandates on their own as an employment measure, so they may have been viewed as redundant and unnecessary. Canada's five big banks all implemented mandatory COVID-19 vaccination policies for a period of nine months starting in August 2021.[22] The banks' implementation of the vaccine mandates coincided with the federal government's announcement of vaccine mandates across many federally regulated industries, and the timing was so coincidental that they were almost certainly coordinated.

Another possibility is that by late January 2022 several provincial governments began to drop vaccine passport requirements, so the federal government's political will to bring in the policy had waned. This was also around the same time that the Freedom Convoy protests were under way. It is possible that the federal government stopped pushing to create additional mandates in the face of strong public resistance. After all, the Freedom Convoy protests began initially as a response to vaccine mandate adjustments for truckers proposed by the federal government in November 2021.

Eventually the federal government announced that it would roll back most of these vaccination requirements effective June 20, 2022.[23] At the same time, the government announced it was suspending its attempts to implement vaccine mandates across all federally regulated industries, more than six months after the announcement that they were "working expeditiously to finalize the new regulations by early 2022." The government announced that employees who had been suspended for failing to get vaccinated would be contacted to return to their positions, but the government would also "not hesitate to make adjustments based on the latest public health advice and science to keep Canadians safe," including by reimplementing vaccine mandates in the fall, if needed.

Provincial government industry mandates

Like the federal government, multiple provincial governments also imposed industry-related vaccine mandates separately from the mandates imposed by private employers. The most common form of provincial industry mandates applied to health care or long-term care industries.

Alberta, British Columbia, Manitoba, New Brunswick, and Quebec all had vaccine mandates that targeted provincial health care workers, although Quebec eventually walked theirs back in the face of labour shortages.[24] The Quebec rollback is significant. The province had taken a very aggressive stance on vaccine mandates for health care settings and initially took the position that they would not accept religious exemptions.[25] The Quebec government even successfully fought a court challenge and injunction launched by unvaccinated health care workers.[26] However, faced with the practical consequences of a shortage of health care workers, Quebec ultimately needed to walk back their aggressive posture.

Nova Scotia, Newfoundland and Labrador, and New Brunswick all went further than the other provinces and made vaccination mandatory for all provincial public servants.

Ontario's Chief Medical Officer required hospitals to implement mandatory vaccination policies, but employees could decline vaccination for any reason if they attended an educational session espousing the safety and efficacy of vaccines against COVID-19.[27] In the case of *Blake v. University Health Network*, several unionized and non-unionized hospital workers sought a temporary injunction against their hospital's vaccination policies.[28] Ultimately, the court ruled that the unionized employees lacked standing to challenge the policy in court. As for the non-unionized employees, they could not meet the legal test to secure an injunction. As a result, the court did not consider the legality of COVID-19 vaccine mandates themselves.

VACCINE MANDATES FOR CANADA'S MILITARY: THE TIDE TURNS

There is an exception to most of the law on mandatory vaccination and Canada's Constitution. While most courts held that the policies were constitutional (or evaded answering the question on technicalities), a July 2023 decision[29] by the Military Grievance External Review Committee found parts of the mandatory vaccine policy for Canadian Armed Forces (CAF) members was unconstitutional.

The Military Grievances External Review Committee is an independent administrative tribunal. The committee reviews military grievances and provides findings and recommendations to the Chief of the Defence Staff and the Canadian Armed Forces member who submitted the grievance. Tribunals are not courts: they do not have the same precedential value. But it is still an important case because there have been so few cases where people hurt by these vaccine mandates were able to hold those who imposed these policies to account.

The committee heard this case because they received numerous grievances from members of the Armed Forces over the mandatory vaccination policy. Between October 2021 and December 2021, a series of directives and amendments to those directives were issued requiring mandatory vaccination for CAF members. CAF members who refused to get vaccinated and were not granted an exemption could be and were subject to discipline, all the way up to discharge. There were CAF members who were discharged or who resigned because of the policy.

The Military Grievances Committee reviewed the constitutionality of the mandatory vaccination directives. The decision of the committee was written by Nina Frid, and she found that the policy was unconstitutional. Frid explained that policies that force people to choose between staying unvaccinated and keeping their jobs engage the *Charter*-protected rights to liberty, which includes the right to direct one's own medical care, and security of the person, which protects bodily integrity. She also found that the limitation of the grievors' right to liberty and security of the person by the CAF vaccination policy is not in accordance with the principles of fundamental justice because the policy, in some aspects, is arbitrary, overly broad, and disproportionate. She wrote in the decision: "I conclude that the grievors' rights protected under section 7 were infringed."[30]

As has been discussed earlier in this book, it is not enough for there to be an infringement of rights—the infringement may still pass constitutional scrutiny if it is "demonstrably justified" in a free and democratic society. In other cases throughout the pandemic, this was where the government succeeded: the courts often find that limits to our rights were justified.

But not in this case.

Frid wrote that the obligation to limit fundamental rights only when necessary and within proportional limits rests with the CAF.

The CAF had the obligation to ensure minimal impairment in the implementation of its vaccination policy, demonstrating that there were no less-impairing measures, other than discharging CAF members, to attain their objective. Like the duty to accommodate, minimal impairment requires the CAF to demonstrate that among the range of reasonable alternatives available, there is no other less-impairing means of achieving the objective in a real and substantial manner. And she finished by saying "I conclude that the CAF has not met its obligation to ensure minimal impairment."[31]

As a result, Frid found that the policies were invalid, and all administrative action taken against CAF members because of the mandatory directives should be rescinded. The decision is not binding, but it will be considered by the Chief of the Defence Staff when he makes decisions on whether discharged soldiers and personnel can be reinstated. This decision could have a significant impact on the members of the forces who were being hurt or had been hurt by the policy.

Another important impact of the decision is that it called out the notion that no one was ever "forced" to get vaccinated. When the pandemic subsided, Trudeau asserted that his government never "forced" anyone to get vaccinated.[32] Grounding passengers and firing public servants and soldiers were mere "incentives." This decision by the Military Grievances Committee pushes back on this notion that no one was ever forced. While service members "theoretically" retained a choice, "the consequences of a refusal are such that this choice is not really a choice," as Frid wrote in her review.

The case could also have relevance for the next big test of vaccine passports, the CCF's appeal in the challenge to the B.C. vaccine mandates being heard in October, 2023. While that appeal deals largely with administrative law principles and a technicality that allowed the government to evade *Charter* review, the Military Grievances Committee decision opens the possibility that judges could follow Frid and find that *Charter* rights are engaged when government leaves a citizen with no meaningful choices.

PRIVATELY IMPOSED VACCINE MANDATES

In addition to government-imposed vaccine passports for public spaces and industry-wide mandates, various private entities created vaccine mandates or imposed vaccine requirements. The conduct of private parties like employers is not a civil liberties issue. The Constitution, including the *Charter*, does not apply to employer/employee relationships. However, for the purposes of this chapter we will briefly consider some noteworthy issues related to privately imposed vaccine passports.

Human rights law

Both the federal government and the provincial governments have enacted human rights legislation that constrains employers from engaging in harmful or discriminatory practices towards employees, potential employees, and customers.

It is important to note, however, that discrimination ordinarily and technically means treating different categories of people differently. Discrimination is not inherently wrongful or immoral: a good example of permissible discrimination is discrimination based on a personal characteristic that relates to the ability of someone to perform their job; for example, professional qualifications, skill sets, test scores, and the like. The government has recognized this and has also enacted provisions to make exceptions for such circumstances. This is known as the *bona fide* requirement.

In basic terms, employers and the providers of goods or services can discriminate when doing so is not arbitrary. For instance, if discriminating is required to fulfil a job competently or to keep employees and customers safe, based on genuine job requirements or genuine concerns that would cause them to want to deny service. This could conceivably include the protection of the health and safety of their employees or customers depending on the circumstances. That is one way vaccine requirements enforced by an employer or service provider could lead to employers and service providers legally denying the same services to both vaccinated and unvaccinated individuals.

Even with a *bona fide* occupational requirement or justification of discrimination, employers and service providers retain a general duty to accommodate. In practice, this means that for discrimination to be legal, employers or service providers must show that accommodating the person being discriminated against would impose undue hardship on their health, safety, or finances. In the context of the COVID-19 pandemic, then, the risks to health and safety presented by unvaccinated people were generally taken to be sufficient to warrant discriminatory practices, as long as reasonable accommodation was offered.

The problem for many who opposed employers' vaccine requirements is whether those requirements would pass as a *bona fide* test. As we have seen in cases involving reasonable limits on mobility rights and religious freedom, courts have been quite willing to accept evidence of COVID-19's danger even by the standards of the much more stringent *Oakes* test. This means that in the context of discrimination by employers or service providers, it would be easy, especially in the earlier stages of the pandemic, for them to justify their discriminatory practices. For one thing, governments at all levels were recommending that people get vaccinated and strongly warning about the risks of COVID-19. For another, it would be easy to establish that the employer demanded a vaccine requirement in good faith. And finally, the accommodations like letting employees work from home and arranging curb side pick-up for customers would easily fit within a duty to accommodate unvaccinated persons.

Here is what further complicates the matter: while human rights codes allow employers to implement with discretion potentially discriminatory policies to protect the health and safety of their workplaces, occupational health and safety legislation puts them under a weighty duty to make robust accommodations. For example, section 25(2)(h) of the Ontario *Occupational Health and Safety Act* provides that "an employer shall," "take every precaution reasonable in the circumstances for the protection of a worker."[33] While this legislation does not explicitly establish a duty to require vaccination in the workplace, it has been used by employers as authority to legitimize the practice.

The Ontario Human Rights Commission released a statement on vaccine mandates in September 2022, stating "the OHRC takes the position that mandating and requiring proof of vaccination to protect people at work or when receiving services is generally permissible under the Human Rights Code (Code) as long as protections are put in place to make sure people who are unable to be vaccinated for Code-related reasons are reasonably accommodated. This applies to all organizations."[34] On the duty to accommodate, the Commission further stated:

> Some people are not able to receive the COVID-19 vaccine for medical or disability-related reasons. Under the Code, organizations have a duty to accommodate them, unless it would significantly interfere with people's health and safety.

In other words, in the view of the OHRC, employer-led (non-government) vaccine mandates are consistent with Ontario human rights law, provided the employer makes reasonable accommodations for those who cannot be vaccinated for medical reasons. For the most part, this analysis has played out in courts. There have been several cases dealing with employer-imposed mandates that have been upheld.[35]

However, as the pandemic wound down this calculus changed. As governments dropped their vaccine mandates and passports, hospitals faced reduced COVID-19 caseloads, new variants became less severe, and vaccination became widespread, the argument that vaccination is a *bona fide* occupational requirement became weaker, especially in the face of disability claims. For example, employment lawyer Ronald Pizzo said in May 2022, "Unless something changes, and there's a flare-up in the vaccine or other unforeseen circumstances, it looks like the whole issue is coming to an end."[36]

As the pandemic receded, there were several successful challenges to employer mandates. For example, in *FCA Canada Inc. v. Unifor, Locals 195, 444, 1285*,[37] decided in June of 2022, a labour arbitrator found that the employer's two-dose vaccine requirement was no longer reasonable.

The employer, FCA Canada Inc., is a wholly-owned subsidiary of Stellantis, a global automaker. The union grieved that the vaccine mandate was once reasonable but was no longer reasonable in the context of June 2022 and the Omicron wave. At the hearing, the union argued that recent scientific studies had shown that two-dose vaccines were no longer effective against transmitting COVID-19, which made the vaccination policy unreasonable and meant that unvaccinated employees on unpaid leave should be fully compensated.[38]

The employer argued that the evolution in the scientific evidence was not as clear and consistent as the union suggested, and that vaccines remained effective in preventing serious illnesses. The employer also relied on the fact that public health guidelines still encouraged vaccination.

The arbitrator reviewed previous decisions upholding the reasonableness of workplace COVID-19 vaccine policies, but ultimately concluded that the policy was no longer reasonable. She wrote that this was based on "the evidence supporting the waning efficacy of that vaccination status and the failure to establish that there is any notable difference in the degree of risk of transmission of the virus as between the vaccinated (as defined in the Policy) and the unvaccinated." The arbitrator went on to hold that "the evidence supports a conclusion that there is negligible difference in the risk of transmission in respect of Omicron as between a two-dose vaccine regimen and remaining unvaccinated." The arbitrator declared the policy to be of no force or effect as of June 25, 2022.

WHAT DOES THE FUTURE HOLD FOR VACCINE PASSPORTS?

As of this writing in mid-2023, governments have ended the policy of vaccine passports, and many employers have likewise given up on vaccine mandates. However, the experience with these policies remains a troubling one. The courts were generally unsympathetic to arguments about the unconstitutionality of these policies, declining to hear most challenges on procedural grounds such as mootness and prematurity.

There was more success in the employment context, but only as the pandemic waned. The extreme approach taken by Quebec was just one step short of mandatory vaccination, a policy that is dangerously authoritarian. It is unfortunate that the courts did not take the opportunity presented by the COVID-19 pandemic to give clear guidance on the rights Canadians have to bodily autonomy.

CHAPTER 11
COVID-19, DEMOCRACY, AND THE RULE OF LAW

In March 2020, during the haze of those early and surreal weeks of lockdown, the federal Liberals were preparing to go to parliament and table a bill that would grant themselves virtually unprecedented, sweeping powers to allocate billions of funds and raise taxes without consulting parliament—up to December 2021. Taxation is enumerated as a parliamentary power under the *Constitution Act (1867)*, and even the *Emergencies Act* does not permit this to be modified.

The proposed bill meant many of the measures carried out under those new powers could be swept in without parliamentary debate and without the elected representatives of Canadians getting a chance to vote for or against the measures. The proposed bill was roundly rejected by all opposition parties. Andrew Scheer, then Conservative Party leader, commented:[1]

> In a crisis, broad all-party agreement is essential, especially when the government has a minority in the House of Commons. And we are prepared to have Parliament sit as needed to transact the business of Parliament.
>
> But we will not give the government unlimited power to raise taxes without a parliamentary vote. We will authorize whatever spending measures are justi-

fied to respond to the situation but we will not sign a blank cheque.

In the face of widespread opprobrium, the Liberals backed down and withdrew the blank-cheque provision from the bill. However, this early attempt at a power grab in the name of flexibility and public safety was, in retrospect, a foreshadowing of the numerous similar actions to come that undermined democracy and the rule of law in Canada.

By the rule of law, for the purposes of our discussion in this chapter, we are referring to the bedrock principle of liberal democracy that says no one in society—neither governments nor citizens—is above the law but all are governed under the law, and under the same rules, regardless of personal characteristics like wealth, connections, political power, race, or religious creed. It means that the rules that govern everyone are stable and predictable. From the perspective of the rule of law, citizens ought to know in advance the legal rules they could be held responsible for following. Furthermore, legal rules should not be changed on an arbitrary whim or applied retroactively, and certain constitutional obligations are binding upon everyone.

The rule of law dictates that people should not be punished or penalized for things they had no way of knowing in advance. It means that when the government applies or changes the law, it follows certain procedural rules that outline how those changes are to be made. And it also means having independent courts that can review legal conflicts to ensure that the law is being applied in a way that is consistent with its meaning and the rule-of-law principles listed above.

In the case *Reference re Secession of Quebec*,[2] the Supreme Court of Canada described the rule of law thus: "At its most basic level, the rule of law vouchsafes to the citizens and residents of the country a stable, predictable and ordered society in which to conduct their affairs. It provides a shield for individuals from arbitrary state action."

Closely tied to the principle of the rule of law is that of constitutionalism, which means that the basic guarantees of the constitution are binding upon all actors in a national body, from citizens to judges to civil servants to the prime minister. At its core, it promises certain legal limits on government powers. This principle is expressed by section 52(1) of the *Constitution Act (1867)*, which holds that "The Constitution of Canada is the supreme law of Canada, and any law that is inconsistent with the provisions of the Constitution is, to the extent of the inconsistency, of no force or effect."

And in the *Quebec Secession Reference*, the Supreme Court explained that a commitment to the rule of law means that "all government action must comply with the law, including the Constitution. [. . .] The Constitution binds all governments, both federal and provincial, including the executive branch. They may not transgress its provisions: indeed, their sole claim to exercise lawful authority rests in the powers allocated to them under the Constitution and can come from no other source."[3]

Unfortunately, the requirements of wide-scale emergencies like pandemics have an observable tendency to hollow out the adherence to the rule of law, on the basis that flexibility, responsiveness, and swift action are more important in the moment than the higher-level importance of the rule of law. This sentiment is sometimes expressed by the maxims "necessity knows no law," or, in Cicero's words, *salus populi suprema lex* (the welfare of the people is the supreme law). However, these sentiments do not form part of our constitutional tradition and would seem to severely undermine the authority of our claim to be a constitutional polity at all.

As Professor Ryan Alford put it;[4]

> [. . .] the framers of our constitutional order never intended that public emergencies should grant the government special powers to go beyond what was permitted by the Constitution, even when there was a danger to the state that we can hardly even imagine: the invasion of Canada.

In this chapter, we will see that departures from the basic requirements of the rule of law and democratic accountability in the name of public safety were sadly the rule and not the exception. This chapter will consider:

- Ontario's third-wave lockdown measures, likely enacted with the knowledge that they were unconstitutional;
- legislatures granting themselves infinitely expanded states of emergency;
- the bank-freezing measures announced along with the invocation of the *Emergencies Act*; and
- the B.C. government's argument that its vaccine-passport program could be remedied by the use of discretion.

FLOUTING THE CHARTER: ONTARIO'S CONSTITUTIONAL CATCH-22

For many Ontarians, Friday, April 26, 2021, stands out as a grim high-water mark of pandemic misery. While our friends and family south of the border were regaling us with stories of joyfully returning to normal life owing to widespread vaccine availability, most of Canada was being pummelled by a brutal third wave driven by the Delta variant. Due to a failure of Canadian government officials to either secure timely deliveries of vaccines or to scale-up domestic vaccine manufacturing, the vaccines were not estimated to become available at least until well into the summer.

On the afternoon of April 26th, in a press conference that was delayed by hours due to last-minute cabinet deliberations, Premier Ford, flanked by Health Minister Christine Elliott and Solicitor General Sylvia Jones, announced a set of draconian measures aimed at curbing the spread of the virus. The measures included instituting a mandatory stay-at-home order and closing outdoor playgrounds.[5] The risk of transmitting COVID-19 in outdoor settings is exceedingly low. A review of the literature in the *Journal of Infectious Diseases*[6] concluded that a low proportion, less than 10 per cent, of transmission globally occurred outdoors. But the figure may indeed be far lower. For example, a study[7] of case numbers in Ireland found that just one in every thousand confirmed COVID-19 cases was traced to outdoor transmission, meaning that 0.1 per cent of total cases was linked to outdoor transmission. Ontario's own science advisory table never recommended that Premier Doug Ford close outdoor recreational amenities. Dr. Peter Jüni, who sits on the table, has said "just as an estimate, that outdoor activities are probably roughly 20 times safer than indoor activities."[8]

From a legal point of view, however, the gravest worry was that the provincial police were now given extraordinary powers to randomly stop vehicles and inquire about an individual's reasons for leaving their home. Police, along with bylaw officers, now had the power to demand that citizens provide their home address and explain why they were outside during the stay-at-home order.

The measures immediately struck alarm bells among civil rights activists: in a province of fifteen million people, it would appear to be a foregone conclusion that police would by necessity engage in some sort of triaging behaviour in questioning individuals outside of their homes. And given what we know about police behaviour, that risked profiling of racialized communities, which already attract a heavy police presence.[9] This issue is discussed in detail in Chapter 7.

This is concerning enough from a civil rights perspective, but reporting at the time also provided strong evidence that the government was thumbing its nose at the rule of law by ignoring strong signals that there were serious constitutional issues with the regulations.

New legislation and regulations go through a legal risk assessment as standard practice, and the cabinet would almost certainly have required a legal risk assessment before approving the enhanced police powers. At the time, CBC reporting confirmed that Attorney General Doug Downey flagged potential constitutional problems during a cabinet meeting, only to be shut down.[10]

We will never know what that risk assessment contained. However, it almost certainly raised some of the same concerns laid out by the Canadian Constitution Foundation and the Canadian Civil Liberties Association, which immediately put out statements that they would challenge these new police powers. Police departments across the province also put out their own statements that they would not use these new controversial (and likely illegal) powers.[11]

But relying solely on police not to enforce an illegal regulation is completely unacceptable from the perspective of the rule of law, since the government should not be enacting unconstitutional laws in the first place, and knowingly so.

Indeed, the catch-22 of the police measures was that they were short-term regulations. The new police powers would likely have expired before a full legal challenge could be heard by the courts. So, it is likely that if the regulations had not been repealed, the government would have argued that any ultimate legal challenge would have been moot.[12] The Ford government's negligence was likely driven in part because it assumed that the courts would not hear such challenges in time, a deeply cynical perspective. Politicians who knowingly enact illegal laws deserve condemnation and have lost moral authority to govern.

The notorious Ontario "carding" measures were, sadly, just one colourful episode in an array of pandemic measures that flouted the ordinary operation of the rule of law.

INDEFINITELY EXTENDED STATES OF EMERGENCY

At the beginning of the pandemic, Ontario entered a state of emergency under its *Emergency Management and Civil Protection Act*. Under section 7.0.1 of the *EMCPA*, the premier or the Lieutenant Governor in Council can declare a state of emergency in the province. However, the state of emergency expires after fourteen days.[13] After declaring an emergency, the Lieutenant Governor in Council can extend this emergency for a further fourteen days. After that, the Act requires an approval of the legislature to extend states of emergencies for twenty-eight days at a time. These built-in sunset clauses are a means of checking the expansive powers contained in the *EMCPA* and ensuring a means of government accountability. It is a way of preventing the normalization of governing by emergency order.

But after only a few months of the state of emergency under the *EMCPA* in the summer of 2020, the Ford government decided to replace the function of the *EMCPA* with a new act called the *Reopening Ontario (A Flexible Response to COVID-19) Act*. Under the new *Reopening Ontario Act*, the government defined the COVID-19 state of emergency to be over in Ontario. At the same time, however, it also transformed the emergency orders made under the *EMCPA* into orders under the *Reopening Ontario Act* and extended many of the powers of the *EMCPA* while eliminating the need for continued legislative approval and without any sunset clauses.

In other words, the *Reopening Ontario Act* allowed the government to extend and retain the bulk of its extraordinary powers obtained through the declaration of an emergency under the *EMCPA*. The *Reopening Ontario Act* allowed the government to sidestep ordinary legislative procedures in enacting extraordinarily orders that restrict civil liberties. The new law also empowered the government to override certain key provisions of various collective union agreements, including especially for nurses and health care professionals, and to regulate businesses. As the founding executive director of the Law Commission of Ontario and former dean of law at the University of Calgary, Patricia Hughes noted that[14] "by shifting from the EMCPA to the more positive and optimistic *Reopening of Ontario Act*, [the Ford government] is able to eliminate even the vestiges of legislative democracy in order to benefit from the processes of executive authority."

In effect, the Ford government cleverly extended its own ability to make COVID-19 health orders without the need for the review processes originally set out by the *EMCPA* and repackaged this extension of executive authority in Ontario as an end to the COVID-19 emergency and a plan to reopen the province.

The *Reopening Ontario Act* was criticized by many proponents of democratic oversight and fundamental freedoms. Christine Van Geyn of the Canadian Constitution Foundation said the "province of Ontario making emergency powers permanent while simultaneously declaring the emergency over? This power grab by the premier is an unjustified

194

violation of *Charter*-protected rights, and citizens should be concerned."[15] The Canadian Civil Liberties Association called the Act an "undemocratic power grab," which gives the premier and his ministers the ability to impose emergency orders that "drastically curtail basic rights and freedoms" without the "need to engage in the legislative process or involve members of the Legislative Assembly."[16] Unlike under the *EMCPA*, where the government had to return to the legislature every twenty-eight days to seek an extension of emergency measures, the measures under *Reopening Ontario* required no renewal for up to a year. The effect was clearly to sideline the ability of elected representatives to check and balance extraordinary legal powers, many of which would be unconstitutional.

It is telling that even a member of Doug Ford's own Progressive Conservative Party was concerned about the controversial piece of legislation. MPP Belinda Karahalios was removed from the Progressive Conservative caucus for voting against the *Reopening Ontario Act*.[17] She was quoted by CBC as stating that "by transferring away the ability for Ontario MPPs to consider, debate, and vote on how emergency powers are used on Ontarians, Bill 195 essentially silences every single Ontario MPP on the most important issue facing our legislature today."[18]

The politics surrounding the *Reopening Ontario Act* illustrate the general trend of federal and provincial governments' concentration of discretionary power to the executive branch—both the executive cabinets and the bureaucrats—to the detriment of legislative bodies and the electorate. Any opposition to the government's concentration of power was swiftly swept under the rug, and COVID-19 orders continued to be made without crucial legislative oversight before the beginning of the COVID-19 pandemic.

ALBERTA'S BILL 10: SIDESTEPPING THE LEGISLATURE

Another example of provincial governments widening the scope of the executive authority was Alberta's Bill 10, *Public Health (Emergency Powers) Amendment Act*. Bill 10 was introduced, passed, and came into force at the lightning-fast speed of only forty-eight hours in April

2020. Only 21 out of 87, members of Alberta's legislative assembly were present to vote on the bill, just enough to pass quorum. Bill 10's emergency powers included two key amendments to the *Public Health Act*—sections 52.1(2)(b) and 52.21(2)(b)—both of which authorized government cabinet ministers to unilaterally create new laws and side-step the legislature when doing so.

Soon after Bill 10 came into force, then-Health Minister Tyler Shandro created a new law under the bill exactly as the observers worried. Minister Shandro amended the *Public Health Act* to authorize the release of "information obtained by the Chief Medical Officer" to "any police service." Ministerial Order 632/2020 states, "I, Tyler Shandro, the Minister of Health . . . do hereby order." Shandro then proceeded to add sections 53(4.2) and (4.3) to the *Public Health Act*. The legislature was not consulted prior to this legislative amendment. No studies were conducted. No debate was allowed. The public was not informed or consulted. For the first time in Canadian history, a law passed by a duly elected democratic legislature was unilaterally altered by a single politician, effectively overriding democracy in an act of executive authority. Shandro's new law, which benefited from the truncated procedures permitted by Bill 10, came into effect immediately upon signing on May 4, 2020. How could citizens reasonably be able to comply with a law they had no advance warning about?[19]

The amendments made under Bill 10 in Alberta did not just grant amazing powers to the minister to make new law unilaterally, it also granted the power to make law retroactively: it punished citizens' past behaviours for failing to comply with the new law, even though they were not illegal at the time. This flies in the face of rule-of-law principles that attempt to make the law stable, predictable, and prospective rather than retroactive. To quote law professor Shaun Fluker at the University of Calgary Faculty of Law:[20]

> These new subsections grant retroactive lawmaking power to ministers, subject to the limitation set out in subsection (2.2). Subsection (2.3) is particularly note-

worthy in that it appears to be curing invalidity in existing ministerial orders issued in relation to COVID-19 prior to the enactment of these amendments.

Subsections 2.2 and 2.3 limited retroactive lawmaking preventing it from creating new offences or taxes that could apply retroactively, or from making retroactive law that applied before the declaration of an emergency in the province of Alberta. Nonetheless, the ability to make retroactive law seems to be an attempt to cure invalidly made law that predated the Bill 10 amendments. According to Professor Fluker:[21]

> The *Public Health (Emergency Powers) Amendment Act* purports to be retroactive law which validates executive orders which themselves purport to be retroactive. This is confusing governance at the worst possible time, to say the least.
>
> Retroactive lawmaking is like getting into Dr. Brown's DeLorean and traveling back in time to change the past, and then returning to the present day. The Alberta legislature has done just this by going back to March 17 when cabinet declared a public health emergency and changing the law governing the exercise of emergency powers under the *Public Health Act*. Measures such as this which stretch the rule of law to its breaking point must be used sparingly, clearly articulated, and thoroughly justified, if these powers are to be seen as legitimate.

In particular, Fluker cited section 11 of the *Public Health (Emergency Powers) Amendment Act*, which declared that an earlier regulation that authorized the use of fines to punish the breaking of the Chief Medical Officer's orders to be valid. He further explained that section 11 makes these orders enforceable even when they have not been published to the Alberta public through the *Alberta Gazette* as would be the usual process.

The Government of Alberta would eventually walk these changes back in the following year with Bill 66, also amending the *Public Health Act*. This new amendment repealed the ability of ministers to unilaterally amend legislation without consulting the provincial legislature. The Justice Centre for Constitutional Freedoms (JCCF) challenged Bill 10 in court; however, their challenge was ultimately dismissed for being moot. The judge tasked with case intake held off on making any judgment about the constitutionality of the legislation, citing a statement by the provincial Minister of Health who said the law would eventually be repealed. The Alberta Court of Appeal summarized the case management judge's view when also deciding not to consider the constitutionality of the impugned amendments:[22]

> The case management judge was, however, alive to the fact that the impugned provisions had not, at that point, actually been repealed. She therefore granted the appellant leave to bring another application for standing if the provisions were not repealed by July 1, 2021.

By the time the Court of Appeal considered the issue, the provisions had already been repealed by Bill 66, leaving the court with no "justiciable issue."[23]

> While we agree with the appellant and the intervenor that there are curiosities about the enactment in question, we are of the view there is no remaining "serious justiciable issue as to the law's invalidity."

Although the British Columbia Civil Liberties Association, an intervenor in the case, and the JCCF argued that the statement by the provincial Minister of Health does not bind the legislature to repeal such legislation, the Court of Appeal reasoned that the case management judge had broad discretion to decline the JCCF's application for public interest standing while waiting to see if the government would repeal the laws as promised by the minister.

THE FREEDOM CONVOY: RECKLESSNESS ON BOTH SIDES

Although the Freedom Convoy is explored in depth in Chapter 3, few Canadians will forget the events of February 14, 2022, when the Trudeau government announced its decision to invoke the *Emergencies Act* in response to the Convoy. Particularly jarring was the announcement of the government's economic measures by Minister Chrystia Freeland. It's worth revisiting part of her speech from that day:[24]

> The government is issuing an order with immediate effect, under the *Emergencies Act*, authorizing Canadian financial institutions to temporarily cease providing financial services where the institution suspects that an account is being used to further the illegal blockades and occupations. This order covers both personal and corporate accounts.
>
> [. . .] we are directing Canadian financial institutions to review their relationships with anyone involved in the illegal blockades and report to the RCMP or CSIS.
>
> As of today, a bank or other financial service provider will be able to immediately freeze or suspend an account without a court order. In doing so, they will be protected against civil liability for actions taken in good faith.

Joanna and Christine were texting in real-time through the press conference and were utterly agog. Did we hear things correctly—that not only was the government giving banks the go-ahead to immediately freeze bank accounts without a warrant, but it was also immunizing them from any civil liability claims?

The measures were a visceral, bone-chilling warning of the coercive power of government to muzzle expression and compel banks, crowdfunding platforms, and other financial institutions to disclose private financial records. As reviewed in Chapters 4 and 6, they could potentially reveal the most intimate details of a person's private life. They were anti-democratic. They flouted even the mere appearance of respecting due process, and on their face would affect people who did not participate in the Convoy, such as spouses of protesters holding joint bank accounts, or ex-spouses of protesters who were unable to receive child support payments.

However, as we argued in previous chapters, it must be noted for the sake of clarity that the Convoy itself was not free from lawlessness. While the *Charter* protects the right to peaceful assembly and free expression, this does not automatically extend to the right to essentially paralyze an entire city's downtown core or prevent businesses from operating. This is to say nothing of the effects that the Convoy had on the civil servants and elected parliamentarians of our nation's capital.

In other words, there was indeed more than a whiff of lawlessness afoot during the Freedom Convoy's occupation of the capital. And as part of their general mandate to keep the peace, police do indeed have wide latitude to enforce laws against public nuisances and obstructing access to roadways. This is why our position has always been that while the Freedom Convoy organizers had a right to demonstrate and express their political opinions to elected officials, a three-week long disruptive demonstration that brought downtown Ottawa to its knees clearly strained the limits of the right to peaceful assembly. Police officers certainly had reasonable ambit under their mandates to clear the parts of the protest that disrupted the normal functioning of the city.

B.C. VACCINE PASSPORTS AND DISCRETIONARY CONSTITUTIONALISM

The B.C. government's vaccine passport program, which failed to create workable exemptions for those medically unable to be vaccinated, was discussed in depth in Chapter 7, which dealt with COVID-19 and inequality. However, the peculiar judgment dismissing the Canadian Constitution Foundation's challenge of this program merits dissection for the purposes of the rule of law.

In his decision, a judge of the B.C. Supreme Court dismissed the CCF's petition on the basis of "prematurity," claiming that the petitioners who were unable to be fully vaccinated for medical reasons had not fully exhausted their possible avenues of redress from the Public Health Office.[25] This is in spite of B.C. Public Health publishing a strictly limited list of acceptable conditions for medical exemptions and declaring that no other conditions would be considered for exemption. Two of the petitioners suffered from conditions that did not appear on the list of government-approved "check boxes" that made a patient eligible to apply for an exemption.

Ultimately, the rule of law requires clear and cogent rules to be published in advance. B.C.'s vaccine passport policy was the antithesis of these requirements, since when it came to the CCF's litigation challenge the government's defence was that individual government agents would have exercised their discretion to allow exemptions, contradicting the wording of the statute. A rule that relies on the discretion of an individual government agent to preserve its constitutionality is the very antithesis of the rule of law's demands.

An unconstitutional public health order such as B.C.'s thus cannot be saved by an assertion by a government lawyer, as happened with the CCF's vaccine passport challenge, that a member of the public could, contrary to the wording of the order, disregard the wording of the vaccine passport order and rely on the government proceeding. In this case, on the theory that the B.C. judge accepted, the Public Health office would, contrary to the order and the binding forms, grant exemptions for unlisted conditions.

This is unacceptable. The government must not be permitted to escape a finding of unconstitutionality by permitting things in practice that their own orders and mandatory forms prohibit. The Supreme Court made it clear that individual discretion may not save an otherwise unconstitutional law in *R. v. Nur*, a 2015 decision that took up the issue of mandatory minimum sentences. The government in that case argued that prosecutorial discretion ensured that mandatory minimums would not amount to "cruel and unusual punishment." The Court rejected this suggestion, concluding that "The discretionary decision of the parole board is no substitute for a constitutional law."[26]

What the rule of law demands is an admission (or court finding) of unconstitutionality and for the order to be amended to make it constitutionally compliant. Unfortunately, the decision at first instance in the B.C. vaccine passport case fell short of this hurdle. The appeal in that case is pending.

IN DEFENCE OF THE RULE OF LAW

It became apparent early on that governments would be zig-zagging away from ordinary procedures for devising laws in response to the pandemic. Indeed, to some extent we are sympathetic to this impulse: fast-moving emergencies require nimble responses. It was appropriate for the government to swiftly ensure that the Canada Emergency Response Benefit (CERB) would be available to Canadians to make sure nobody went without food or shelter in exchange for the government requiring them to stay home and, in many cases, not work.

However, as this chapter has clearly shown, this principle of prioritizing expediency over due process went completely haywire during the pandemic, with almost no scrutiny of due proportionality between the gravity of the emergency and its impact on individual rights. In the case of the B.C. vaccine passport policy, for example, the government seems to have outright conceded that their original position of barring exemptions for medical conditions was a bridge too far but declined to set out clear public guidelines. In the case of the *Emergencies Act*, the government skirted around clear statutory guidelines with the effect of imposing unprecedented restrictions on people's liberty and livelihoods. We should be vigilant to ensure that in future public health emergencies governments may not cut corners without consequences.

CHAPTER 12
CANADA'S FUTURE

The subtitle of this book is "How Canadian Governments' Responses to COVID-19 Changed Civil Liberties Forever." This is not hyperbole. The pandemic forever changed Canada's culture of civil liberties and created a large set of case law in the context of an emergency where the courts deferred to governments trampling on long-held rights.

On case law, courts declined opportunities to clarify the law, dismissing many cases on procedural grounds. The B.C. court has so far accepted the procedural argument that the CCF's challenge to discriminatory vaccine passports was premature because the government was secretly allowing exemptions that its own regulations did not permit. The Ontario court dismissed a challenge to protests during lockdowns on the procedural ground that the politician who brought the challenge lacked standing. A challenge to Ontario vaccine passports and a challenge to the federal vaccine mandate for planes and trains were also dismissed for mootness. The government even tried to argue that the legal challenge to the Trudeau government's historic and illegal invocation of the never-before-used *Emergencies Act* was moot and should be dismissed. Mootness means that there is no longer a live issue before the courts—that outside facts have resolved the dispute. For example, the government has frequently argued to dismiss COVID-era legal challenges because COVID-19 policies are no longer in force. However, this argument ignores the fact that important legal guidance from the courts on these novel issues could be required for any future pandemic or national crisis.

Courts also declined to even find that rights were engaged; a Newfoundland court would not accept that restrictions on social gatherings engaged the right to freedom of assembly. An Ontario court questioned whether the right to enter Canada was engaged by prohibitively expensive quarantine hotels created basically overnight. We should worry about what all of this says about the courts' willingness and ability to push back against government overreach in the future.

The pandemic showed the weakness of the courts in responding quickly to rights violations, and it showed the government's awareness of that. When the Ontario provincial government enacted a strict stay-at-home order with wide-reaching police powers, the Ontario cabinet proceeded with these unconstitutional measures, even in the face of their own knowledge of their unconstitutionality. The temporary nature of the stay-at-home order meant that courts would not even hear a legal challenge before the measures expired, at which point the government could evade review by arguing mootness. What changed the Ford government's mind on the stay-at-home order and the police powers was not the courts, but the public response. This was a rare instance where the civic culture showed a prioritization of civil liberties over government restrictions in the name of safety.

For the most part, the pandemic revealed the existing weakness of Canada's culture of civil liberties and may have permanently weakened that culture further. Groupthink infected many parts of society, not just the courts. There was only one acceptable way to think about the pandemic for an extended period. Those of us who called for restraint and questioned the severity of the restrictions were called "COVID-deniers" and "anti-vaxxers." In what world would police arresting young men for playing hockey or barging in on Christmas dinners be acceptable, other than one where groupthink is strongly enforced? Or where you are shouted down for questioning the use of government "snitch lines" to report on neighbours for insufficient social distancing or questioning why governments are denying teens with pericarditis access to restaurants.

But perhaps the most chilling case from the COVID-19 era in Canada was the Trudeau government's use of the *Emergencies Act* in response to the 2022 Freedom Convoy. The glass on the *Emergencies Act* has been broken. Bank accounts were frozen because people were protesting. We now need to brace ourselves for this extraordinary tool to be used again and prepare for the normalization of emergency governing. We still take our boots off at the airport following the mid-aughts war on terror. We still need to separate our toiletries into tiny bottles in see-through bags. What remnants of the pandemic will now exist forever? Crisis is always the greatest opportunity for governments to seize new powers and limit rights, so the Canadian public and the courts must be watchful for what the next emergency will bring.

By reading this book you are playing a part in that role as a watcher. Many Canadians would like to forget the three pandemic years. To throw them into a "memory hole" and move forward. But we cannot forget, because if we do, the governments of this country will be even better positioned to do this to us again.

WHAT SHOULD YOU DO NEXT?

Thank you so much for taking the time to read this book with an open mind, for serving the vital purpose of remembering what the pandemic years did to civil liberties. Remembering is one of the most important means of guarding against government abuse in the future. If you are looking for something more to read next, allow us to offer some suggestions.

1. If reading *Pandemic Panic* better equipped you to respond to current and present threats to your civil liberties, then you would also benefit from examining our other writings and content. All of our most recent articles are sent out in our free weekly newsletter, the *Freedom Update*. Subscribers are also the first to hear about our new litigation and other projects in defence of civil liberties.

    We also use the newsletter to share all our video content from our YouTube channel and the fundamental freedom episodes of Christine's national broadcast television series, *Canadian Justice*.

    You can subscribe to the *Freedom Update* by signing up at: theCCF.ca/FreedomUpdates/.

2. If you are convinced, as we are, that our elected representatives—municipally, provincially, and federally—need to be much more vigilant in pro-

tecting our fundamental rights and freedoms than they were throughout the COVID-19 crisis, then you can and should communicate this to them via respectful but clearly worded correspondence, perhaps using the material in *Pandemic Panic* to describe or support your concern.

3. Think globally but act locally. Change starts at the local level. Spread the word to your community about what you've learned in this book. You are now your community's resident expert on constitutional rights and their treatment during the pandemic. Consider gifting a copy of *Pandemic Panic* to a friend or family member who could benefit from the information in this book. You could even organize a local book club to discuss it.

4. Continue educating yourself about your guaranteed rights under the Constitution of Canada. One great free resource to start with is the CCF's complimentary constitutional law course, where you'll learn about the fundamental freedoms of the constitution from a curated list of Canada's top legal experts and scholars. Sign up for free at theCCF.ca/learn/.

ENDNOTES

CHAPTER 1

1. We are grateful for the help of our student research and editing assistants, Mark O'Brien and David Jo.

2. Emily Oster, "Let's Declare a Pandemic Amnesty," *The Atlantic* (31 October 2022), online: <https://www.theatlantic.com/ideas/archive/2022/10/covid-response-forgiveness/671879/>.

3. David Leonhardt, "A Misleading C.D.C. Number," *The New York Times* (11 May 2021), online: <https://www.nytimes.com/2021/05/11/briefing/outdoor-covid-transmission-cdc-number.html>.

4. Joel Dryden, "Police Arrest 21-Year-Old at Skating Rink After Bylaw Officers Say Crowd Violated COVID-19 Regulations," *CBC News* (20 December 2020), online: https://www.cbc.ca/news/canada/calgary/calgary-skating-rink-arrest-1.5848904.

5. Jocalyn Clark, Sharon E. Straus, Adam Houston, and Kamran Abbasi, "The World Expected More of Canada," *British Medical Journal 2023*; 382, p. 1634, online: <https://www.bmj.com/content/382/bmj.p1634>.

6. "COVID Misery Index" (last updated 10 January 2022), online: *The Macdonald-Laurier Institute* <https://www.macdonaldlaurier.ca/covid-misery-index/>.

CHAPTER 2

1. Tim Durkin, "No More Lockdown daily rally draws hundreds," *Quinte News* (16 April 2021), online: <https://www.quintenews.com/2021/04/16/260351/>.

2. "Evidence Suggests Outdoor COVID-19 Transmission is Low. Here's What You Need To Know," *CBC Radio* (23 April 2021), online: <https://t.co/LvDtabzRVQ>.

3. The Canadian Constitution Foundation, Press Release, "Defending the Right to Protest: Robert Bristol" (11 May 2021), online: <https://theccf.ca/?case=defending-the-right-to-protest-robert-bristol>.

4. The Canadian Constitution Foundation, Press Release, "CCF Victory: Charges Dropped Against Lone Protestor In Kingston," (24 June 2021), online: <https://theccf.ca/ccf-victory-charges-dropped-against-

lone-protestor-in-kingston/>.

5. There is no doubt that Bristol's section 2(b) right to freedom of expression was engaged.

6. *The Forgotten Fundamental Freedoms of the Charter*, edited by Dwight Newman, Derek Ross, Brian Bird, and Sarah Mix-Ross (Toronto: LexisNexis Canada, 2020).

7. *Roach v. Canada (Minister of State for Multiculturalism and Citizenship)*, 1994 CanLII 3453 (FCA), [1994] 2 FC 406, <https://canlii.ca/t/4nm5>.

8. *Bérubé c. Ville de Québec*, 2019 QCCA 1764 at paras 43-46.

9. This is a translation from French.

10. This is a translation from French.

11. As it was called then.

12. *Ontario (AG) v. Dieleman*, 1994 CanLII 7509 (ON SC) at para 700 <https://canlii.ca/t/1wc2r>.

13. Trevor Lawson, Lara Nathans, Adam Goldenberg, Marco Fimiani, David Boire-Schwab, Grace Waschuk, Charlotte Simard-Zakaib, Gabriel Querry, Caroline-Ariane Bernier, Todd Pribanic-White, Lauren Weaver, Hannah Young, Awanish Sinha, "COVID-19: Emergency Measures Tracker" (26 May 2022), online (blog article): *McCarthy Tétrault* <https://www.mccarthy.ca/en/insights/articles/covid-19-emergency-measures-tracker>.

14. Basil S. Alexander, "Exploring a More Independent Freedom of Peaceful Assembly in Canada" (2018) 8:1 UWO J Leg Stud 4, <https://www.canlii.org/en/commentary/doc/2018CanLIIDocs66>.

15. Kristopher E. G. Kinsinger, "Restricting Freedom of Peaceful Assembly During Public Health Emergencies" (2021) 30:1 Constitutional Forum 19, <https://canlii.ca/t/t30m>.

16. Section 1 is an important part of our *Charter* and will be referred to throughout this book. To determine if the violation of a right is justified, the courts generally apply a test called the *Oakes Test*. The Oakes test requires all of the following to be met:

    There must be a *pressing and substantial objective*

    The means must be *proportional*: (a) the legislative means must be rationally connected to the legislative objective; (b) there must be minimal impairment of rights; (c)there must be overall proportionality between the infringement and the objective.

17. Kristopher E. G. Kinsinger, "Restricting Freedom of Peaceful Assembly During Public Health Emergencies" (2021) 30:1

Constitutional Forum 19, <https://canlii.ca/t/t30m> at 22 and 23.

18. *R. v. Hillier*, Court File: CV-22-00682682-0000, hearing July 27 and 28, 2023.

19. *Koehler v. Newfoundland and Labrador*, 2021 NLSC 95, <https://canlii. ca/t/jgp6w>.

20. Ibid. at paras 45–46, <https://canlii.ca/t/jgp6w>.

21. *Ontario (AG) v. 2192 Dufferin Street*, 2019 ONSC 615 at para 54, <https://canlii.ca/t/hx6b2>.

22. *Bérubé c. Ville de Québec*, 2019 QCCA 1764 at paras 43–46.

23. "Men Fined at Edmonton Protest Over COVID-19 Restrictions Have Tickets Withdrawn," *The Canadian Press* (3 September 2020), online: <https://globalnews.ca/news/7314445/tickets-withdrawn-alberta-legislature-protest-covid-19-restrictions/>.

24. Dan Diamond, "Suddenly, Public Health Officials Say Social Justice Matters More Than Social Distance," *Politico* (4 June 2020), online: <https://www.politico.com/news/magazine/2020/06/04/public-health-protests-301534>; Ryan Tumilty, "Trudeau Defends Decision to Attend Protest Despite Advice to Avoid Large Crowds During COVID-19," *The National Post* (8 June 2020), online: <https://nationalpost.com/news/trudeau-defends-decision-to-attend-protest-despite-advice-to-avoid-large-crowds-during-covid-19>; "Over 1,000 Health Experts Sign Letter Supporting Anti-Black Racism Protests Despite COVID-19 Risks," *CBC Radio* (8 June 2020), online: <https://www.cbc.ca/radio/asithappens/as-it-happens-monday-edition-1.5603024/over-1-000-health-experts-sign-letter-supporting-anti-black-racism-protests-despite-covid-19-risks-1.5603025>.

25. The *Beaudoin* case also involved a group of religious petitioners, and that aspect of the case will be considered in further detail in Chapter 9, on freedom of religion.

26. *Beaudoin v. British Columbia, 2021 BCSC 248 at para 145,* <https://www. bccourts.ca/jdb-txt/sc/21/02/2021BCSC0248.htm>.

27. *Beaudoin v. British Columbia,* 2021 BCSC 248 at paras 147 and 249, <https://www.bccourts.ca/jdb-txt/sc/21/02/2021BCSC0248.htm>.

28. Roman Baber, "Lockdowns are deadlier than Covid. I wrote a respect-ful letter to Premier Ford, asking to end the Lockdown. Look @ the data—the virus is real but the crisis is mostly in LTC. Let's focus on LTC & hospital capacity, but ending the Lockdown is best for our health. #onpoli #cdnpoli" (15 January 2021) at 6:15), online: Twitter <https://twitter.com/Roman_Baber/status/1350039239090601984>.

29. Joshua Freeman, "Ford Turfs York Centre MPP Who Wrote Open Letter Saying 'Lockdown Is Deadlier Than COVID," *CP 24 News* (15 January 2021), online: <https://www.cp24.com/news/ford-turfs-york-centre-mpp-who-wrote-open-letter-saying-lockdown-is-deadlier-than-covid-1.526822>.

30. Rob Ferguson, "Court Rejects Former Tory MPP's Challenge of COVID-19 Lockdown Measures," *The Toronto Star* (20 August 2021), online: <https://www.thestar.com/politics/provincial/2021/08/20/court-rejects-former-tory-mpps-challenge-of-covid-19-lockdown-measures.html>.

31. *Baber v. Ontario (AG)*, 2022 ONCA 245 (CanLII), <https://canlii.ca/t/jp101>.

32. *R v. Lecompte*, [2000] CanLII 8782 (QC CA), <https://canlii.ca/t/1f8sd >.

33. *Guelph (City of) v. Soltys*, 2009 ONSC at para 26, < https://canlii.ca/t/2557w>.

34. Ibid., <https://www.canlii.org/en/on/onsc/doc/2009/2009canlii42449/2009canlii42449.html>.

35. *Highway Traffic Act*, RSO 1990, c H.8, s 134.1, <https://www.ontario.ca/laws/statute/90h08/v108#BK235>.

36. Ryan Alford, "The Danger of Politicizing the Policing of Protests: Ryan Alford for Inside Policy," *The Macdonald-Laurier Institute* (16 February 2022), online: <https://macdonaldlaurier.ca/danger-politicizing-policing-protests-ryan-alford-inside-policy/>.

37. "2020 Canadian Pipeline and Railway Protests," *Wikipedia*, online: <https://en.wikipedia.org/wiki/2020_Canadian_pipeline_and_railway_protests>.

CHAPTER 3

1. Sarah Turnbull, "GoFundMe Head Testifies Over Freedom Convoy Fundraising, Says Most Donors Were Canadian," *CTV News* (3 March 2022), online: <https://www.ctvnews.ca/politics/gofundme-head-testifies-over-freedom-convoy-fundraising-says-most-donors-were-canadian-1.5804094>.

2. "'Freedom Convoy' Organizers Tamara Lich, Chris Barber Will Face Trial In Sept. 2023," *The Canadian Press* (30 August 2022), online: <https://globalnews.ca/news/9094544/tamara-lich-chris-barber-trial-freedom-convoy-charges/>.

3. CTV News, "Tamara Lich: Full Testimony at Emergencies Act

Inquiry" (4 November 2022), online (video): YouTube <https://www.youtube.com/watch?v=iW_UHmmXL9E>.

4. Catharine Tunney, "Convoy Organizer Tamara Lich Accused of Having a 'Selective' Memory of Whether She Was Told To Leave Protest," *CBC News* (4 November 2022), online: <https://www.cbc.ca/news/politics/tamara-lich-mackenzie-bulford-1.6640630>.

5. The Public Order Emergency Commission, "Day 2 of Public Hearings" (14 October 2022), online (video): *Public Order Emergency Commission Webcast* <https://publicorderemergencycommission.ca/public-hearings/day-2-october-14/>.

6. For a more extensive look at the Freedom Convoy see; Andrew Lawton, *The Freedom Convoy: The Inside Story of Three Weeks that Shook the World* (Toronto: Sutherland House, 2022). Also see POEC timeline: Canada, The Public Order Emergency Commission, *Overview Report: Timeline of Certain Key Events* (Commission Counsel), <https://publicorderemergencycommission.ca/files/overview-reports/COM.OR.00000004.pdf>.

7. "Public Health Agency of Canada Involved in 'Error' on Trucker Vaccine Rules: CP Sources," *CBC News* (21 January 2022), online: <https://www.cbc.ca/news/politics/phac-truck-vaccine-mandate-communications-error-1.6322988>.

8. Michael Lee, "Canada's Vaccine Mandate for Cross-Border Truckers is Now in Effect," *CTV News* (15 January 2022), online: <https://www.ctvnews.ca/canada/canada-s-vaccine-mandate-for-cross-border-truckers-is-now-in-effect-1.5741561>.

9. Andrew Lawton, *The Freedom Convoy: The Inside Story of Three Weeks That Shook the World* (Toronto: Sutherland House, 2022) at 3.

10. Andrew Lawton, *The Freedom Convoy: The Inside Story of Three Weeks That Shook the World* (Toronto: Sutherland House, 2022) at 5.

11. Michael Lee, "Canada's Vaccine Mandate for Cross-Border Truckers is Now in Effect," *CTV News* (15 January 2022), online: <https://www.ctvnews.ca/canada/canada-s-vaccine-mandate-for-cross-border-truckers-is-now-in-effect-1.5741561>.

12. Canada, The Public Order Emergency Commission, *Report of the Public Inquiry Into the 2022 Public Order Emergency,* vol 1 (The Honourable Paul S. Rouleau) at 43, <https://publicorderemergency-commission.ca/files/documents/Final-Report/Vol-1-Report-of-the-Public-Inquiry-into-the-2022-Public-Order-Emergency.pdf>.

13. Ibid.

14. Rachel Gilmore, "'Fringe Minority' in Truck Convoy with 'Unacceptable Views' Don't Represent Canadians: Trudeau," *Global News* (26 January 2022), online: <https://globalnews.ca/news/8539610/trucker-convoy-covid-vaccine-mandates-ottawa/>.

15. *We the Fringe Apparel* <https://wethefringeapparel.com/>.

16. Aaron Wherry, "Rouleau's Report Redeems the Emergencies Act— But It's Not the End of the Story," *CBC News* (17 February 2023), online: <https://www.cbc.ca/news/politics/rouleau-trudeau-poilievre-wherry-1.6752996>.

17. Megan DeLaire, "Trudeau Says He Now Regrets 'Fringe' Views Remark About 'Freedom Convoy' Protesters," *CTV News* (17 February 2023), online: <https://www.ctvnews.ca/politics/trudeau-says-he-now-regrets-fringe-views-remark-about-freedom-convoy-protesters-1.6278913>.

18. Ibid.

19. Canada, The Public Order Emergency Commission, *Report of the Public Inquiry Into the 2022 Public Order Emergency*, vol 1 (The Honourable Paul S. Rouleau) at 49, <https://publicorderemergencycommission.ca/files/documents/Final-Report/Vol-1-Report-of-the-Public-Inquiry-into-the-2022-Public-Order-Emergency.pdf>.

20. Ibid. at 50.

21. Canada, The Public Order Emergency Commission, *Report of the Public Inquiry Into the 2022 Public Order Emergency*, vol 1 (The Honourable Paul S. Rouleau) at 54, <https://publicorderemergencycommission.ca/files/documents/Final-Report/Vol-1-Report-of-the-Public-Inquiry-into-the-2022-Public-Order-Emergency.pdf>.

22. Michael Woods and Ted Raymond, "'All Options Are On the Table' To End Truckers' Protest: Ottawa Police Chief," *CTV News* (31 January 2022), online: <https://ottawa.ctvnews.ca/all-options-are-on-the-table-to-end-truckers-protest-ottawa-police-chief-1.5760880>.

23. Canada, The Public Order Emergency Commission, Report of the Public Inquiry Into the 2022 Public Order Emergency, vol 1 (The Honourable Paul S. Rouleau) at 50, <https://publicorderemergency-commission.ca/files/documents/Final-Report/Vol-1-Report-of-the-Public-Inquiry-into-the-2022-Public-Order-Emergency.pdf>.

24. Mike Blanchfield and Laura Osman, "Judge Grants Interim Injunction Against Loud Honking at Ottawa Protest," *The Toronto Star* (7 February 2022), online: <https://www.thestar.com/politics/2022/02/07/ottawa-residents-protesters-scheduled-to-clash-in-court.html>.

25. Josh Pringle, "Top Canadian Defence Officials Condemn Protesters Dancing on Tomb of the Unknown Soldier," *CTV News* (30 January 2022), online: <https://ottawa.ctvnews.ca/top-canadian-defence-officials-condemn-protesters-dancing-on-tomb-of-the-unknown-soldier-1.5760168>.

26. "Woman Who Danced on Tomb of the Unknown Soldier Won't Face Criminal Charges," *CTV News* (28 April 2022), online: <https://www.cbc.ca/news/canada/ottawa/ottawa-tomb-unknown-soldier-police-1.6434275>.

27. Cadillac Fairview Corporation Limited, News Release. "Statement Regarding the Ongoing Closure of CF Rideau Centre" (6 February 2022), online: *Cision PR Newswire* <https://www.newswire.ca/news-releases/statement-regarding-the-ongoing-closure-of-cf-rideau-centre-826894547.html>.

28. Stephanie Taylor and David Fraser, "Former Ottawa Police Chief Peter Sloly Defends Intelligence Reading of 'Freedom Convoy,'" *CTV News* (28 October 2022), online: <https://toronto.citynews.ca/2022/10/28/emergencies-act-inquiry-peter-sloly/>.

29. Ryan Alford, "The Danger of Politicizing the Policing of Protests: Ryan Alford for Inside Policy," *The Macdonald-Laurier Institute* (16 February 2022), online: <https://macdonaldlaurier.ca/danger-politicizing-policing-protests-ryan-alford-inside-policy/>.

30. Ibid.

31. Tonda MacCharles and Alex Ballingall, "'Freedom Convoy' Didn't Need Help From Foreigners to Overwhelm Ottawa Police, Inquiry Told," *The Toronto Star* (18 October 2022), online: <https://www.thestar.com/politics/federal/2022/10/18/ottawa-police-chief-peter-sloly-hesitant-with-freedom-convoy-because-of-g20-experience-in-toronto-documents-show.html>.

32. Canada, The Public Order Emergency Commission, *Report of the Public Inquiry Into the 2022 Public Order Emergency,* vol 1 (The Honourable Paul S. Rouleau), <https://publicorderemergencycommission.ca/files/documents/Final-Report/Vol-1-Report-of-the-Public-Inquiry-into-the-2022-Public-Order-Emergency.pdf>.

33. Tonda MacCharles and Alex Ballingall, "Ottawa Police Chief Warned He'd 'Crush' Anyone Who Interfered with His 'Freedom Convoy' Response, Deputy Testifies," *The Toronto Star* (20 October 2022), online: <https://www.thestar.com/politics/federal/2022/10/20/emergencies-act-inquiry-set-to-hear-from-more-police-witnesses-thursday.html>.

34. Canada, The Public Order Emergency Commission, *Report of the Public Inquiry Into the 2022 Public Order Emergency*, vol 1 (The Honourable Paul S. Rouleau) at 66, <https://publicorderemergencycommission.ca/files/documents/Final-Report/Vol-1-Report-of-the-Public-Inquiry-into-the-2022-Public-Order-Emergency.pdf>.

35. Alistair Steele, "Ottawa's Request for 1,800 More Officers Caught RCMP Off Guard, Lucki Testifies," *CBC News* (15 November 2022), online: <https://www.cbc.ca/news/canada/ottawa/convoy-commission-officer-request-rmcp-1.6652121>.

36. Ibid.

37. Canada, The Public Order Emergency Commission, *Report of the Public Inquiry Into the 2022 Public Order Emergency*, vol 1 (The Honourable Paul S. Rouleau) at 66–68, <https://publicorderemergencycommission.ca/files/documents/Final-Report/Vol-1-Report-of-the-Public-Inquiry-into-the-2022-Public-Order-Emergency.pdf>.

38. The Public Order Emergency Commission, "Day 7 of Public Hearings" (21 October 2022), online (video): *Public Order Emergency Commission Webcast* <https://publicorderemergencycommission.ca/public-hearings/day-7-october-21/>.

39. Ibid.

40. Canada, The Public Order Emergency Commission, *Report of the Public Inquiry Into the 2022 Public Order Emergency*, vol 1 (The Honourable Paul S. Rouleau) at 56, <https://publicorderemergencycommission.ca/files/documents/Final-Report/Vol-1-Report-of-the-Public-Inquiry-into-the-2022-Public-Order-Emergency.pdf>.

41. Canada, The Public Order Emergency Commission, *Report of the Public Inquiry Into the 2022 Public Order Emergency*, vol 1 (The Honourable Paul S. Rouleau) at 58–59, <https://publicorderemergencycommission.ca/files/documents/Final-Report/Vol-1-Report-of-the-Public-Inquiry-into-the-2022-Public-Order-Emergency.pdf>.

42. Canada, The Public Order Emergency Commission, *Report of the Public Inquiry Into the 2022 Public Order Emergency*, vol 1 (The Honourable Paul S. Rouleau) at 64. <https://publicorderemergencycommission.ca/files/documents/Final-Report/Vol-1-Report-of-the-Public-Inquiry-into-the-2022-Public-Order-Emergency.pdf>.

43. The Public Order Emergency Commission, "Day 12 of Public Hearings" (28 October 2022), online (video): *Public Order Emergency Commission Webcast*, <https://publicorderemergencycommission.ca/public-hearings/day-12-october-28/>.

44. Ryan Tumilty and Christopher Nardi, "Trudeau Accused Ford of

'Hiding From His Responsibility' During Freedom Convoy," *The National Post* (18 October 2022), online: <https://nationalpost.com/news/politics/trudeau-accused-ford-of-hiding-from-his-responsiblity-during-freedom-convoy>.

45. Stephanie Levitz, "Doug Ford 'Abandoned' Ontario's Second-Largest City, Emergencies Act Report Finds," *The Toronto Star* (17 February 2023), online: <https://www.thestar.com/politics/federal/2023/02/17/doug-ford-abandoned-ottawas-residents-emergencies-act-report-finds.html>.

46. The Public Order Emergency Commission, "Day 23 of Public Hearings" (15 November 2022), online (video): *Public Order Emergency Commission Webcast* <https://publicorderemergencycommission.ca/public-hearings/day-23-november-15/>.

47. Jennifer La Grassa, "Ambassador Bridge Blockade Stalled Billions in Trade—And There Could Be Other Effects: Expert," *CBC News* (15 February, 2022), online: <https://www.cbc.ca/news/canada/windsor/ambassador-bridge-protest-cost-1.6351312>.

48. "Freedom Convoy: Canada Trucker Protests Force Car Plant Shutdowns," *BBC News* (10 February, 2022), online: <https://www.bbc.com/news/world-us-canada-60331882>.

49. Rob Drinkwater, "Jason Kenney Says Truckers' Coutts Border Blockade Violates Traffic Laws and Must End," *The Globe and Mail* (30 January 2022; last updated 31 January 2022), online: <https://www.theglobeandmail.com/canada/article-kenney-says-truckers-border-blockade-violates-traffic-laws-and-must/>.

50. Ibid.

51. Ibid.

52. Caley Gibson, "RCMP Arrest 13 People, Seize Weapons and Ammunition Near Coutts Border Blockade," *Global News* (14 February 2022), online: <https://globalnews.ca/news/8618494/alberta-coutts-border-protest-weapons-ammunition-seized/ ; https://web.archive.org/web/20220214181820/https://www.myprincegeorgenow.com/155991/eleven-people-arrested-weapons-seized-at-coutts-alberta-border-blockade/>.

53. Jana Pruden, "RCMP Charge Four Men With Plotting to Murder Officers in Connection With Coutts Border Protest," *The Globe and Mail* (15 February 2022; last updated 17 February 2022), online: <https://www.theglobeandmail.com/canada/alberta/article-rcmp-charge-four-men-with-plotting-to-murder-officers-in-connection/>.

54. "'You Shouldn't Need More Tools' To Clear Bridge Protest in Wind-

sor: Trudeau to Ford," *The City News* (9 November 2022), online: <https://ottawa.citynews.ca/2022/11/09/you-shouldnt-need-more-tools-to-clear-bridge-protest-in-windsor-trudeau-to-ford-6075279/>.

55. "Trucker Convoy: Counter-Protesters Block Convoy Traffic; Convoy Organizers Plan To 'Consolidate' Efforts Around Parliament Hill; Arrests in Windsor as Ambassador Bridge Cleared," *The Ottawa Citizen* (13 February 2022), online: <https://ottawacitizen.com/news/trucker-convoy-protest-enters-day-17-in-ottawa-arrests-in-windsor>.

56. Melanie Borrelli, "42 Arrests, 37 Vehicle Seizures Made By Police in Windsor Protest," *CTV News* (14 February 2022; last updated 15 February 2022), online: <https://windsor.ctvnews.ca/42-arrests-37-vehicle-seizures-made-by-police-in-windsor-protest-1.5780883>.

57. Ryan Tumilty and Christopher Nardi, "Tamara Lich Told 'Very Controversial' Pat King Not To Go To Ottawa Protest, She Tells Inquiry," *The Edmonton Journal* (3 November 2022; last updated on 5 November 2022), online: <https://edmontonjournal.com/news/politics/tamara-lich-told-very-controversial-pat-king-not-to-go-to-ottawa-protest-she-tells-inquiry/wcm/6880a94d-9965-499e-b98e-c3b78d82f57e>.

58. Rachel Gilmore, "'Fringe Minority' In Truck Convoy With 'Unacceptable Views' Don't Represent Canadians: Trudeau," *Global News* (26 January 2022), online: <https://globalnews.ca/news/8539610/trucker-convoy-covid-vaccine-mandates-ottawa/>.

59. Matt Gurney, "Dispatch From the Ottawa Front: Hot Dogs, Horns and Hard Men" (7 February 2022), online (blog): *The Line* <https://theline.substack.com/p/dispatch-from-the-ottawa-front-hot>.

60. Aedan Helmer, "Newsmakers 2022: The Freedom Convoy," *Ottawa Citizen* (30 December 2022) online: <https://ottawacitizen.com/news/newsmakers-2022-the-freedom-convoy>.

61. Matt Gurney, "Dispatch From the Ottawa Front: Hot Dogs, Horns and Hard Men" (7 February 2022), online (blog): *The Line* <https://theline.substack.com/p/dispatch-from-the-ottawa-front-hot>.

62. Patricia D'Cunha, "In Ottawa, A Tale Of Two Protests . . . And A Dangerous Ending," *CityNews Vancouver* (10 February 2022), online: <https://vancouver.citynews.ca/2022/02/10/ottawa-protests-big-story-podcast/>, Big Story Podcast, featuring Matt Gurney from The Line.

63. The Public Order Emergency Commission, "Day 2 of Public Hearings" (14 October 2022), online (video): *Public Order Emergency Commission Webcast* <https://publicorderemergencycommission.ca/public-hearings/day-2-october-14/>.

64. "Woman Who Danced on Tomb of the Unknown Soldier Won't Face Criminal Charges," *CBC News* (28 April 2022), online: >https://www.cbc.ca/news/canada/ottawa/ottawa-tomb-unknown-soldier-police-1.6434275>.

65. Kelsey Patterson, "UPDATE: Convoy Protesters Seeking Food Accused of Harassing Ottawa Soup Kitchen Staff," *CityNews Ottawa* (30 January 2022), online: <https://ottawa.citynews.ca/local-news/convoy-protesters-sought-food-from-ottawa-homeless-shelters-soup-kitchen-5008615>.

66. Pat King, "Trudeau Is Going To Catch A Bullet . . . Only Way This Ends Is With Bullets," online (video): *Streamable* <https://streamable.com/8jjmns>.

67. CBC News, "King Is Questioned About His 'Trudeau Is Going To Catch A Bullet' Video" (2 November 2022), online (video): <https://www.cbc.ca/player/play/2098311747651>.

68. Christopher Nardi and Catherine Lévesque, "OPP Saw No Evidence Freedom Convoy Posed Direct Threat to National Security: Intelligence Officer," *The National Post* (19 October 2022), online: <https://nationalpost.com/news/politics/opp-sent-ottawa-police-intelligence-warning-freedom-convoy-would-stay-long-term>.

69. For example, one protester carried a mock Canadian flag, but the maple leaf symbol had been replaced by a swastika made of needles, an apparent suggestion that vaccine mandates are a Nazi or authoritarian tool.

70. The Public Order Emergency Commission, "Day 12 of Public Hearings" (28 October 2022), online (video): *Public Order Emergency Commission Webcast* <https://publicorderemergencycommission.ca/public-hearings/day-12-october-28/>.

CHAPTER 4

1. CBC News, "Trudeau Invokes Emergencies Act for First Time Ever in Response to Protests" (14 February 2022), online (video): YouTube <https://www.youtube.com/watch?v=M1iXToPJFcs>.

2. Ibid.

3. Marie Woolf, "RCMP Gave Police Info on Ottawa Protesters With a List of Accounts to Freeze," *CBC News* (8 March 2022), online: <https://www.cbc.ca/news/politics/rcmp-names-banks-freeze-1.6376955>.

4. Ibid.

5. Andrew Lawton, *The Freedom Convoy: The Inside Story of Three Weeks*

That Shook the World (Toronto: Sutherland House, 2022) at 155.

6. 117 Ibid. at 157.

7. Mack Lamoureux, "At 3:30 or so in the morning protestors are shovelling snow on the barricades to make police advancements in the AM harder. The mood is odd and serious. Many cars and trucks inside this area have already bailed so what they're protecting is shrinking" (19 February 2022 at 3:35), online: Twitter, <https://twitter.com/MackLamoureux/status/1494953799554945032>.

8. Mack Lamoureux, "Inside the End of the 'Freedom Convoy' Occupation of Ottawa," *Vice News* (22 February 2022), online: <https://www.vice.com/en/article/z3nwp8/inside-end-of-freedom-convoy-ottawa>.

9. Ibid.

10. The Public Order Emergency Commission, "Day 17 of Public Hearings" (4 November 2022), online (video): *Public Order Emergency Commission Webcast* <https://publicorderemergencycommission.ca/public-hearings/day-17-november-4/>.

11. Lisa Joy, "Wounded Veteran Says Was His 'Duty' to Protect Ottawa Protesters," *SaskToday* (11 November 2022), online: <https://www.sasktoday.ca/central/local-news/wounded-veteran-says-was-his-duty-to-protect-ottawa-protesters-6090218>;The Public Order Emergency Commission, "Day 17 of Public Hearings" (4 November 2022), online (video): *Public Order Emergency Commission Webcast* <https://publicorderemergencycommission.ca/public-hearings/day-17-november-4/>.

12. The Public Order Emergency Commission, "Day 17 of Public Hearings" (4 November 2022), online (video): *Public Order Emergency Commission Webcast* <https://publicorderemergencycommission.ca/public-hearings/day-17-november-4/>; Lisa Joy, "Wounded Veteran Says Was His 'Duty' to Protect Ottawa Protesters," *SaskToday* (11 November 2022), online: <https://www.sasktoday.ca/central/local-news/wounded-veteran-says-was-his-duty-to-protect-ottawa-protesters-6090218>.

13. Honking for Freedom, "Statement of Intent" (19 February 2022 at 11:54), online: Twitter <https://twitter.com/Honking4Freedom/status/1495079282376327171>.

14. Tyler Dawson and Bryan Passifiume, "Identities of Nearly All the People Arrested at the Freedom Convoy Protest Remain Secret," *The National Post* (11 March 2022), online: <https://nationalpost.com/news/canada/identities-of-nearly-all-the-people-arrested-at-the-freedom-convoy-protest-remain-secret>.

15. Eamon Barrett, "Pepper Spray, Tow Trucks, and Bitcoin Seizures: How

Canada Finally Ended the Weeks-Long Freedom Convoy Protests in Ottawa," *Fortune* (21 February 2022), online: <https://fortune.com/2022/02/21/canada-ottawa-freedom-convoy-protest-ends-truckers-arrest-covid-vaccine-mandate/>.

16. Aedan Helmer, "'Take those shackles off': Tamara Lich released on bail, again" (July 27, 2022). *Ottawa Citizen*, online: <https://ottawacitizen.com/news/local-news/take-those-shackles-off-tamara-lich-released-on-bail-again>.

17. The Canadian Press, "Protest Organizer Tamara Lich Deemed Risk to Reoffend and Denied Bail in Ottawa," *The National Post* (22 February, 2022), online: <https://nationalpost.com/news/canada/canadian-press-newsalert-ottawa-protest-organizer-tamara-lich-denied-bail>.

18. Laura Osman, "'Freedom Convoy' Organizer Tamara Lich Granted Bail," *Global News* (7 March 2022), online: <https://globalnews.ca/news/8664743/tamara-lich-bail-freedom-convoy/>.

19. Canada, The Public Order Emergency Commission, *Report of the Public Inquiry Into the 2022 Public Order Emergency*, vol 3 (The Honourable Paul S. Rouleau) at 137, <https://publicorderemergencycommission.ca/files/documents/Final-Report/Vol-3-Report-of-the-Public-Inquiry-into-the-2022-Public-Order-Emergency.pdf>.

20. Peter Zimonjic, "Most Bank Accounts Frozen Under the Emergencies Act Are Being Released, Committee Hears," *CBC News* (22 February 2022), online: <https://www.cbc.ca/news/politics/emergency-bank-measures-finance-committee-1.6360769>.

21. Christopher Nardi and Catherine Lévesque, "Bureaucrats Who Froze Bank Accounts of Freedom Convoy Leaders Weren't Trying to 'Get At The Family,'" *The National Post* (17 November 2022), online: <https://nationalpost.com/news/politics/bureaucrats-who-froze-bank-accounts-of-freedom-convoy-leaders-werent-trying-to-get-at-the-family>.

22. Cabinet also created the power to cancel truckers' insurance. Ultimately that power was not used, because law-enforcement officials were concerned that suspending insurance might make it difficult for protesters to leave, since they would not be able to drive their uninsured vehicles. The RCMP believed that using this tool would have done more harm than good. See Canada, The Public Order Emergency Commission, *Report of the Public Inquiry Into the 2022 Public Order Emergency*, vol 3 (The Honourable Paul S. Rouleau) at 137, <https://publicorderemergencycommission.ca/files/documents/Final-Report/Vol-3-Report-of-the-Public-Inquiry-into-the-2022-Public-Order-Emergency.pdf>.

23. Christopher Nardi and Catherine Lévesque, "Bureaucrats Who Froze Bank Accounts of Freedom Convoy Leaders Weren't Trying to 'Get At The Family,'" *The National Post* (17 November 2022), online: <https://nationalpost.com/news/politics/bureaucrats-who-froze-bank-accounts-of-freedom-convoy-leaders-werent-trying-to-get-at-the-family>.https://nationalpost.com/news/politics/bureaucrats-who-froze-bank-accounts-of-freedom-convoy-leaders-werent-trying-to-get-at-the-family>.

24. Christine Van Geyn and Joanna Baron, "Opinion Even After Being Revoked, the Emergencies Act Is Creating a Chill on Charities," *The National Post* (8 March 2022), online: <https://nationalpost.com/opinion/opinion-even-after-being-revoked-the-emergencies-act-is-creating-a-chill-on-charities>.

25. The *War Measures Act* was a statute of the Parliament of Canada that provided for the declaration of war, invasion, or insurrection, and the types of emergency measures that could thereby be taken. The Act was brought into force three times in Canadian history: during the First World War, the Second World War, and the 1970 October Crisis. The Act was questioned for its suspension of civil liberties and personal freedoms, including suspensions enacted only for Ukrainians and other Europeans during Canada's first national internment operations of 1914–1920, the Second World War›s Japanese Canadian internment, and in the October Crisis. In 1988, it was repealed and replaced by the *Emergencies Act*.

26. *Emergencies Act*, RSC 1985, c 22 (4th Supp), s 3.

27. 1988 House of Commons Debates (*Hansard*) 33 Parl 2nd Session Vol 12 at p. 14765.

28. Marsha McLeod and Janice Dickson, "Emergencies Act Was Not Needed to Bring Convoy Protests to an End, Retired OPP Official Tells Inquiry," *The Globe and Mail* (21 October 2022), online: <https://www.theglobeandmail.com/politics/article-article-emergencies-act-opp/>.

29. Catharine Tunney, "Retired OPP Officer Says He Doesn't Think Emergencies Act was Needed to Clear Freedom Convoy Protesters," *CBC News* (21 October 2022), online: <https://www.cbc.ca/news/politics/pardy-opp-sloly-1.6624651>.

30. Stephanie Taylor, "Was the Emergencies Act Needed to Stop Convoy Blockades? What the Inquiry Has Heard," *Sudbury Local* (28 October 2022), online: <https://www.sudbury.com/beyond-local/was-the-emergencies-act-needed-to-stop-convoy-blockades-what-the-inquiry-has-heard-6021162>.

31. Canada, The Public Order Emergency Commission, *Report of the Public Inquiry Into the 2022 Public Order Emergency*, vol 1 (The Honourable Paul S. Rouleau) at 115, <https://publicorderemergency-commission.ca/files/documents/Final-Report/Vol-1-Report-of-the-Public-Inquiry-into-the-2022-Public-Order-Emergency.pdf>.

32. Ibid. at 113.

33. Christopher Nardi and Catherine Lévesque, "Ottawa Police Had a Plan and Tow Trucks Ready to Roll Day Before Emergencies Act Invoked," *The National Post* (26 October 2022), online: <https://nationalpost.com/news/politics/police-had-a-plan-and-tow-trucks-ready-day-before-emergencies-act-invoked>.

34. The Public Order Emergency Commission, "Day 30 of Public Hearings" (30 November 2022), online (video): *Public Order Emergency Commission Webcast* <https://publicorderemergencycommission.ca/public-hearings/day-30-november-24/>; testimony of Katie Telford, Brian Clow, and John Brodhead.

35. Canada, The Public Order Emergency Commission, *Report of the Public Inquiry Into the 2022 Public Order Emergency*, vol 3 (The Honourable Paul S. Rouleau) at 76–77 and 134, <https://publicorderemergency-commission.ca/files/documents/Final-Report/Vol-3-Report-of-the-Public-Inquiry-into-the-2022-Public-Order-Emergency.pdf>; see also the testimony of Trish Ferguson from the Public Order Emergency Commission, "Day 20 of Public Hearings" (9 November 2022), online (video): *Public Order Emergency Commission Webcast* https://publicord-eremergencycommission.ca/public-hearings/day-20-november-9/.

36. *Emergencies Act*, *RSC* 1985, c 22 (4th Supp), Emergencies Act, s 16.

37. *Canadian Security Intelligence Service Act*, RSC 1985, c C-23 [*CSIS Act*].

38. Canada, The Public Order Emergency Commission, *Report of the Public Inquiry Into the 2022 Public Order Emergency*, vol 1 (The Honourable Paul S. Rouleau) at 119, <https://publicorderemergency-commission.ca/files/documents/Final-Report/Vol-1-Report-of-the-Public-Inquiry-into-the-2022-Public-Order-Emergency.pdf>.

39. The Public Order Emergency Commission, "Day 27 of Public Hearings" (21 November 2022), online (video): *Public Order Emergency Commission Webcast* <https://publicorderemergencycommission.ca/public-hearings/day-27-november-21/>.

40. The News Forum, "Reactions to the Emergencies Act Inquiry Report" (13 March 2023), online (video): YouTube <https://www.youtube.com/watch?v=GKr3L7NXTcI&t=4s>; For the full video, see The News Forum, "The Rouleau Report & the Emergencies Act" (13 March

2023), online (video): *The News Forum* <https://www.newsforum.tv/canadian-justice-1/videos/the-rouleau-report-the-emergencies-act>. https://www.newsforum.tv/videos/the-rouleau-report-038-the-emergencies-act #thenewsforum

41. The News Forum, "Reactions to the Emergencies Act Inquiry Report" (13 March 2023), online (video): YouTube <https://www.youtube.com/watch?v=GKr3L7NXTcI&t=4s>; for a full video, see The News Forum, "The Rouleau Report & the Emergencies Act" (13 March 2023), online (video): *The News Forum* <https://www.newsforum.tv/canadian-justice-1/videos/the-rouleau-report-the-emergencies-act>. https://www.newsforum.tv/videos/the-rouleau-report-038-the-emergencies-act #thenewsforum

42. Marsha McLeod and Marieke Walsh, "Trudeau's Use of Emergencies Act was Appropriate, Inquiry Finds," *The Globe and Mail* (17 February 2023), online: <https://www.theglobeandmail.com/politics/article-emergencies-act-inquiry-trudeau-final-report/>.

43. A version of this section was previously published in *C2C Journal*. See Christine Van Geyn, "The Last Guardrail of Accountability: The Legal Challenge to the Trudeau Government's Use of the Emergencies Act," *C2C Journal* (21 April 2023), online: <https://c2cjournal.ca/2023/04/the-last-guardrail-of-accountability-the-legal-challenge-to-the-trudeau-governments-use-of-the-emergencies-act/>.

44. The Canadian Civil Liberties Association, Press Release, "CCLA Reacts to Minister Freeland's Testimony at POEC" (24 November 2022), online: <https://ccla.org/press-release/ccla-reacts-to-minister-freelands-testimony-at-poec/>.

CHAPTER 5

1. "She Was Denied Entry for Her Mother's Funeral. Now She's Taking the N.L. Government to Court," *CBC News* (15 May 2020), online: <https://www.cbc.ca/news/canada/newfoundland-labrador/kim-taylor-constitutional-challenge-1.5571322>.

2. *Public Health Protection and Promotion Act*, SNL 2022, c P-30.1, s 60, 4.

3. The claim also dealt with section 7, life liberty and security of person; *Public Health Protection and Promotion Act*, SNL 2022, c P-30.1, s 60, 6-8.

4. *Taylor v. Newfoundland and Labrador*, 2020 NLSC 125.

5. *Public Health Protection and Promotion Act*, SNL 2022, c P-30.1, s 60, 247.

6. Ibid. s 60, 365.

7. *Public Health Protection and Promotion Act*, SNL 2022, c P-30.1, s 60, 373.

8. *Taylor v. Newfoundland and Labrador*, 2020 NLSC 125 at para 492.

9. Ibid. at para 384.

10. *United States of America v. Cotroni; United States of America v. El Zein*, [1989] 1 SCR 1469.

11. "Coronavirus Outbreak: Hajdu Stresses Shutting Down Borders Over Illness 'Not Effective At All,'" *Global News* (17 February 2020), online: <https://globalnews.ca/video/6560512/coronavirus-outbreak-hajdu-stresses-shutting-down-borders-over-illness-not-effective-at-all>.

12. Joanna Baron, "Hotel Canada: A Stay to Remember," *Law & Liberty* (10 May 2021), online: <https://lawliberty.org/hotel-canada-a-stay-to-remember/>.

13. The cost varied: in many cases it was higher.

14. Michelle Rempel, "Today @carefreeland said "people shouldn't travel" when pushed on reports of sexual assault at a federal quarantine facility. I asked @PattyHajdu if this meant the victim deserved it. She disgustingly said, "Every woman deserves to live a life free of violence, BUT . . ." Watch" (25 February 2021), online: Twitter <https://twitter.com/MichelleRempel/status/1365032919866118147>.

15. Joanna Baron, "Hotel Canada: A Stay to Remember," *Law & Liberty* (10 May 2021), online: <https://lawliberty.org/hotel-canada-a-stay-to-remember/>.

16. Joanna Baron, "Joanna Baron: Unconstitutional Travel Bans Are Causing Real Harm." *The National Post* (9 June 2020), online: <https://nationalpost.com/opinion/joanna-baron-unconstitutional-travel-bans-are-causing-real-harm>.

17. A version of this section was previously published in Law & Liberty. See Joanna Baron, "Hotel Canada: A Stay to Remember", Law & Liberty (10 May 2021), online: <https://lawliberty.org/hotel-canada-a-stay-to-remember/>.

18. Bryann Aguilar, "Rod Philips Informed Ford's Senior Staff He Would Be in St. Barts Days Before Trip, Email Shows," *CTV News* (29 April 2021; last updated 30 April 2021), online: <https://toronto.ctvnews.ca/rod-phillips-informed-ford-s-senior-staff-he-would-be-in-st-barts-days-before-trip-emails-show-1.5408510>.

19. Shane Gibson, "Politicians Travelling Amid COVID-19 Should Fear Voters, Manitoba Professor Says," *Global News* (5 January 2021),

online: <https://globalnews.ca/news/7554922/politicians-travelling-coronavirus-manitoba-professor/>.

20. Lauren Gardner, "Meanwhile, in Canada: Politicians Face Fury of Nation After Holiday Travel," *Politico* (6 January 2021; last updated 7 January 2021), online: <https://www.politico.com/news/2021/01/06/canada-fury-coronavirus-holiday-travel-455257>.

21. Ibid.

22. "Ontario's Finance Minister Resigns After Returning From Caribbean Vacation," *CBC News* (31 December 2020; last updated 1 January 2021), online: <https://www.cbc.ca/news/canada/toronto/ford-rod-phillips-st-barts-vacation-1.5858285#:~:text=Rod%20Phillips%20resigned%20as%20Ontario's,municipal%20affairs%20travelled%20to%20Hawaii>.

23. Transport Canada, News Release, "New pre-departure COVID-19 testing requirements come into effect for all air travellers flying into Canada" (6 January 2021), online: *Government of Canada* https://www.canada.ca/en/transport-canada/news/2021/01/new-pre-departure-covid-19-testing-requirements-come-into-effect-for-all-air-travellers-flying-into-canada.html.

24. Catharine Tunney, "Hotel Quarantine Measures for Air Travellers Come Into Effect Feb. 22: Trudeau, *CBC News* (12 February 2021), online: <https://www.cbc.ca/news/politics/travel-restrictions-border-1.5911845>.

25. Although it should be emphasized that Australia's experience was far from a clear success story. In Australia, a second wave of COVID-19 was reported to have been triggered by hotel security, who contracted the virus from a guest and then introduced it into the community. Guest-to-guest transmission in Australia's quarantine hotels was also reported; see: Catharine Tunney, "Hotel Quarantine Measures for Air Travellers Come Into Effect Feb. 22: Trudeau," *CBC News* (12 February 2021), online: <https://www.theguardian.com/world/2020/aug/22/appalling-and-inconsistent-how-melbournes-hotel-quarantine-unleashed-a-second-wave>.

26. See: John Paul Tasker, "COVID-19 Transmission on Flights 'Extremely Rare,' Dr. Tam Says," *CBC News* (10 November 2020), online: <https://www.cbc.ca/news/politics/covid-transmission-flights-extremely-rare-1.5797065; https://airlines.iata.org/analysis/extremely-low-risk-of-viral-transmission-inflight>.

27. See, for example: Jon Victor, "Travellers Booking COVID-19 Quarantine Hotels Report Long Wait Times, Lack of Options," *Global News* (28 February 2021), online: <https://globalnews.ca/

news/7668282/problems-travellers-quarantine-hotels/>; Christine Rankin, "Canada's 'Broken' Quarantine Hotel Booking System Means Family Could Face a Hefty Fine," *CBC News* (23 February 2021), online: <https://www.cbc.ca/news/canada/hamilton/quarantine-covid19-burlington-1.5922962>; Meera Bains, "Travellers Struggle to Book Quarantine Hotels in B.C., as Phone Lines Back Up," *CBC News* (22 February 2021), online: <https://www.cbc.ca/news/canada/british-columbia/travellers-struggle-book-quarantine-hotels-bc-1.5923821>; Jeremiah Rodriquez, "Travellers Complain of Unanswered Calls, Long Wait Times to Book Quarantine Hotels," *CTV News* (21 February 2021), online: <https://www.ctvnews.ca/health/coronavirus/travellers-complain-of-unanswered-calls-long-wait-times-to-book-quarantine-hotels-1.5318119>.

28. Iman Kassam and Selena Ross, "Man Charged with Sexual Assault at Montreal Quarantine Hotel; Woman Says She Felt 'Helpless,'" *CTV News* (24 February 2021), online: <https://montreal.ctvnews.ca/man-charged-with-sexual-assault-at-montreal-quarantine-hotel-woman-says-she-felt-helpless-1.5323176>.

29. Sean Davidson, "Ontario Woman Forced to Pay $3,458 Hotel Quarantine Bill for One-Night Stay After Returning to Canada From Father's Funeral," *CTV News* (1 March 2021), online: <https://toronto.ctvnews.ca/ontario-woman-forced-to-pay-3-458-hotel-quarantine-bill-for-one-night-stay-after-returning-to-canada-from-father-s-funeral-1.5329229>.

30. Sean Davidson, "Ontario Family Charged $2,448 for Quarantine Hotel Claim They Were Forced to Pay Adult Rate for Eight-Year-Old Son," *CTV News* (11 March 2021), online: <https://toronto.ctvnews.ca/ontario-family-charged-2-448-for-quarantine-hotel-claim-they-were-forced-to-pay-adult-rate-for-eight-year-old-son-1.5343436>.

31. The News Forum, "Canadian Justice | Hotel Quarantine Nightmares" (16 March 2021), online (video): YouTube <https://www.youtube.com/watch?v=2OSucrfWumc>.

32. Adrian Humphreys, "Quarantine Hotels on Trial as Federal Court Hears Constitutional Challenge of COVID Restrictions," *The National Post* (1 June 2021), online: <https://nationalpost.com/news/canada/quarantine-hotels-on-trial-as-federal-court-hears-constitutional-challenge-of-covid-restrictions>.

33. The Canadian Constitution Foundation, Press Release, "Canadian Constitution Foundation Launches Legal Challenge of Federal Quarantine Hotel Policy" (8 March 2021), online: <https://theccf.ca/canadian-constitution-foundation-launches-legal-challenge-of-

federal-quarantine-hotel-policy/>.

34. Stephanie Taylor, "Expert Panel Recommends Liberal Government End COVID-19 Quarantine Hotel Stay," *CP24* (27 May 2021), online: <https://www.cp24.com/news/expert-panel-recommends-liberal-government-end-covid-19-quarantine-hotel-stay-1.5445825>.

35. The Canadian Constitution Foundation, News Release, "Release: Canadian Constitution Foundation Achieves Victory in Quarantine Hotel Challenge for Compassionate Travel" (31 May 2021), online: <https://theccf.ca/release-ccf-achieves-victory-in-quarantine-hotel-challenge-for-compassionate-travel/>.

36. Government of Canada factum, para. 20

37. *Canadian Constitution Foundation v. Canada (AG)*, 2021 ONSC 2117 (CanLII), <https://www.canlii.org/en/on/onsc/doc/2021/2021onsc2117/2021onsc2117.html>.

38. *Canadian Constitution Foundation v. Canada (AG)*, 2021 ONSC 4744 <https://www.canlii.org/en/on/onsc/doc/2021/2021onsc4744/2021onsc4744.html

39. Ibid. at para 26.

40. Ibid. at para 43.

41. Ibid. at para 20.

42. Ibid.

43. Ibid. at para 42.

44. *Canadian Constitution Foundation v. Canada (AG)*, 2021 ONSC 2117 at para 15 (CanLII), <https://www.canlii.org/en/on/onsc/doc/2021/2021onsc2117/2021onsc2117.html>.

45. Avis Favaro, Elizabeth St. Philip, Alexandra Mae Jones, "Health experts warn of dangers of B.1.1.7 variant as it emerges in more provinces," CTV News (February 2, 2021), online: <https://www.ctvnews.ca/health/coronavirus/health-experts-warn-of-dangers-of-b-1-1-7-variant-as-it-emerges-in-more-provinces-1.5293379

46. Matt Robinson, "Five Things to Know About the P1 variant spreading in B.C.," *Vancouver Sun* (April 5, 2021), online: <https://vancouversun.com/news/local-news/covid-19-five-things-to-know-about-the-brazilian-p-1-variant-spreading-in-b-c

47. Craig Momney and Jayme Doll, "Documents Show Federal Government Spent More Than $6M on Calgary Quarantine Hotel," *Global News* (31 January 2023), online: <https://globalnews.ca/news/9450452/calgary-quarantine-hotel-costs-michelle-rempel-garner/>.

48. Elise von Scheel, "Quarantine Hotel Co-Owner misappropriated almost $16m of public funds, lawsuit alleges," CBC News (14 September 2023), online: <https://www.cbc.ca/news/canada/calgary/calgary-quarantine-hotel-civil-lawsuit-1.6964389>.

49. Ontario Daily Epidemiological Summary, December 2021, <https://www.publichealthontario.ca/en/Data-and-Analysis/Infectious-Disease/COVID-19-Data-Surveillance/Archives/Daily-Epi-Summary>

50. Caitlin Owens, "Age is still a huge coronavirus risk factor", Axios (19 October 2021), online: <https://www.axios.com/2021/10/19/age-coronavirus-risk-vaccines>.

51. "Honourable Brian Peckford, Nikkanen, Baigent et al. v. Minister of Transport and Canada," *The Justice Centre for Constitutional Freedoms* (28 January 2022), online: <https://www.jccf.ca/court_cases/honourable-brian-peckford-nikkanen-baigent-et-al-vs-minister-of-transport-and-canada/>.

52. *The Honourable A. Brian Peckford, Leesha Nikkanen, Ken Baigent, Drew Belobaba, Natalie Grcic, and Aedan Macdonald v. Canada (AG)* (20 October 2022), Ottawa On CA FCTD T-168-22 (motion granted) <https://www.jccf.ca/wp-content/uploads/2022/10/T-168--22_20221020_J_E_O_OTT_20221020151632_GG2-1.pdf>.

53. The Justice Centre for Constitutional Freedoms, News Release, "Bernier, Peckford File Written Appeal Argument on "Mootness" at Federal Court of Appeal" (24 April 2023), online: <https://www.jccf.ca/bernier-peckford-file-written-appeal-argument-on-mootness-at-federal-court-of-appeal/>.

CHAPTER 6

1. Ted Raymond and Jeremie Charron, "Gatineau Police Issue Fines, Arrest Two During Confrontation Over Private Gathering on New Year's Eve," *CTV News* (2 January 2021), online: <https://ottawa.ctvnews.ca/gatineau-police-issue-fines-arrest-two-during-confrontation-over-private-gathering-on-new-year-s-eve-1.5251296>.

2. Nusakan, "Il faut que ça devienne viral. RT en masse les amis. La lumière doit être fait sur cet événement" (1 January 2021), online: Twitter <https://twitter.com/Nusakan007/status/1345150743129501700>.

3. Nusakan, "According to the man who initially published the video, police came to their house because it was an "illegal gathering." The man resisted the police officers after they pulled his mother outside, using accessive [*sic*] force" (2 January 2021), online: Twitter <https://twitter.com/Nusakan007/status/1345371995723202563>; Ted Raymond and

Jeremie Charron, "Gatineau Police Issue Fines, Arrest Two During Confrontation Over Private Gathering on New Year's Eve," *CTV News* (2 January 2021), online: <https://ottawa.ctvnews.ca/gatineau-police-issue-fines-arrest-two-during-confrontation-over-private-gathering-on-new-year-s-eve-1.5251296>.

4.   The Office of the Prime Minister of Canada Justin Trudeau, News Release, "Prime Minister Announces New Mobile App to Help Notify Canadians of COVID-19 Exposure" (18 June 2020), online: <https://pm.gc.ca/en/news/news-releases/2020/06/18/prime-minister-announces-new-mobile-app-help-notify-canadians-covid>.

5.   Jason Herring, "Alberta government blocking federal COVID Alert app, Trudeau says," *The Calgary Herald* (30 October 2020), online: <https://calgaryherald.com/news/local-news/alberta-government-blocking-federal-covid-alert-app-trudeau-says>.

6.   Richard Zussman, "B.C.'s Top Doctor Says COVID-19 App Would 'Cause More Concern' If Activated in the Province," *Global News* (27 October 2020), online: <https://globalnews.ca/news/7424544/bc-bonnie-henry-covid-19-app-concern-coronavirus/>.

7.   Pierre Saint-Arnaud, "COVID Alert app cost feds $20M but results 'did not meet expectations': new data," The Canadian Press (July 5, 2021), online: <https://globalnews.ca/news/8003920/covid-alert-app-expensive-ineffective/>.

8.   The Government of Ontario, "COVID Alert Impact Data," online: *Ontario Data Catalogue* <https://data.ontario.ca/dataset/covid-alert-impact-data>.

9.   The Government of Ontario, "Ontario COVID-19 Data Tool" (retrieved on 17 June 2022), online: *Public Health Ontario* <https://www.publichealthontario.ca/en/data-and-analysis/infectious-disease/covid-19-data-surveillance/covid-19-data-tool>.

10.   The Government of Canada, "COVID-19 Epidemiology Update: Key Updates" (retrieved on 17 June 2022), online: <https://health-infobase.canada.ca/covid-19/>.

11.   Patricia Kosseim, News Release, "COVID Alert and Your Privacy" (31 July 2020), online: *Information and Privacy Commissioner of Ontario* <https://www.ipc.on.ca/covid-alert-and-your-privacy/>; Information and Privacy Commissioner of Ontario, News Release, "COVID Alert and Your Privacy" (31 July 2020), online: <https://www.ipc.on.ca/covid-alert-and-your-privacy/>.

12.   It is also significant that the government discontinued the app. Many other jurisdictions have maintained citizen tracing apps as the

pandemic has waned.

13. The Canada Border Services Agency, "ArriveCAN now and in the future" (last modified 31 January 2023), online: <https://www.canada.ca/en/border-services-agency/services/arrivecan.html>.

14. Sophia Harris, "Ottawa Admits Some Travellers Were Incorrectly Told To Quarantine Due To ArriveCAN App Glitch," *CBC News* (22 July 2022), online: <https://www.cbc.ca/news/business/arrivecan-app-quarantine-glitch-1.6528312>.

15. The International Network of Civil Liberties Organizations, "Under Surveillance: (Mis)use of Technologies in Emergency Responses: Global lessons from the Covid-19 pandemic" (December 2022), online (pdf): https://files.inclo.net/content/pdf/79/INCLO-Under%20Surveillance-Report.pdf.

16. Bill Curry, "Spending on ArriveCan App Projected to Top $54-Million, Double the Amount Ottawa First Divulged," *The Globe and Mail* (6 October 2022), online: https://www.theglobeandmail.com/politics/article-arrivecan-app-spending-government/.

17. Ibid.

18. Hannah Alberga, "Toronto Tech Companies Cloned ArriveCan in Under 48 Hours to Show the Government Overpaid Millions," *CTV News* (11 October 2022), online: https://toronto.ctvnews.ca/toronto-tech-companies-cloned-arrivecan-in-under-48-hours-to-show-the-government-overpaid-millions-1.6104652.

19. "Feds Admit Cell Surveillance" (21 December 2021), online (blog): <https://www.blacklocks.ca/feds-admit-cell-surveillance/>.

20. Swikar Oli, "Canada's Public Health Agency Admits It Tracked 33 Million Mobile Devices During Lockdown," *The National Post* (24 December 2021; last updated 27 December 2021), online: https://nationalpost.com/news/canada/canadas-public-health-agency-admits-it-tracked-33-million-mobile-devices-during-lockdown.

21. The House of Commons Canada, "Collection and Use of Mobility Data by the Government of Canada and Related Issues: Report of the Standing Committee on Access to Information, Privacy and Ethics" (May 2022), online (pdf): https://www.ourcommons.ca/Content/Committee/441/ETHI/Reports/RP11736929/ethirp04/ethirp04-e.pdf.

22. Bryan Short, "How the Federal Government Failed to Protect Our Mobility Data" (2 May 2022), online (blog): *OpenMedia* https://openmedia.org/article/item/how-the-federal-government-failed-to-protect-our-mobility-data.

23. Marie Woolf, "MPs Back Motion to Halt COVID-19 Phone Data Collection Over Privacy Concerns," *Global News* (8 February 2022), online: https://globalnews.ca/news/8604596/phac-covid-phone-data-privacy/.

24. The House of Commons Canada, "Collection and Use of Mobility Data by the Government of Canada and Related Issues: Report of the Standing Committee on Access to Information, Privacy and Ethics" (May 2022), online (pdf): https://www.ourcommons.ca/Content/Committee/441/ETHI/Reports/RP11736929/ethirp04/ethirp04-e.pdf.

25. The News Forum, "Government Surveillance" (August 17, 2023) at 00h:16m:04s, online (video): https://www.newsforum.tv/videos/government-surveillance.

26. Bryan Short, "How the Federal Government Failed to Protect Our Mobility Data" (2 May 2022), online (blog): *OpenMedia* https://openmedia.org/article/item/how-the-federal-government-failed-to-protect-our-mobility-data.

27. Irelyne Lavery, "Doug Ford Has Ordered the Closure of Outdoor Amenities at Parks to Stop COVID-19. Health Experts Say That's a Bad Move," *The Toronto Star* (21 April 2021), online: <https://www.thestar.com/news/gta/2021/04/20/doug-ford-has-ordered-the-closure-of-outdoor-amenities-at-parks-to-stop-covid-19-health-experts-say-thats-a-bad-move.html>.

28. The Government of Ontario, News Release, "Ontario Strengthens Enforcement of Stay-at-Home Order" (16 April 2021), online: *Government of Ontario Newsroom* <https://news.ontario.ca/en/release/61192/ontario-strengthens-enforcement-of-stay-at-home-order>.

29. O. Reg. 8/21 under *Emergency Management and Civil Protection Act*, RSO 1990, c E.9. <https://www.ontario.ca/laws/regulation/210008/v3>.

30. See, for example: *R. v. Hufsky*, [1988] 1 SCR 621 and *R. v. Ladoucer*, [1990] 1 SCR 1257. For an evolving issue, see Luamba c. Procureur général du Québec, 2022 QCCS 3866 https://www.canlii.org/fr/qc/qccs/doc/2022/2022qccs3866/2022qccs3866.html

31. Mike Crawley, "The Inside Story of Doug Ford's COVID-19 Climbdowns," *CBC News* (22 April 2021), online: <https://www.cbc.ca/news/canada/toronto/covid-19-ontario-doug-ford-cabinet-police-playgrounds-1.5997381>.

32. Christine Van Geyn, "Ford Government Had to Have Known Its New Police Powers Were Wrong: Politicians Who Knowingly Enact Illegal Laws Deserve Condemnation, and Have Lost Moral Authority to

Govern," *The National Post* (22 April 2021), online: https://national-post.com/opinion/christine-van-geyn-ford-government-had-to-have-known-its-new-police-powers-were-wrong.

33. The Canadian Constitution Foundation, Press Release, "Canadian Constitution Foundation Condemns New Ontario Police Powers as "Police State" (16 April 2021), online: https://theccf.ca/canadian-constitution-foundation-condemns-new-ontario-police-powers-as-police-state/.

34. The Canadian Civil Liberties Association, "Know Your Rights for Ontarians" (23 April 2021), online: <https://ccla.org/fundamental-freedoms/democratic-rights/know-your-rights-for-ontarians/>.

35. The Canadian Constitution Foundation, "Know Your Rights," online: https://theccf.ca/knowyourrights/.

36. Nick Westoll, "COVID-19: Ontario's Temporary Increased Police Powers Raise Concerns About Random Stops, Carding," *Global News* (16 April 2021), online: <https://globalnews.ca/news/7765412/covid-19-ontario-temporary-police-powers-carding/>; Colin Perkel, "Many Ontario Police Forces Won't Use New COVID-19 Powers to Conduct Random Stops," *Global News* (17 April 2021), online: https://global-news.ca/news/7765907/ontario-police-forces-new-covid-19-powers/.

37. Andrew Lawton, "FINAL TALLY: Of Ontario's 45 provincially-mandated police forces (44 municipal/regional + OPP), all but three came out against random and unwarranted stops. Two services—Chatham-Kent and Deep River—didn't comment. Just one, the OPP, came out in favor" (17 April 2021), online: Twitter https://twitter.com/AndrewLawton/status/1383585291793944577.

38. Adam Carter, "Ford Apologizes After Public Backlash to Enhanced Police Powers, Playground Closures," *CBC News* (22 April 2021), online: <https://www.cbc.ca/news/canada/toronto/doug-ford-ontario-covid-19-news-conference-1.5997521>.

39. Mike Crawley, "The Inside Story of Doug Ford's COVID-19 Climbdowns," *CBC News* (22 April 2021), online: <https://www.cbc.ca/news/canada/toronto/covid-19-ontario-doug-ford-cabinet-police-playgrounds-1.5997381>.

40. O. Reg. 8/21 under *Emergency Management and Civil Protection Act*, RSO 1990, c E.9. <https://www.ontario.ca/laws/regulation/210008/v4>.

41. The Ontario Human Rights Commission, News Release, "OHRC statement on Government's Expansion of Police Powers During COVID Stay-At-Home Order" (21 April 2021), online: <https://www.ohrc.on.ca/en/news_centre/ohrc-statement-

government%E2%80%99s-expansion-police-powers-during-covid-stay-home-order>.

42. Claire Loewen, "Quebec Police Won't Be Allowed to Enter Homes Without Consent or a Warrant, Public Security Minister Says," *CBC News* (23 September 2020), online: https://www.cbc.ca/ news/canada/montreal/guilbault-police-covid-19-warrant-ticket-gatherings-1.5735339.

43. Ibid.

44. Adam Kovac, "Sûreté du Québec Hand Out Ticket for Illegal Gathering in Incident Caught on Video," *CTV News* (26 December 2020; last updated 26 December 2020), online: https://montreal.ctvnews.ca/ surete-du-quebec-hand-out-ticket-for-illegal-gathering-in-incident-caught-on-video-1.5245624.

45. The Canadian Civil Liberties Association, "COVID-19 and Law Enforcement in Canada: The Second Wave" (May 2021) at pages 28–29, online (pdf): <https://ccla.org/wp-content/uploads/2021/06/2021-05-13-COVID-19-and-Law-Enforcement-The-second-wave.pdf>.

46. "Quebec Coroner to Investigate How Homeless Man Died Outside, Steps From Closed Shelter," *CBC News* (18 January 2021 last updated 19 January 2021), online: <https://www.cbc.ca/news/canada/montreal/ death-homeless-man-montreal-1.5877205>.

47. Jonathan Montpetit, "Feds Push Legault to Ease Curfew Rules, Say Homeless Man's Death in Montreal was Avoidable," *CBC News* (20 January 2021; last updated 21 January 2021), online: https://www. cbc.ca/news/canada/montreal/quebec-curfew-rules-homeless-marc-miller-1.5881022.

48. Ibid.

49. Kalina Laframboise, "Quebec will Exempt Homeless from COVID-19 Curfew After Court Finds Rule Endangered Safety," *Global News* (27 January 2021), online: https://globalnews.ca/ news/7602260/quebec-homeless-population-curfew-exemption-reaction/.

50. Ibid.

51. The Canadian Civil Liberties Association, "COVID-19 and Law Enforcement in Canada: The Second Wave" (May 2021) at page 34, online (pdf): <https://ccla.org/wp-content/uploads/2021/06/2021-05-13-COVID-19-and-Law-Enforcement-The-second-wave.pdf>.

52. Christopher J. Schneider, "Assholes in the News: Policing in the Age of the COVID-19 Pandemic" (2021) 10 *Annual Rev of*

Interdisciplinary Justice Research 59, online: (https://canlii.ca/t/t9hq).

53. George Orwell, *Nineteen Eighty-Four (first published 1949)*, from Book 2, Chapter 3, online: 1984: Book 2, Chapter 3 Summary | Shmoop (https://www.shmoop.com/study-guides/literature/1984/summary/book-2-chapter-3)

54. Simon Smith, "Should I report my neighbour for breaking COVID rules?" *The Signal* (21 November 2020), online: <https://signalhfx.ca/should-i-report-my-neighbour-for-breaking-covid-rules/>.

55. Alexander McClelland and Alex Luscombe, "Policing the Pandemic: Counter-mapping Policing Responses to COVID-19 across Canada" (2021) 10 *Annual Rev of Interdisciplinary Justice Research* 195 at 213, online: (https://canlii.ca/t/t9hw).

56. Ibid. at 214.

57. Eric Mykhalovskiy et al. "Human Rights, Public Health and COVID-19 in Canada" (2020) 111 *Can J Public Health* at 978 (https://link.springer.com/article/10.17269/s41997-020-00408-0).

58. Christopher Nardi, "COVID-19 Pandemic Is Turning Canada Into a Nation of Snitches," *The National Post* (16 April 2020), online: <https://nationalpost.com/news/it-has-become-the-civic-duty-covid-19-pandemic-is-turning-us-into-a-nation-of-snitches>.

59. Brenda McPhail, "FAQ: Vaccine Passports" (13 April 2021; last updated 17 August 2021), online (blog): *Canadian Civil Liberties Association* <https://ccla.org/privacy/surveillance-technology/faq-vaccine-passports/>.

60. The Office of the Privacy Commissioner of Canada, News Release, "Privacy and COVID-19 Vaccine Passports: Joint Statement by Federal, Provincial and Territorial Privacy Commissioners" (19 May 2021; last updated on 8 October 2021), online: <https://www.priv.gc.ca/en/opc-news/speeches/2021/s-d_20210519/>.

61. Sarah Rieger, "Portpass App May Have Exposed Hundreds of Thousands of Users' Personal Data," *CBC News* (28 September 2021), online: <https://www.cbc.ca/news/canada/calgary/portpass-privacy-breach-1.6191749>.

62. Robson Fletcher, "Private Proof-of-Vaccine App Portpass Continues to Expose Personal Data Even After Relaunch and Updates," *CBC News* (28 October 2021), online: <https://www.cbc.ca/news/canada/calgary/portpass-app-proof-of-vaccination-unsecured-data-update-1.6229034>.

63. "QR Codes Removed From Sask. Vaccination Records Due to Privacy Breach," *CTV News Regina* (24 September 2021), online: <https://

regina.ctvnews.ca/qr-codes-removed-from-sask-vaccination-records-due-to-privacy-breach-1.5599830>.

CHAPTER 7

1. 2752953 Ontario Inc. operating as NorthXFit and *Sascha King v. Ontario (AG)*, ONSC, Court File No. CV-21-00000090-0000.

2. Ryan O'Connor, "PARTIAL VICTORY: Ontario has amended the lockdown rules following the court challenge of our client, @ NorthXFitness, to gym and fitness class closures which argues, in part that banning disabled Ontarians from the gym violates their Charter rights" (5 February 2021), online: Twitter https://twitter.com/rpoconnor/status/1357837143645782016.

3. Note: these laws predated the *Charter*

4. *Andrews v. Law Society of British Columbia*, [1989] 1 SCR 143.

5. Ibid.

6. *Withler v. Canada (AG)*, 2011 SCC 12. See also *Quebec (AG) v. A*, 2013 SCC 5.

7. *Fraser v. Canada (AG)*, 2020 SCC 28.

8. Ibid. at para 69.

9. Ibid. at para 178.

10. Ibid. at para 227.

11. See, for example: https://www.utflr.ca/blog/fraser-section-15; https://nationalmagazine.ca/en-ca/articles/law/in-depth/2020/an-equitable-outcome; Jonnette Watson Hamilton and Jennifer Koshan, "Courting Confusion? Three Recent Alberta Cases on Equality Rights Post-Kapp" (2010) *Alberta Law Rev. 927, 2010 CanLIIDocs 296,* <https://canlii.ca/t/2cxr>.

12. See for example: Bruce Pardy, "Substantive Equality: Some People Are More Equal Than Others" (6 February 2019), online (blog): *The Advocates for the Rule of Law* <http://www.ruleoflaw.ca/substantive-equality-some-people-are-more-equal-than-others/>.

13. See for example: *R v. Sharma*, 2022 SCC 39, https://decisions.scc-csc.ca/scc-csc/scc-csc/en/item/19540/index.do.

14. For greater clarity, when we use the term "vaccine passport" or "proof of vaccine policy," we are referring to a *government* requirement that an individual show proof of vaccination in order to access a public space or service. This book does not deal with the voluntary decision

by a business to require its employees to be vaccinated. While such requirements can raise employment discrimination and human rights law concerns, they do not engage constitutional rights and are therefore beyond the scope of this book.

15. Brenda McPhail, "FAQ: Vaccine Passports" (13 April 2021; last updated 17 August 2021), online (blog): *Canadian Civil Liberties Association* <https://ccla.org/privacy/surveillance-technology/faq-vaccine-passports/>.

16. Jon Woodward, "Toronto Restaurant Says It Won't Accept Medical Exemptions," *CTV News* (26 September 2021), online: https://toronto.ctvnews.ca/toronto-restaurant-says-it-won-t-accept-medical-exemptions-1.5601281.

17. "Confused About Proof-of-Vaccination for Travel? Your Questions Answered," *CBC News* (8 October 2021; last updated 13 October 2021), online: https://www.cbc.ca/news/canada/canada-proof-of-vaccine-travel-1.6203642.

18. Mike Lloyd, Hana Mae Nassar, and Denise Wong, "COVID-19: Vaccine Passports Come with Risks, Warns B.C. Ombudsperson," *CityNews Vancouver* (26 Mat 2021), online: https://vancouver.citynews.ca/2021/05/26/covid-19-vaccine-passports-bc-ombudsperson/.

19. Punditclass (8 September 2021 at 11:26), online: Twitter <https://twitter.com/punditclass/status/1435625580305666049>. Note that this tweet is no longer available.

20. Allison Jones, "'Statistically Curious' that 2 Ontario PC Caucus Members Have Medical Exemptions: Horwath," *Global News* (4 October 2021), online: https://globalnews.ca/news/8241918/horwath-statistically-curious-ontario-pc-covid-vaccine-medical-exemptions/.

21. The Canadian Constitution Foundation, Press Release, "Manitoba Government Creates Medical Exemptions for Vaccine Passport Following CCF Letter" (16 September 2021), online: https://theccf.ca/manitoba-government-creates-medical-exemptions-for-vaccine-passport-following-ccf-letter/.

22. Letter from the Canadian Civil Liberties Association to the Honorable Brian Pallister, "Letter to Manitoba Re: Vaccine Passports" (17 June 2021), online: *Canadian Civil Liberties Association* https://ccla.org/privacy/surveillance-technology/vaccine-passports/letter-to-manitoba-re-vaccine-passports/.

23. Sean Fine, "Legal Questions Around Rights Linger as Some Provinces Bring in COVID-19 Vaccine Passports," *The Globe and Mail* (8 September 2021), online: <https://www.theglobeandmail.

com/canada/article-legal-questions-around-rights-linger-as-some-provinces-bring-in-covid/>.

24. Devon McKendrick, "Manitoba Finalizes Process for Medical Exemption From COVID-19 Vaccine," *CTV News* (6 October 2021), online: <https://winnipeg.ctvnews.ca/manitoba-finalizes-process-for-medical-exemption-from-covid-19-vaccine-1.5613790>.

25. The Canadian Constitution Foundation, Press Release, "Manitoba Government Creates Medical Exemptions for Vaccine Passport Following CCF Letter" (16 September 2021), online: <https://theccf.ca/manitoba-government-creates-medical-exemptions-for-vaccine-passport-following-ccf-letter/>.

26. Ibid.

27. Christine Van Geyn, "British Columbia's Vaccine Passport Policy Is the Worst in Canada," *C2C Journal* (19 October 2021), online: https://c2cjournal.ca/2021/10/british-columbias-vaccine-passport-policy-is-the-worst-in-canada/.

28. Mike Lloyd, Hana Mae Nassar, and Denise Wong, "COVID-19: Vaccine Passports Come with Risks, Warns B.C. Ombudsperson," *CityNews Vancouver* (26 May 2021), online: https://vancouver.citynews.ca/2021/05/26/covid-19-vaccine-passports-bc-ombudsperson/.

29. The only initial exemption was for children under twelve, who at the time were ineligible for vaccination.

30. The Canadian Constitution Foundation, "Petition to the Court" (22 December 2021), online (pdf): https://theccf.ca/wp-content/uploads/2021.12.22-Petition-BC-Vaccine-Passport-case-Filed-Copy-Redacted.pdf.

31. Ibid.

32. The Canadian Constitution Foundation, "Petition to the Court" (22 December 2021), online (pdf): https://theccf.ca/wp-content/uploads/2021.12.22-Petition-BC-Vaccine-Passport-case-Filed-Copy-Redacted.pdf.

33. Twinkle Ghosh, "Health Canada Adds Bell's Palsy Warning to Pfizer Labels, But Says Vaccine Is Safe," *Global News* (6 August 2021), online: https://globalnews.ca/news/8092666/health-canada-bells-palsy-warning-pfizer-covid-vaccine/.

34. Public Health Ontario, "Surveillance Report: Adverse Events Following Immunization (AEFIs) for COVID-19 in Ontario: December 13, 2020 to February 26, 2023" (2023), online (pdf): https://www.publichealthontario.ca/-/media/documents/ncov/epi/

covid-19-aefi-report.pdf?la=en.

35. Hannah Alberga, "Ontario Confirms There Are Only Two Valid Medical Exemptions from COVID-19 Vaccines," *CTV News* (3 September 2021), online: <https://toronto.ctvnews.ca/ontario-confirms-there-are-only-two-valid-medical-exemptions-from-covid-19-vaccines-1.5572833>.

36. The College of Physicians and Surgeons of British Columbia, "Guidance re: valid contraindications and deferrals to COVID-19 vaccination" (15 September 2021), online (pdf): https://www.cpsbc.ca/files/pdf/2021-09-15-Guidance-re-COVID-19-Vaccine-Contraindications-and-Deferrals.pdf.

37. *Kassian v. British Columbia*, 2022 BCSC 1603.

38. Laura Osman, "Lack of Demographic Data Leaving Potential Gaps in COVID-19 Vaccine Policy," *CTV News* (8 November 2021), online: <https://www.ctvnews.ca/health/coronavirus/lack-of-demographic-data-leaving-potential-gaps-in-covid-19-vaccine-policy-1.5657391>.

39. The Canadian Press, "Black Canadians More Likely to be Hesitant About COVID-19 Vaccines, Survey Suggests," *CBC News* (15 July 2021), online: <https://www.cbc.ca/news/health/black-canadians-vaccine-hesitancy-covid19-1.6102770>.

40. "COVID-19 Vaccine Confidence Black Canadian Perspectives," *Innovative Research Group* (14 July 2021), online: <https://innovativeresearch.ca/vaccine-confidence-among-black-canadians/>.

41. Azza Eissa et al. "Increasing SARS-CoV-2 Vaccination Rates Among Black People in Canada" (2021) 193:31 Canadian Medical Association J E1220-E1221, online: <https://www.cmaj.ca/content/193/31/E1220>.

42. "Study: COVID-19 vaccine willingness among Canadian population groups" (26 March 2021), online: *Statistics Canada* <https://www150.statcan.gc.ca/n1/daily-quotidien/210326/dq210326b-eng.htm>; "COVID-19 vaccine willingness among Canadian population groups" (26 March 2021), online: *Statistics Canada* <https://www150.statcan.gc.ca/n1/pub/45-28-0001/2021001/article/00011-eng.htm> (Both links use the same data but the second link provides a more detailed breakdown.)

43. "COVID-19 Vaccination Coverage Survey" (9 July 2021), online: *Statistics Canada* <https://www150.statcan.gc.ca/n1/daily-quotidien/210709/dq210709b-eng.htm>.

44. "COVID-19 vaccine uptake and intent: Canadian Community Health Survey (CCHS) insight" (last modified 29 October 2022), online: *Statistics Canada* <https://www.canada.ca/en/public-health/services/

publications/vaccines-immunization/covid-19-vaccine-uptake-intent-canadian-community-health-survey.html#a4>.

45. Government of Canada, "COVID-19 vaccination coverage by ethnicity: Insight from the Canadian Community Health Survey (CCHS), Available at https://www.canada.ca/en/public-health/services/immunization-vaccines/vaccination-coverage/covid-19-vaccination-coverage-ethnicity-insight-canadian-community-health-survey.html.

46. James Iveniuk and Scott Leon, "An Uneven Recovery: Measuring COVID-19 Vaccine Equity in Ontario," *Wellesley Institute* (16 April 2021), online: <https://www.wellesleyinstitute.com/wp-content/uploads/2021/04/An-uneven-recovery-Measuring-COVID-19-vaccine-equity-in-Ontario.pdf>.

47. Brenda McPhail, "FAQ: Vaccine Passports" (13 April 2021; last updated 17 August 2021), online (blog): *Canadian Civil Liberties Association* <https://ccla.org/privacy/surveillance-technology/faq-vaccine-passports/>.

48. Kristin Voigt, "COVID-19 Vaccination Passports: Are They a Threat to Equality?" (2022) 15:1 *Public Health Ethics* at 55, online: <https://academic.oup.com/phe/article/15/1/51/6576090#359526938>.

49. Max Fisher, "Vaccine Passports, Covid's Next Political Flash Point," *The New York Times* (1 March 2021; last updated 8 May 2021), online: <https://www.nytimes.com/2021/03/02/world/europe/passports-covid-vaccine.html>.

50. Ian Mosby and Jaris Swidrovich, "Medical Experimentation and the Roots of COVID-19 Vaccine Hesitancy Among Indigenous Peoples in Canada" (2021) 193:11 *Canadian Medical Association Journal* E381-3, online: <https://www.cmaj.ca/content/193/11/E381>.

51. Centre for Ethics, "Sophia Moreau and Sabine Tsuruda, The Moral and Legal Risks of Immunity Passports" (12 May 2020), online (video): YouTube <https://www.youtube.com/watch?v=RHgdYUb_Vt4>.

52. Ibid.

53. Massey College, "Ethics Series—A Pandemic of Ethical Issues: Public Health and Vaccinations" (21 October 2021), online (video): YouTube <https://www.youtube.com/watch?v=OBzKSYj1rJ0>.

54. Ibid.

55. O. Reg. 8/21 under *Emergency Management and Civil Protection Act*, RSO 1990, c E.9. <https://www.ontario.ca/laws/regulation/210008/v3>.

56. O. Reg 58/16 under *Police Services Act* RSO 1990, c P. 15. https://www.ontario.ca/laws/regulation/160058.

57. Franca G. Mignacca, "Quebec Premier Refuses to Provide Curfew Exemptions for Homeless People, Despite Calls Following Man's Death," *CBC News* (19 January 2021), online: https://www.cbc.ca/news/canada/montreal/montreal-mayor-valerie-plante-calls-for-help-open-door-shelter-death-1.5878872.

58. Jacob Serebrin, "Civil Liberties Association Condemns Quebec COVID-19 Curfew, Private Gathering Ban," *The Star* (1 January 2022), online: https://www.thestar.com/news/canada/2022/01/01/quebec-reports-17122-new-covid-19-cases-8-deaths-as-hospitalizations-rise-by-98.html.

59. Franca G. Mignacca, "Quebec Premier Refuses to Provide Curfew Exemptions for Homeless People, Despite Calls Following Man's Death," *CBC News* (19 January 2021), online: https://www.cbc.ca/news/canada/montreal/montreal-mayor-valerie-plante-calls-for-help-open-door-shelter-death-1.5878872.

60. Hannah Jackson, "Mask Mandates in Canada: A Province-by-Province Look at the Rules and Exemptions," *CTV News* (8 December 2021), online: <https://www.ctvnews.ca/health/coronavirus/mask-mandates-in-canada-a-province-by-province-look-at-the-rules-and-exemptions-1.5698936>.

61. The Canadian Constitution Foundation, Press Release, "Release: CCF Raises Concerns About Mandatory Masks Order" (29 June 2020), online: <https://theccf.ca/release-ccf-raises-concerns-about-mandatory-masks-order/>.

62. Jordyn Read, "Family Asked to Leave Disney Store After Child with Autism Couldn't Keep Mask On," *CTV News* (5 August 2020), online: https://london.ctvnews.ca/family-asked-to-leave-disney-store-after-child-with-autism-couldn-t-keep-mask-on-1.5051857.

63. See for example; *Beaudin v. Zale Canada Co. o/a Peoples Jewellers* (16 August 2021), AHRC 155 (CanLII) <https://www.canlii.org/en/ab/abhrc/doc/2021/2021ahrc155/2021ahrc155.html>; *Szeles v. Costco Wholesale Canada Ltd.* (16 August 2021), AHRC 154 (CanLII) <https://www.canlii.org/en/ab/abhrc/doc/2021/2021ahrc154/2021ahrc154.html>; *Sox v. Knott Insurance and Registries (Gibbons)* (21 October 2021), AHRC 182 (CanLII) <https://www.canlii.org/en/ab/abhrc/doc/2021/2021ahrc182/2021ahrc182.html>; *Gariano v. West Edmonton Mall Property Inc.* (31 May 2022), AHRC 63 (CanLII); <https://www.canlii.org/en/ab/abhrc/doc/2022/2022ahrc63/2022ahrc63.html>; *The Customer v. The Store* (March 2021), BCHRT 39 <http://www.bchrt.

bc.ca/shareddocs/decisions/2021/mar/39_The_Customer_v._The_
Store_2021_BCHRT_39.pdf>; *Coelho v Lululemon Athletica Canada
Inc.* (17 November 2021), BCHRT 156 <http://www.bchrt.bc.ca/
shareddocs/decisions/2021/nov/156_Coelho_v._Lululemon_Athleti-
ca_Canada_Inc_2021_BCHRT_156.pdf>; *Sharma v. Toronto (City of)*
(27 November 2020), HRTO 949 (CanLII) <https://www.canlii.org/
en/on/onhrt/doc/2020/2020hrto949/2020hrto949.html>.

CHAPTER 8

1. Sheera Frenkel, Ben Decker, and Davey Alba, "How the '*Plandemic*'
    Movie and Its Falsehoods Spread Widely Online," *The New York Times*
    (21 May 2020), online: <https://www.nytimes.com/2020/05/20/tech-
    nology/plandemic-movie-youtube-facebook-coronavirus.html>.

2. Richard Bruns, Divya Hosangadi, Marc Trotochaud, and Tara Kirk
    Sell, "COVID-19 Vaccine Misinformation and Disinformation
    Costs an Estimated $50 to $300 Million Each Day" (2021), online
    (pdf): Center for Health Security at Johns Hopkins Bloomberg
    School of Public Health <https://www.centerforhealthsecurity.org/
    our-work/pubs_archive/pubs-pdfs/2021/20211020-misinformation-
    disinformation-cost.pdf>.

3. Isaac Schorr, "New York Times COVID Reporter Calls Discussion of
    Lab-Leak Theory 'Racist,'" *National Review* (26 May 2021), online:
    <https://www.nationalreview.com/news/new-york-times-covid-
    reporter-calls-discussion-of-lab-leak-theory-racist/>.

4. Daniel Engber, "The Lab Leak Will Haunt Us Forever," *The Atlantic*
    (28 February 2023), online: <https://www.theatlantic.com/science/
    archive/2023/02/covid-pandemic-origin-china-lab-leak-theory-
    energy-department/673230/>.

5. Maria Cramer and Knvul Sheikh, "Surgeon General Urges the Public
    to Stop Buying Face Masks," *The New York Times* (29 February 2020),
    online: https://www.nytimes.com/2020/02/29/health/coronavirus-
    n95-face-masks.html.

6. Inderveer Mahal, "Why Theresa Tam Changed Her Stance On Masks,"
    Maclean's (22 May 2020), online: https://macleans.ca/opinion/why-
    theresa-tam-changed-her-stance-on-masks/.

7. *R. v. Keegstra*, [1990] 3 SCR 697.

8. Blair Rhodes. "Province gets injunction to block all anti-public health
    order protests," *CBC News* (14 May 2021), online: <https://www.
    cbc.ca/news/canada/nova-scotia/province-gets-injunction-to-block-
    planned-anti-mask-rally-1.6026894>.

9. Office of the Premier, News Release, "Injunction Granted to Stop Anti-Vaccine, Anti-Lockdown Protests" (14 May 2021), online: <https://novascotia.ca/news/release/?id=20210514006>.

10. *Nova Scotia (AG) v. Freedom Nova Scotia*, 2021 NSSC 170 (CanLII), https://www.canlii.org/en/ns/nssc/doc/2021/2021nssc170/2021nssc170.html.

11. Ibid., at para 27.

12. *Ingram v. Alberta (Chief Medical Officer of Health)*, 2020 ABQB 806 (CanLII), <https://www.canlii.org/en/ab/abqb/doc/2020/2020abqb806/2020abqb806.html>.

13. *Nova Scotia (AG) v. Freedom Nova Scotia*, 2021 NSSC 170 at para 25 (CanLII), https://www.canlii.org/en/ns/nssc/doc/2021/2021nssc170/2021nssc170.html.

14. *Nova Scotia (AG) v. Freedom Nova Scotia*, 2021 NSSC 170 at para 27 (CanLII), https://www.canlii.org/en/ns/nssc/doc/2021/2021nssc170/2021nssc170.html.

15. Ibid at para. 34.

16. Ibid at para. 33.

17. *Nova Scotia (AG) v. Freedom Nova Scotia* (14 May 2021), Halifax NS NSSC 506040 (injunction) <https://s3.amazonaws.com/tld-documents.llnassets.com/0026000/26771/nova%20scotia%20injunction%20may%2017%202021.pdf>; see also *Nova Scotia (AG) v Freedom Nova Scotia*, 2021 NSSC 170 at para 3 (CanLII), https://www.canlii.org/en/ns/nssc/doc/2021/2021nssc170/2021nssc170.html.

18. *Nova Scotia (AG) v. Freedom Nova Scotia and the Canadian Civil Liberties Association* (2021), Halifax NS NSSC 506040 (brief of the Canadian Civil Liberties Association) at para 4, https://ccla.org/wp-content/uploads/2021/08/CCLA-20210625-Brief-re-mootness.pdf.

19. *Nova Scotia (AG) v. Freedom Nova Scotia and the Canadian Civil Liberties Association* (2021), Halifax NS NSSC 506040 (brief of the Canadian Civil Liberties Association) at para 5, https://ccla.org/wp-content/uploads/2021/08/CCLA-20210625-Brief-re-mootness.pdf.

20. Edward Conway "Experts: COVID injunction (anticipatory) (is this expert an advocate?) (NSSC)," *CanLII Connects* (3 October 2021), online: <https://canliiconnects.org/en/commentaries/75329>.

21. Bjorg Thorsteinsdottir, Preston Reynolds, Lisa Rucker, Elizabeth Dzeng, and Randy Goldberg, "Are Physicians Hypocrites for Supporting Black Lives Matter Protests and Opposing Anti-Lockdown Protests? An Ethical Analysis" (27 August 2020), online

(blog): *The Hastings Center* <https://www.thehastingscenter.org/ are-physicians-hypocrites-for-supporting-black-lives-matter-protests- and-opposing-anti-lockdown-protests-an-ethical-analysis/> [emphasis added]; Wesley J. Smith, "Another Edition of 'Why We Don't Trust Experts,'" *National Review* (30 August 2020), online: https://www. nationalreview.com/corner/public-health-experts-double-standard/.

22. CBN News, "'Gestapo Nazi': Dramatic Video Shows Canadian Pastor Being Arrested Again Over the Weekend" (4 January 2022), online (video): YouTube <https://www.youtube.com/watch?v=jPvXbIPZEKc>.

23. Meghan Grant, "Pandemic-Denying Mayoral Candidate Kevin J. Johnston's Jail Sentence Delayed Because of COVID-19 Case Surge," *CBC News* 20 September 2021), online: <https://www.cbc.ca/news/ canada/calgary/kevin-j-johnston-mayoral-candidate-contempt- sentence-delay-1.6182571>.

24. Meghan Grant, "Anti-Mask Activists Ordered by Calgary Judge to Preach Science, Too," *CBC News* (13 October 2021), online: <https:// www.cbc.ca/news/canada/calgary/pawlowski-brother-street-church- christopher-scott-contempt-1.6209420>.

25. *Alberta Health Services v. Pawlowski*, 2021 ABQB 813 at para 2.

26. Ibid. at para 38.

27. Ibid. at para 46.

28. Jon Brown, "Canadian Pastor Defiant as Judge Orders Him to Parrot 'Medical Experts' From Pulpit: 'I Will Not Obey,'" *Fox News* (16 October 2021), online: <https://www.foxnews.com/world/canadian- pastor-ordered-judge-cite-medical-experts-pulpit>.

29. Ian Burns, "Probation Order in Alberta COVID-19 Protest Case Raising Free Speech Concerns," *Law360* (20 October 2021), online: <https://www.law360.ca/articles/30594/probation-order-in-alberta- covid-19-protest-case-raising-free-speech-concerns>.

30. Ibid.

31. Joel Dryden, Alberta appeal court sets aside contempt sanctions against pastor, brother and cafe owner, July 22, 2022, online: <https:// www.cbc.ca/news/canada/calgary/artur-dawid-pawlowski-christopher- scott-alberta-appeals-1.6529072>

32. Richard Moon, *The Constitutional Protection of Free Expression* (Toronto: University of Toronto Press, 2000) at 185.

33. Charles Taylor in *Human Agency and Language: Philosophical Papers 1* (Cambridge: Cambridge University Press, 1985), at 256-257.

34. Danielle Smith, "Premier to Pawlowski: 'Can you just leave this with me?'" (April 2023), online (podcast): *CBC News* <https://www.cbc.ca/player/play/2187582531862>.

35. Bill Graveland, "'Intended to incite': Calgary pastor found guilty on two border blockade charges"(May 2, 2023), Calgary *CTV News* <https://calgary.ctvnews.ca/intended-to-incite-calgary-pastor-found-guilty-on-two-border-blockade-charges-1.6379742#:~:text=A%20judge%20has%20found%20Calgary,two%20weeks%20in%20early%202022>.

36. Kulvinder Kaur MD, "If you have not yet figured out that we don't need a vaccine, you are not paying attention." #FactsNotFear, online: Twitter https://twitter.com/dockaurg/status/1290697863777918977.

37. College of Physicians and Surgeons of Ontario, News Release, "Statement on Public Health Misinformation" (30 April 2021), online: <https://www.cpso.on.ca/News/Key-Updates/Key-Updates/COVID-misinformation>. Note that this post is no longer available.

38. College of Physicians and Surgeons of British Columbia and First Nations Health Authority, News Release, "Joint Statement on Misleading COVID-19 Information" (6 May 2021), online: <https://www.cpsbc.ca/news/joint-statement-fnha-misleading-covid-19-information>.

39. "Declaration of Canadian Physicians for Science and Truth," online: <https://canadianphysicians.org/> [content no longer available online, content accessed at https://bpa-pathology.com/declaration-of-canadian-physicians-for-science-and-truth/ on August 29, 2023]

40. *The College of Physicians and Surgeons of Ontario (Inquiries, Complaints and Reports Committee) v. Dr. Kulvinder Kaur Gill* (2021), 2, online: https://www.bennettjones.com/-/media/Files/BennettJones/Blogs/SUMMARY-of-the-Decision-of-the-Inquiries-Complaints-and-Reports-Committee.pdf.

41. Ibid.

42. Ibid.

43. Ibid.

44. *Peterson v. College of Psychologists of Ontario, 2023 ONSC 4685.*

45. Stephanie Taylor, "Mandatory Vaccinations Emerge as First Big Wedge Issue in Pandemic Election Race," *Montreal Gazette* (16 August 2021), online: <https://montrealgazette.com/pmn/news-pmn/canada-news-pmn/mandatory-vaccinations-emerge-as-first-big-wedge-issue-in-pandemic-election-race>.

46. Rachel Gilmore, "'Fringe Minority' in Truck Convoy with

'Unacceptable Views' Don't Represent Canadians: Trudeau,"
Global News (26 January 2022), online: <https://globalnews.ca/
news/8539610/trucker-convoy-covid-vaccine-mandates-ottawa/>.

47. Chris Fox, "Ontario Hospital Association Says Anti-Vaccine Protests
     Outside Hospitals Went Too Far," *CTV News* 3 September 2021),
     online: <https://toronto.ctvnews.ca/ontario-hospital-association-says-
     anti-vaccine-protests-outside-hospitals-went-too-far-1.5572629>.

48. Canadian Press, "'It's Terrifying': Police on Hand as Pandemic Protest-
     ers Picket Hospitals," *CityNews* (14 September 2021), online <https://
     kitchener.citynews.ca/2021/09/14/its-terrifying-police-on-hand-as-
     pandemic-protesters-picket-hospitals-4326357/>.

49. Bill C-3, *An Act to amend the Criminal Code and the Canada
     Labour Code,* 1st Sess, 44th Parl, 2021. <https://www.parl.ca/
     DocumentViewer/en/44-1/bill/C-3/first-reading>.

50. Michael Spratt, "Trudeau's New Law to Protect Health Care Workers
     Will Make No Real Difference and It Might Make Things Worse" (3
     December 2021), online (blog): *Michael Spratt* <https://www.michael-
     spratt.com/opinion/trudeaus-new-law-to-protect-health-care-workers-
     will-make-no-real-difference-and-it-might-make-things-worse/>.

CHAPTER 9

1. John Chidley-Hill, "Toronto Church Files Constitutional Challenge
    Over COVID-19 Restrictions," *CBC News* (9 December 2020),
    online: <https://www.cbc.ca/news/canada/toronto/covid-ont-
    church-1.5835451>.

2. *Toronto International Celebration Church v. The Queen,* 2020 (Motion
    record, Affidavit of Peter Youngren), Court File No. CV 2000-
    652728-0000.

3. Ibid.

4. Ibid.

5. Ibid.

6. Trevor Lawson, Lara Nathans, Adam Goldenberg, Marco Fimiani,
    David Boire-Schwab, Grace Waschuk, Charlotte Simard-Zakaib,
    Gabriel Querry, Caroline-Ariane Bernier, Todd Pribanic-White,
    Lauren Weaver, Hannah Young, Awanish Sinha, "COVID-19:
    Emergency Measures Tracker" (26 May 2022), online (blog article):
    McCarthy Tétrault <https://www.mccarthy.ca/en/insights/articles/
    covid-19-emergency-measures-tracker>.

7. *Toronto International Celebration Church v. Ontario (AG)*, 2020 ONSC 8027 at paras 1–6.

8. Jennifer Pagliaro, "'We Believe That We Are an Essential Service': Toronto Church Challenges Gathering Limits in Court, Arguing They Are Unconstitutional," *The Toronto Star* (8 December 2020), online: <https://www.thestar.com/news/city_hall/2020/12/07/we-believe-that-we-are-an-essential-service-toronto-church-challenges-gathering-limits-in-court-arguing-they-are-unconstitutional.html>.

9. *Toronto International Celebration Church v. The Queen*, 2020 (Motion record, Affidavit of Peter Youngren), Court File No. CV 2000-652728-0000.

10. "Ontario Church Lockdowns Intervention," online: *The Canadian Constitution Foundation* <https://theccf.ca/?case=ontario-church-lockdowns-intervention>.

11. *Toronto International Celebration Church v. The Queen*, 2020 (Motion record, Endorsement of Myers J), Court File No. CV 2000-652728-0000.

12. *Toronto International Celebration Church v. The Queen*, 2020 (Motion record, Affidavit of Peter Youngren), Court File No. CV 2000-652728-0000.

13. Ibid. (Motion record, Affidavit of Betty Berzowski), Court File No. CV 2000-652728-0000.

14. Ibid. (Motion record, Affidavit of Perzol Joan Descanzo), Court File No. CV 2000-652728-0000.

15. Trevor Lawson, Lara Nathans, Adam Goldenberg, Marco Fimiani, David Boire-Schwab, Grace Waschuk, Charlotte Simard-Zakaib, Gabriel Querry, Caroline-Ariane Bernier, Todd Pribanic-White, Lauren Weaver, Hannah Young, Awanish Sinha, "COVID-19: Emergency Measures Tracker" (26 May 2022), online (blog article): *McCarthy Tétrault* <https://www.mccarthy.ca/en/insights/articles/covid-19-emergency-measures-tracker>.

16. *Attorney General of Ontario v. Trinity Bible Chapel*, Factum of the intervener, the Association for Reformed Political Action (ARPA) Canada, Court File No: C70528, at para. 2, online: https://arpacanada.ca/publication/trinity-bible-chapel-v-ontario-appeal/.

17. Ibid. at para. 6.

18. Ibid. at para. 31.

19. Ibid. at para. 30.

20. David Williams, "How Coronavirus Spread From One Member to

87% of the Singers at a Washington Choir Practice," *CNN* (13 May 2020), online: https://www.cnn.com/2020/05/13/us/coronavirus-washington-choir-outbreak-trnd/index.html>.

21. *Toronto International Celebration Church v. Ontario (AG)*, 2020 ONSC 8027 (CanLII), <https://www.canlii.org/en/on/onsc/doc/2020/2020onsc8027/2020onsc8027.html>.

22. *Harper v. Canada*, 2000 SCC 57, para. 9

23. *RJR-MacDonald Inc. v. Canada (AG)*, [1995] 3 SCR 199.

24. *Toronto International Celebration Church v Ontario (AG)*, 2020 ONSC 8027 at para 21.

25. Ibid. at para 16.

26. *Toronto International Celebration Church v. Ontario (AG)*, 2020 ONSC 8027 at para 18.

27. Ibid. at para 19.

28. Ibid. at para 23.

29. Ibid. at para 30.

30. Beaudoin v. British Columbia, 2021 BCSC 512 (CanLii: https://www.canlii.org/en/bc/bcsc/doc/2021/2021bcsc512/2021bcsc512.html)

31. Ibid. at para. 58.

32. Ibid at para. 100.

33. Ibid. at para. 216.

34. *Gateway Bible Baptist Church et al. v. Manitoba et al.*, 2021 MBQB 219 at paras 79 to 81.

35. Ibid.

36. Ibid. at para 82.

37. *Taylor v. Newfoundland and Labrador*, 2020 NLSC 125.

38. *Gateway Bible Baptist Church et al. v. Manitoba et al.*, 2021 MBQB 219 at para 50.

39. Ibid. at para 200.

40. Ibid.

41. *R. v. Oakes*, [1986] 1 SCR 103 at para. 14.

42. *Beaudoin v. British Columbia*, 2021 BCSC 512 (CanLII), <https://www.canlii.org/en/bc/bcsc/doc/2021/2021bcsc512/2021bcsc512.html>.

43. *Gateway Bible Baptist Church et al. v. Manitoba et al.*, 2021 MBQB 219 at paras 206, 210, 214, 245, 252 and 276.

44. "Great Barrington Declaration," online: *Great Barrington Declaration* <https://gbdeclaration.org/>.

45. *Gateway Bible Baptist Church et al. v. Manitoba et al.*, 2021 MBQB 219 at para 313.

46. Ibid. at paras 332 to 336.

47. Ibid. at paras 313, 314, and 316.

48. *Gateway Bible Baptist Church et al. v. Manitoba et al.*, 2021 MBQB 219 at para 336.

49. John Saunders, "Furor Erupts as Police Seize Spanked Children," *The Globe and Mail* (7 July 2001), online: https://www.theglobeandmail.com/news/national/furor-erupts-as-police-seize-spanked-children/article4150244/; Randy Richmond and Megan Stacey, "Henry Hildebrandt: From Religious Firebrand to COVID-19 Provocateur," *The London Free Press* (9 January 2021), online: <https://lfpress.com/news/local-news/henry-hildebrandt-from-religious-firebrand-to-covid-19-provocateur>.

50. Luc Rinaldi, "The Anti-Vax Crusaders," *Toronto Life* (14 October 2021), online: <https://torontolife.com/life/the-anti-vax-crusaders/>.

51. Henry Hildebrandt, "Live from Ottawa. Freedom convoy 2022" (28 January 2022), posted on *Pastor Henry Hildebrandt*, online: Facebook <https://www.facebook.com/watch/live/?ref=watch_permalink&v=1373622219764398>.

52. Luc Rinaldi, "The Anti-Vax Crusaders," *Toronto Life* (14 October 2021), online: <https://torontolife.com/life/the-anti-vax-crusaders/>.

53. Randy Richmond, "Police videotape Aylmer church's drive-in Sunday service as COVID-19 clash continues," *London Free Press* (April 27 2020), online: <https://lfpress.com/news/local-news/police-videotape-aylmer-churchs-drive-in-sunday-service-as-covid-19-clash-continues>

54. Luc Rinaldi, "The Anti-Vax Crusaders," *Toronto Life* (14 October 2021), online: <https://torontolife.com/life/the-anti-vax-crusaders/>.

55. Ibid.

56. Ibid.

57. Austin Grabish, " Church fighting pandemic restrictions is cult-like, former worshippers, expert allege" (June 17, 2021), *CBC News*, online: https://www.cbc.ca/news/canada/manitoba/church-of-god-restoration-manitoba-1.6066688.

58. *R v. The Church of God (Restoration) Aylmer*, 2021 ONSC 3452 at paras 4 to 9 (CanLII), https://www.canlii.org/en/on/onsc/doc/2021/2021onsc3452/2021onsc3452.html.

59. Ibid. at para 7.

60. Ibid. at para 24.

61. Ibid. at para 27.

62. *R. v. The Church of God (Restoration) Aylmer*, 2021 ONSC 3452 (CanLII), https://www.canlii.org/en/on/onsc/doc/2021/2021onsc3452/2021onsc3452.html.

63. Ibid. at 38.

64. *Ontario v. Trinity Bible Chapel et al.*, 2022 ONSC 1344 at para 95.

65. Ibid.

66. Ibid. at para 99.

67. Ibid. at paras 99–100.

68. *R. v. Oakes*, [1986] 1 SCR 103

69. *Ontario v. Trinity Bible Chapel et al.*, 2022 ONSC 1344 at para 125 and 127.

70. Ibid. at para 131.

71. Ibid. at para 136.

72. Ibid. at para 139.

73. Ibid. at para 144.

74. Ibid. at para 149.

75. *Ontario v. Trinity Bible Chapel et al.*, 2022 ONSC 1344 at para 120.

76. Ibid. at para 155.

77. *Ontario v. Trinity Bible Chapel et al.*, 2022 ONSC 1344 at para 132.

78. *South Bay United Pentecostal Church et al. v. Gavin Newsom, Governor of California*, et al., 590 U.S. (2020).

79. *Ontario v. Trinity Bible Chapel et al.*, 2022 ONSC 1344 at para 129; *Gateway Bible Baptist Church et al. v. Manitoba et al.*, 2021 MBQB 219 at 283.

80. *Roman Catholic Diocese of Brooklyn, New York v. Andrew M. Cuomo, Governor of New York*, 592 U.S. (2020), No. 20A87.

81. Ibid. at p 4.

82. Ibid., Gorsuch concurrence p. 2.

83. *Ontario v. Trinity Bible Chapel et al.*, 2022 ONSC 1344 at para 153.

84. *Religious Freedom Restoration Act*, 107 Stat. 1488, 42 USC §2000bb *et seq.* (1993).

CHAPTER 10

1. Verity Stevenson and Isaac Olson, "Unvaccinated Quebecers Will Have to Pay a Health Tax, Legault Says," *CBC News* (11 January 2022; last updated 12 January 2022), online: <https://www.cbc.ca/news/canada/montreal/unvaccinated-health-contribution-quebec-1.6311054>

2. Ibid.

3. Ibid.

4. Joanna Baron, "Joanna Baron: Quebec's Vaccination Tax Must Be Condemned Outright," *The Hub* (14 January 2022), online: <https://thehub.ca/2022-01-14/quebecs-vaccination-tax-must-be-condemned-outright/>.

5. Verity Stevenson and Isaac Olson, "Unvaccinated Quebecers Will Have to Pay a Health Tax, Legault Says," *CBC News* (11 January 2022; last updated 12 January 2022), online: <https://www.cbc.ca/news/canada/montreal/unvaccinated-health-contribution-quebec-1.6311054>

6. Brooklyn Neustaeter, "Quebec Wants to Tax the Unvaccinated, But Experts Say It Could Backfire," *CTV News* (12 January 2022), online: <https://www.ctvnews.ca/health/coronavirus/quebec-wants-to-tax-the-unvaccinated-but-experts-say-it-could-backfire-1.5737101>.

7. The Canadian Press, "Quebec's Tax on the Unvaccinated Could Worsen Inequity, Advocates Say" *The National Post* (11 January 2022), online: <https://nationalpost.com/pmn/news-pmn/canada-news-pmn/quebecs-tax-on-the-unvaccinated-could-enhance-inequity-black-health-alliance>.

8. Jenna Pearl, "Doctors Opposing the Quebec Unvaccinated Tax Proposed 6 Other Ways to Boost Vaccinations," Mtl Blog, (25 January, 2022), online (blog): *MTL Blog* <https://www.mtlblog.com/doctors-opposing-the-quebec-unvaccinated-tax-proposed-6-other-ways-to-boost-vaccinations>.

9. Verity Stevenson and Isaac Olson, "Unvaccinated Quebecers Will Have to Pay a Health Tax, Legault Says," *CBC News* (11 January 2022; last updated 12 January 2022), online: <https://www.cbc.ca/news/canada/montreal/unvaccinated-health-contribution-quebec-1.6311054>.

10. Darrell Bricker, "Strong Majority of Canadians Support Vaccination Mandates; Open to Measures Including Vaccine Passports" (19 August 2021), online (blog): *Ipsos* <https://www.ipsos.com/en-ca/news-polls/majority-of-canadians-support-vaccination-mandates>.

11. The U.S. Food and Drug Administration, News Release, "FDA Takes Key Action in Fight Against COVID-19 by Issuing Emergency Use

Authorization for First COVID-19 Vaccine" (11 December 2020), online: <https://www.fda.gov/news-events/press-announcements/fda-takes-key-action-fight-against-covid-19-issuing-emergency-use-authorization-first-covid-19>.

12. The Newsroom, "Pfizer Did Not Know Whether COVID Vaccine Stopped Transmission Before Rollout" (12 October 2022), online (video): YouTube <https://www.youtube.com/watch?v=mnxlxzxoZx0>.

13. Tristan Hopper, "Why Canada's Hospital Capacity Was So Easily Overwhelmed by the COVID Pandemic," *The National Post* (17 January 2022), online: <https://nationalpost.com/news/canada/why-canadas-hospital-capacity-was-so-easily-overwhelmed-by-the-covid-pandemic>.

14. Although some municipalities in Nunavut implemented their own vaccine passport bylaws. See for example: "Rankin Inlet to bar unvaccinated people from municipal buildings. Proof-of-vaccination bylaw takes effect next week" (November 22, 2021), *Nunatsiaq News*, online: <https://nunatsiaq.com/stories/article/rankin-inlet-to-bar-unvaccinated-people-from-municipal-buildings/>; additionally, Nunavut did issue vaccination QR codes that complied with federal requirements for vaccination for travel. See, for example; "COVID-19 vaccination certificates with QR codes now available in Nunavut" (October 12, 2021), *CTV News*, online: https://www.ctvnews.ca/health/coronavirus/covid-19-vaccination-certificates-with-qr-codes-now-available-in-nunavut-1.5620260.

15. Antoni Nerestant, "Quebec Expands Vaccine Passports to Liquor, Cannabis Stores, With 3rd Dose Requirement on the Way," *CBC News* (6 January 2022), online: <https://www.cbc.ca/news/canada/montreal/vaccination-passport-saq-sqdc-covid-hospitalizations-1.6305992>.

16. Brendan Kelly, "Quebec Retailers Worry New Vaccine Passport Rule Will Cause Tension," *The Montreal Gazette* (21 January 2022), online: <https://montrealgazette.com/news/local-news/quebec-retailers-worry-new-vaccine-passport-rule-will-cause-tension>.

17. Kalina Laframboise, "Quebec to End COVID-19 Vaccine Passport System on March 14," *Global News* (15 February, 2022), online: <https://globalnews.ca/news/8621158/quebec-covid-vaccine-passport-restrictions-eased/>.

18. Discussed in greater detail in Chapter 7.

19. The Justice Centre for Constitutional Freedoms, News Release, "Justice Centre Challenges the Ontario Vaccine Pass in Court Tuesday, July 26," Justice Centre for Constitutional Freedoms, (22 July, 2022), online

<https://www.jccf.ca/justice-centre-challenges-the-ontario-vaccine-pass-in-court-tuesday-july-26/>.

20. Treasury Board of Canada Secretariat, News Release, "Government of Canada to Require Vaccination of Federal Workforce and Federally Regulated Transportation Sector" (13 August 2021), online: *The Government of Canada* Treasury Board of Canada Secretariat, August 13, 2021 <https://www.canada.ca/en/treasury-board-secretariat/news/2021/08/government-of-canada-to-require-vaccination-of-federal-workforce-and-federally-regulated-transportation-sector.html>

21. The proposed changes were to Part II of the *Canada Labour Code*; The Government of Canada, News Release, "Government of Canada Will Require Employees in All Federally Regulated Workplaces to Be Vaccinated Against COVID-19" (7 December 2021), online: *Employment and Social Development Canada* <https://www.canada.ca/en/employment-social-development/news/2021/12/government-of-canada-will-require-employees-in-all-federally-regulated-workplaces-to-be-vaccinated-against-covid-19.html>.

22. Vanmala Subramaniam, "Canada's Big Five Banks Move Away From Mandatory COVID-19 Vaccine Policy," *The Globe and Mail* (31 May, 2022), online: <https://www.theglobeandmail.com/business/article-bay-street-backs-away-from-vaccine-mandates/>.

23. Treasury Board of Canada Secretariat, News Release, "Suspension of the Vaccine Mandates for Domestic Travellers, Transportation Workers and Federal Employees" (14 June 2022), online: *The Government of Canada* <https://www.canada.ca/en/treasury-board-secretariat/news/2022/06/suspension-of-the-vaccine-mandates-for-domestic-travellers-transportation-workers-and-federal-employees.html>.

24. Laura Stone, Jeff Gray, Eric Andrew-Gee, et al. "Quebec Scraps Vaccine Mandates for Health Care Workers, Ontario Won't Require Them," *The Globe And Mail* (3 November, 2021), online: <https://www.theglobeandmail.com/canada/article-ontario-expands-booster-shots-to-people-70-and-older-wont-be-mandatory/>.

25. The Canadian Press, "Vaccination : Pas D'exemption Religieuse Pour le Personnel de la Santé au Québec," *CBC News* (7 October, 2021), online: <https://ici.radio-canada.ca/nouvelle/1830019/vaccination-obligatoire-sante-religion-quebec>.

26. Pierre Saint-Arnaud, "Court Hears Request to Put Off Quebec's Vaccine Mandate for Health-Care Workers," *The Toronto Star* (27 October, 2021), online: <https://www.thestar.com/news/canada/2021/10/27/court-hears-stay-request-of-quebecs-vaccine-mandate-for-health-care-workers.html>.

27. The Government of Ontario, News Release, "Ontario Makes COVID-19 Vaccination Policies Mandatory for High-Risk Settings," Government of Ontario Newsroom (17 August, 2021), online: *Government of Ontario News Room* <https://news.ontario.ca/en/release/1000750/ontario-makes-covid-19-vaccination-policies-mandatory-for-high-risk-settings>.

28. *Blake v. University Health Network*, 2021 ONSC 7139 (CanLII), <https://canlii.ca/t/jk25x>.

29. Government of Canada, "Annex I: Constitutionality of the Canadian Armed Forces COVID-19 vaccination policy," July 18, 2023. Available online at: https://www.canada.ca/en/military-grievances-external-review/services/covid19-vaccination-policy-analysis/annex-i-constitutionality.html

30. Ibid.

31. Ibid.

32. "Trudeau says he didn't force anyone to get vaccinated," (April 27, 2023), online: Sun: https://torontosun.com/news/national/trudeau-says-he-didnt-force-anyone-to-get-vaccinated

33. *Occupational Health and Safety Act*, RSO 1990, c O.1, s 25 (2)(h), <https://www.ontario.ca/laws/statute/90o01#BK47>.

34. The Ontario Human Rights Commission, News Release, "OHRC Policy Statement on COVID-19 Vaccine Mandates and Proof of Vaccine Certificates," Ontario Human Rights Commission (September 22, 2021), online: <https://www.ohrc.on.ca/en/news_centre/ohrc-policy-statement-covid-19-vaccine-mandates-and-proof-vaccine-certificates>.

35. See, for example: CC Partners "A Complete Rundown of COVID-19 Vaccine Policy Decisions in Ontario" (19 January 2022; last updated on 30 September 2022), online (blog): <https://www.ccpartners.ca/blog/details/the-employers-edge/2022/01/19/a-complete-rundown-of-covid-19-vaccine-policy-decisions-in-ontario>; *United Food and Commercial Workers Union, Canada Local 333 v. Paragon Protection Ltd (Policy Grievance)*, [2021] OLAA No 435.

36. Annabel Oromoni, "Employers Will Need to Revoke Immunization Demands as the Government Drops Vaccine Mandates: Lawyer," *Canadian Lawyer* (14 March 2022), online: <https://www.canadianlawyermag.com/practice-areas/labour-and-employment/employers-will-need-to-revoke-immunization-demands-as-the-government-drops-vaccine-mandates-lawyer/364918>.

37. *FCA Canada Inc. v. Unifor, Locals 195, 444, 1285*, 2022 CanLII 52913 (ON LA), <https://www.canlii.org/en/on/onla/doc/2022/

2022canlii52913/2022canlii52913.html>.

38. Khushi David, "Arbitrator Rules Employer's Two-Dose COVID Vaccine Requirement Not Reasonable (Anymore . . .)" (30 June 2022), online (blog): *CC Partners* <https://www.ccpartners.ca/blog/details/the-employers-edge/2022/06/30/arbitrator-rules-employer-s-two-dose-covid-vaccine-requirement-not-reasonable-(anymore-)>.

CHAPTER 11

1. Peter Zimonjic, "Liberals Back Down on Proposed Bill to Broadly Tax and Spend Without Parliamentary Approval," *CBC News* (23 March 2020), online: <https://www.cbc.ca/news/politics/house-commons-covid-emergency-bill-1.5507499>.

2. *Reference re Secession of Quebec*, 1998 CanLII 793 (SCC), [1998] 2 SCR 217.

3. Ibid. para. 72.

4. Ryan Alford, "Emergency Powers and the Rule of Law: Why Inquiries Matter," *The Macdonald-Laurier Institute* (4 August 2022), online: <https://macdonaldlaurier.ca/emergency-powers-and-the-rule-of-law-why-inquiries-matter/>.

5. Bryann Aguilar, "Ontario Gives Police Authority to Stop People, Vehicles, Ask Purpose of Travel," *CTV News* (16 April 2021), online: <https://toronto.ctvnews.ca/ontario-gives-police-authority-to-stop-people-vehicles-ask-purpose-of-travel-1.5390805>.

6. Tommaso Celeste Bulfone, Mohsen Malekinejad, George W Rutherford, Nooshin Razani, "Outdoor Transmission of SARS-CoV-2 and Other Respiratory Viruses: A Systematic Review" (2020) 223:4 *The Journal of Infectious Diseases*.

7. Hannah Alberga, "Outdoor Transmission of COVID-19 is Far Lower Than Statistics Suggest, Expert Says," *CTV News* (12 May 2021), online: <https://toronto.ctvnews.ca/outdoor-transmission-of-covid-19-is-far-lower-than-statistics-suggest-expert-says-1.5425049>.

8. Muriel Draaisma, "Science Experts Didn't Recommend Ontario Ban Outdoor Amenities, COVID-19 Panel Member Says," *CBC News* (19 April 2021), online: <https://www.cbc.ca/news/canada/toronto/ontario-outdoor-recreational-amenities-ban-covid-19-science-advisory-table-did-not-recommend-1.5993818>.

9. Christine Van Geyn, "Christine Van Geyn: Ford Government Had to Have Known Its New Police Powers Were Wrong," *The National Post* (22 April 2021), online: <https://nationalpost.com/opinion/christine-

van-geyn-ford-government-had-to-have-known-its-new-police-powers-were-wrong>.

10. Mike Crawley, "The Inside Story of Doug Ford's COVID-19 Climb-downs," *CBC News* (22 April 2021), online: https://www.cbc.ca/news/canada/toronto/covid-19-ontario-doug-ford-cabinet-police-playgrounds-1.5997381.

11. Andrew Lawton, "FINAL TALLY: Of Ontario's 45 provincially-mandated police forces (44 municipal/regional + OPP), all but three came out against random and unwarranted stops. Two services—Chatham-Kent and Deep River—didn't comment. Just one, the OPP, came out in favor" (17 April 2021), online: Twitter https://twitter.com/AndrewLawton/status/1383585291793944577.

12. Enacting the regulations was also financially negligent, since the government risked having to defend the new police powers in court, spending taxpayer money to defend a law they knew was illegal.

13. *Emergency Management and Civil Protection Act*, R.S.O. 1990, c. E.9, s 7.0.1 <https://www.ontario.ca/laws/statute/90e09/v9>.

14. Patricia Hughes, "Democracy, Emergency and the Reopening Ontario Act," *Slaw* (4 August 2020), online: <https://www.slaw.ca/2020/08/04/democracy-emergency-and-the-reopening-ontario-act/>.

15. Christine Van Geyn, "Opinion: Ontario's Semi-Emergency COVID-19 Bill Is An Attack on Our Rights," *The National Post* (20 July 2020), online: <https://nationalpost.com/opinion/opinion-ontarios-semi-emergency-covid-19-bill-is-an-attack-on-our-rights>.

16. "The Ontario Government Is Making a Grab for More Permanent Emergency Powers While Cutting Democratic Controls" (10 July 2020), online (blog): *The Canadian Civil Liberties Association* <https://ccla.org/fundamental-freedoms/democratic-rights/ccla-to-ontario-mpps-resist-the-premiers-undemocratic-power-grab/>.

17. Jackie Sharkey, "Cambridge MPP Belinda Karahalios Booted from PC Caucus After Voting Against COVID-19 Emergency Bill," *CBC News* (21 July 2020), online: <https://www.cbc.ca/news/canada/kitchener-waterloo/belinda-karahalios-cambridge-progressive-conservative-1.5658084>.

18. Ibid.

19. Jay Cameron, "Ministers as Kings—Alberta's Bill 10 a Dangerous Overreach," *Western Standard*, (11 June, 2020), online: <https://www.westernstandard.news/opinion/cameron-ministers-as-kings-alberta-s-bill-10-a-dangerous-overreach/article_3c2a29fc-3173-5c05-a610-44f98f4232ab.html>.

20. Shaun Fluker, "COVID-19 and Retroactive Law-Making in the Public Health (Emergency Powers) Amendment Act (Alberta)," *ABlawg* (6 April, 2020), online: <https://ablawg.ca/2020/04/06/covid-19-and-retroactive-law-making-in-the-public-health-emergency-powers-amendment-act-alberta>.

21. Ibid.

22. *Justice Centre for Constitutional Freedoms v. Alberta*, 2021 ABCA 415 (CanLII), at para 8 <https://canlii.ca/t/jlbnn>.

23. Ibid. at para 11.

24. Remarks by the Deputy Prime Minister and Minister of Finance regarding the *Emergencies Act*, Government of Canada, Department of Finance Canada, Minister Chrystia Freeland (February 14 2022 [sic]) online: <https://www.canada.ca/en/department-finance/news/2022/02/remarks-by-the-deputy-prime-minister-and-minister-of-finance-regarding-the-emergencies-act.html>

25. *Kassian v. British Columbia (AG)*, 2022 BCSC 1603, <https://theccf.ca/wp-content/uploads/Justice-Hinkson-re-Kassian-v.-British-Columbia-09-12.pdf>.

26. *R v. Nur*, 2015 SCC 15 at para 98.